Constructive
Typology
and
Social
Theory

Sociology Series

John F. Cuber, *Editor*
Alfred C. Clarke, *Associate Editor*

Constructive Typology and Social Theory

John C. McKinney

DUKE UNIVERSITY

APPLETON-CENTURY-CROFTS

DIVISION OF MEREDITH PUBLISHING COMPANY

E 62336

PRINTED IN THE UNITED STATES OF AMERICA

To Florentina

Acknowledgments

For some fifteen years I have been interested in the process of typification, the methodological problems of type construction, and the utilization of typologies. Over that period of time I have published, either alone or in collaboration, a number of analyses related in one way or another to the general problem of type construction. These included: "The Role of Constructive Typology in Scientific Sociological Analysis," *Social Forces,* 28 (March, 1950), pp. 235-240; "Constructive Typology and Social Research" in John Doby *et al.,* editors, *An Introduction to Social Research* (Harrisburg: Stackpole Press, 1954), pp. 139-198; (with Charles P. Loomis) "Systemic Differences Between Latin American Communities of Family Farms and Large Estates," *American Journal of Sociology,* 61 (March, 1956), pp. 404-412; "Methodology, Procedures, and Techniques in Sociology," in Howard Becker and Alvin Boskoff, editors, *Modern Sociological Theory* (New York: Dryden Press, 1957), pp. 186-235; "The Polar Variables of Type Construction," *Social Forces,* 35 (May, 1957), pp. 300-306; (with Charles P. Loomis) *"Gemeinschaft* and *Gesellschaft* as Related to Other Typologies," in Ferdinand Tönnies, *Gemeinschaft und Gesellschaft: Community and Society,* as translated and introduced by Charles P. Loomis (East Lansing: Michigan State University Press, 1957), pp. 12-29; (with Charles P. Loomis) "The Typological Tradition" in Joseph Roucek, editor, *Contemporary Sociology* (New York: Philosophical Library, 1958), pp. 557-582; and (with Alan C. Kerckhoff) "Toward a Codification of Typological Procedure," *Sociological Inquiry,* 32 (Winter, 1962), pp. 128-135.

I mention these previous efforts in the typological domain because the present volume represents both an outgrowth and a development of an intellectual journey which has been sustained by these varied attacks upon typological problems. Although this volume has its roots in and rests upon the earlier efforts, it is clearly intended to supersede all of my previous works on typology. In terms of development, however, it represents a phase of continuity rather than a definitive stopping place. I can express the hope that the developmental process can be continued.

There have been three people who have been most instrumental in launching me on this intellectual journey: the late Professor Paul M. Honigsheim of Michigan State University, Professor Charles P. Loomis of Michigan State University, and the late Professor Howard P. Becker of the University of Wisconsin. Professor Honigsheim first interested me in matters typological and it was in his seminars that I first addressed myself to the problem complex. The various collaborations with Professor Loomis, which are specified above, sustained and strengthened my interest in typologies. Our joint presentation of a seminar in social theory for several years in the early and mid-fifties contributed greatly to my experience and enriched my understanding of the relevant problems. My contacts and exchanges with Professor Becker during the fifties were invaluable. At one time we had planned to coauthor a volume on constructive typology and by 1957 had accomplished much of the preliminary planning for such an undertaking. However, we experienced many delays and disruptions because of other commitments which each of us had to fulfill; and then his untimely death brought the proposed work to a halt. The present volume is in lieu of, but could not be a substitute for, the proposed joint publication. My heavy indebtedness to all three of these men is gratefully acknowledged.

In less diffuse ways a number of people have rendered aid in developing this book. I am indebted to Professors Paul F. Lazarsfeld and Talcott Parsons for reading and commenting on an early draft of the manuscript. Their criticisms were manifold and cogent. My attempts to come to terms with their criticisms have, I think, resulted in a manuscript considerably improved over its earlier version. Of course, neither Professor Lazarsfeld nor Professor Parsons can be held accountable for any of the inadequacies of the volume. I benefited greatly from their assessments, but responsibility for final content and form is entirely my own.

Mr. Paul J. Baker and Mr. Charles W. Peek, III, in their capacity as graduate research assistants were very helpful in the screening and development of the annotated bibliography. Mrs. Sandra F. Mascitelli, as editorial assistant, played an invaluable role with respect to getting the manuscript into its final form. Her efforts have unquestionably made this a far more readable book than it otherwise could have been.

Finally, the financial assistance of the Duke University Research Council is gratefully acknowledged. Their contributions at strategic times were most instrumental in bringing the writing project to a satisfactory conclusion.

J. C. M.
Duke University

Foreword

The social scientist finds himself in continuous effort to combine two ideals: vision and precision. Clearly, he needs precise instruments if he wants to develop testable propositions. But the social world is very complex and doesn't provide us with the well delineated objects from which the natural sciences start. Thus, he also needs a great deal of creative imagination—of vision—to decide on the objects about which such propositions should be developed.

Since the beginning of sociology typologies have been one of the most important ways of creating the objects of social analysis. We couldn't think of our social science without also thinking of *Gemeinschaft* and *Gesellschaft*, of Bureaucracy or of Mass Society. The introduction of each of these notions has been a turning point in the history of sociology. The originators of these ideas belong properly among the heroes of our intellectual heritage.

But one must distinguish between the privileges of the pioneers and the duties of the followers. It is not enough for us to accept the innovations of the masters: we have to analyze what they did, we must be able to convert their visions into articulated procedures which can become part of the day to day activities of the social research community.

A few years ago I was invited to address an international congress on the "relation between philosophy of science and empirical social research." * I listed a number of topics which required the collaboration of these two groups. At the top of my list I put the need to explicate the idea of constructive typologies. At that time

---

* *Logic, Methodology and Philosophy of Science.* Nagel, Suppes, Tarski, eds. Stanford University Press: Stanford, Calif. (1962), p. 463.

I referred to Professor McKinney's extensive preliminary work as a major source for such a scrutiny; it is a pleasure indeed to see that he has now approached this task on a broad plane.

A large number of questions have to be answered. In what sense is a constructive type different from a combination of separate variables? What is the relation between abstract type and concrete cases? Under what conditions is a constructive typology dynamic, that is, leading to predictions of change? What distinguishes it from simpler classificatory devices? What is the relation of a constructive typology to a theory of social systems?

Professor McKinney courageously tackles all of these problems. He draws on a large number of concrete examples at the same time as he attends to methodological analysis. His central theme, if I understand him correctly, is this: the constructive typology stands at the juncture of vision and precision, and that juncture is a basic concern for all of us. We might give this dilemma very different names: macrosociology versus microsociology, atomistic versus polistic approaches; synchronic versus diachronic analysis. At one time these were matters of controversy; today we know that they are challenges for synthesis. One of the main merits of this book is that it does look for such a synthesis.

In spite of it, Professor McKinney should not expect complete consent. Readers within his own camp might have different ideas on the way one should present the line from Max Weber over Howard Becker to this modern version of the ideal type tradition. Other readers, conditioned to, say, the generalized logic of survey analysis, might want to give the constructive typologies a less central place in the totality of social research methodology. But all of them, I am sure, will be grateful to the author for providing us with a fine map into which each of us can draw our special predilections. And after all, that is the main purpose of any methodological effort: to give us a frame of reference within which we can perform our productive efforts with ever increasing clarity.

Paul F. Lazarsfeld
Columbia University

Contents

Introduction

The procedural use of *constructive typology* has a long and productive history within the realm of scientific endeavor. The constructed type has been a useful tool in the hands of both the social scientist and the historian. The device has played an undeniable role in the growth of scientific knowledge despite the fact that it has frequently been misused, misinterpreted, or not even recognized by its users. A very great amount of historical and social scientific work has been done wherein the constructed type has remained merely an implicit aspect of the enterprise. There has also been a great deal of historical and social scientific work which explicitly recognized and developed the constructed type, particularly in recent years, but in much of this work the construction and adaptation of the type has not been carried out in the most rigorous and fruitful manner. On the other hand, there is already an extensive body of literature, with quite obviously more to come, which reflects the purposive attempt of researchers to maximize the *potential* of the constructive typological procedure. This volume will necessarily refer to a small sample of the literature now available in English or in English translation.

The direction of attention to the methodological problems involved in typological procedure must be credited to the social sciences, more specifically to a number of the leading German sociologists of the late nineteenth and early twentieth centuries. This despite the fact that the method itself is as old as science. Such analysts of social phenomena as Tönnies, Simmel, Sombart, Troeltsch, and Weber played leading roles in making the procedure of typology explicit. Of that group it was Max Weber who made

1

the greatest contribution to the delineation of the procedure and also to the use of it in both historical and social scientific analysis. It must be carefully noted, however, that Weber's "model" of "ideal-typing" does not blanket the constructive typological procedure as we broadly conceive of it, but is merely a special case emphasizing certain aspects of type construction. Constructive typology is herein viewed as the generic mode of typification encompassing all special typological procedures. This transfer of attention from the special form of the *ideal type* to the more general and comprehensive form of the *constructed type* is primarily, although by no means entirely, based upon the work of Howard Becker.

In this book concern is with the applicability of the constructed type within a scientific or generalizing frame of reference. Science, including social science, is continually in search of what is conceived of as being the identical, the general, and recurrent aspects of the phenomena with which it is concerned. It is the pragmatic assumption of science that the world in its physical, biological, and social aspects is both intelligible and explicable. It is intelligible in the sense that uniformities may be stated, and explicable in the sense that these uniformities stand the test of further experience. The uniformity of nature is a basic assumption of science, and all that science can do is to demonstrate specific uniformities that justify keeping the assumption. The demonstration of uniformities involves the comprehension of the data of experience, which in turn involves the conceptual creation of order out of a vast diversity of experiences. This entails the analytic elimination of the unique, and the *construction* of a *conceptual* order of things wherein the repetitive and interrelated aspects of phenomena are exposed.

The scientific search for uniformities is a selective search that necessarily eliminates much of the data of experience: explicitly, the unique and the irrelevant with respect to the problem or problems under consideration. The elimination of certain elements of data and aspects of knowledge from scientific consideration is entirely legitimate insofar as it is recognized that science does not represent the totality of knowledge but only that part of knowledge concerned with uniformities or regularities, expressed in probability terms in the form of predictive statements. Science is oriented toward the prediction of what might happen under what circumstances. It is a mode of conceptualization wherein results are predicted on the basis of the combination of a particular set of factors under a given set of circumstances. The theoretical prediction is then justified by the results obtained. This method is obviously selective and abstractive, since one can never make a complete statement about all that is involved in anything that happens. In one sense or another, everything is involved in everything that happens. To leave it at that, however, would constitute leaving the experienced world as entirely idiosyncratic and incomprehensible. Science conceptually eliminates the idiosyncratic and achieves comprehension by predicting and thereby tentatively *establishing the regularities and sequences involved in a postulated uniform order of phenomena.*

To achieve scientific prediction, which means the *construction* of order out of diversity, general out of unique, and recurrent out of occurrent, methodology is essential. It is obvious that observation is never simply a matter of opening the eyes and ears and exposing one's self to what is occurring. Scientific observation is always directed by an interest, a problem, a concern, with an exception to a rule, a theory, or a conceptual scheme. *What* is to be observed is a matter of scientific interest and abstraction with regard to problem relevance. *How* it is to be observed is a matter of methodology, and methodology consists essentially in the logic and normative rules of procedure.

Constructive typology is an aspect of scientific methodology generally, but in turn has its own logic and normative rules of procedure, however ill-defined they may be at this time. The construction of types is not confined to any particular science; it is a procedure applicable to the data of any science. The particular type-constructs as substantive entities, however, are not interchangeable among the sciences in view of their necessary restriction to their domain of problem relevance. Within this frame of reference we then define the constructed type as a *purposive, planned selection, abstraction, combination, and (sometimes) accentuation of a set of criteria with empirical referents that serves as a basis for comparison of empirical cases.*

With this definition as our "bench mark," it is possible to assert that *all* types are constructed, and that moreover the scientist typically constructs the units with which he operates. This is true of the physical as well as the social sciences. One only has to glance at any of the special sciences to realize the tremendous importance of constructs to their endeavor. For example, the perfect lever, perfect gas, frictionless motion, perfect vacuum, perfect surfaces, straight cylinders and spheres, and other similar constructs have contributed heavily to the physicist's knowledge in his problem domain. Economics is deeply indebted to its "economic man" from which the classical economic theory was derived. The essential concepts of perfect competition, the perfectly mobile factors of supply and demand, the perfect monopoly, or such classificatory labels as capitalist and socialist systems, money, credit, or barter economies are all constructed types. The sociologist is dependent upon such notions as competition, conflict, accommodation, assimilation, socialization, superordination, subordination, institutionalization, community, society, caste and class, sacred and secular, rural and urban, democracy-autocracy, bureaucracy, the deviant, solidarity, primary group; these and many more may be constructed types. Even the ideographic historian, whose aim differs from that of the scientist and who is legitimately concerned with the "unique and individual," constantly utilizes constructed types. When he talks of epochs, eras, and periods, he has constructed them. When the historian speaks of the Greek city-society, the feudal system, the manorial system, early Protestantism, the medieval Papacy, the Calvinistic ethic, the estates within the state, and countless other things, he is utilizing, usually without awareness, the procedure of constructed typology in his own particular way.

The preceding small sample of usage of constructed types by just a few disciplines should demonstrate the point that they are both useful and prevalent. The scientific orientation is essentially a constructive orientation, and constructed types are a particular kind of construct. Despite the demonstrated prevalence and utility of typifications and typologies, there is a considerable degree of ambiguity and a marked lack of codification with respect to typological procedure. Consequently, we should like to put forward a series of propositions with respect to the constructed type. A major task of this book will be to examine relevant theoretical and empirical evidence with respect to these propositions and thereby explore the role, actual and potential, of constructed typologies in the social research process.

The construction of types, as a methodological approach, is not confined to any particular science; it is a procedure that is applicable to the data of any science. The particular type-constructs as substantive entities, however, are not interchangeable among the sciences in view of their restriction to a domain of problem relevance.

The constructed type is a means of reducing diversities and complexities of phenomena to a generally coherent level. Consequently it does not describe or represent any course of action, situation, etc., in uniqueness, but does represent an objectively probable (empirically relevant) course of action, situation, etc.

The constructed type is a pragmatically devised system of characteristics, made up of abstracted elements and formed into a unified conceptual pattern wherein there may be an intensification of one or more attributes for purposes of utility.

The constructed type has its empirical base in the particularities of history, broadly construed. Consequently, the historian has much to offer the scientific typologist in view of the fact that scientific constructs presuppose a knowledge of the particulars from which they are drawn.

A generalizing constructed type can be drawn from only two different places: from theory or more general types that have already received substantial empirical verification, or constructed directly from the particulars of an historical situation.

There are seemingly six major "axes" around which types are constructed. The variables of type construction involve these polarities: ideal–extracted, general–specific, scientific–historical, timeless–time-bound, universal–local and generalizing–individualizing.

Although examinations of empirical cases may never reveal anything more than approximations or deviations from the constructed type, it is essential for maximum problem relevance and utility that the type should be formulated as being objectively probable.

The type focuses on uniformity. Consequently type usage leads to the development of hypotheses about variations or deviations, because variant forms can only be comprehended through the notion of uniformity.

A manifest function of all types is to identify and simplify; consequently the constructed type performs the task of guiding the initial selection of data relative to the problematic areas of the sciences.

A scientific function of the constructed type is to order the concrete data so that they may be described in terms that make them comparable, so that the experience had in one case, despite its uniqueness, may be made to reveal with some degree of probability what may be expected in others; hence the type is a heuristic device constructed primarily for comparative and predictive rather than descriptive purposes.

The constructed type is a simplification of the concrete; therefore all individual concrete occurrences will deviate from the type in some respect. These deviations will be relative—to each other and to the constructed type. Hence the type can serve as a basis for the measurement (potential or actual) of the degree of deviation.

A primary contribution of the constructed type is that it serves as a basis for comparison of concrete occurrences. Since both enumeration and measurement are subcomponents of comparison, the adaptation of quantifying techniques to typological procedure represents a natural line of development.

The constructed type isolates the behavior that is theoretically significant. It does not in itself say anything about the frequency of that behavior (a function of enumeration), nor does it say anything about the degree of deviation (a function of measurement). Consequently quantitative control is a desirable adjunct of the constructed type, for it enhances the predictive power of the theoretical device.

The use of the constructed type as a predictive scheme demands that it be testable under empirical conditions. Hence the logic of the experimental method is the logic of the explanatory use of the constructed type. *The fact that most of the comparisons necessary to this logic must be made with reference to "naturally" occurring events, and cannot be produced at will, is a handicap to the social scientist, but does not deny him explanation in the scientific sense.*

Prediction on the basis of the constructed type can be either retrospective or prospective. Hence the type "setup" may be sought for in the data of history as well as in that of the contemporary or future scene.

The constructed type is a special kind of concept in that it consists of a set of characteristics wherein the relations between the characteristics are held constant for the purposes at hand. Hence the type is a pragmatically constructed "system."

The constructed type as a conceptual device represents an attempt to advance concept formation in the social sciences from the stage of description and empirical generalization to the construction of theoretical systems.

As a system, the type has the character of a theoretical model that is susceptible of empirical interpretation.

The constructed type is a heuristic expedient that serves as a means by which concrete occurrences can be compared and comprehended within a system of general categories presumably underlying the types.

Insofar as the constructed type is derived from, or can be related to, a generalized scheme, it can perform the functions of orienting empirical research to systematic theory and, conversely, grounding systematic theory in empirical research.

It is not suggested that the following chapters constitute anything more than a preliminary and primitive exploration of matters relevant to the preceding propositions. Unquestionably the propositions, individually and as a set, require a considerably more sophisticated investigation and analysis than can be made at the present before the role of typological procedure in the social sciences can be specified with any high degree of accuracy. Moreover, it should be noted that the definition of constructed type used consistently throughout this volume is in no sense proposed as a final definition. It has been pragmatically developed and proposed as a working device. With this definition as base referent we can proceed with what amounts to a conducted tour of the ideas and procedures implied in the notion of constructed types. It is the thesis of this volume that constructive typology can be best understood as an aspect of a pragmatic research methodology. The establishment of that thesis awaits a more compelling and definitive attack upon the preceding and related propositions than is currently possible. At best, one can hope that the present volume is instrumental in accelerating the process of that scholarly attack and thereby induces its own rapid obsolescence.

Concepts, Constructs, and Constructed Types

All concepts are constructs that have been *developed* out of experience. "Raw" experience is never really raw even at the moment of perception. Human beings, having become human through symbolic interaction, naturally and necessarily categorize and structure their experience in terms of *concepts*. When science begins to analyze and classify its data, it is taking a definite and formal step away from reality at the perceptual level. All phenomena are unique in their concrete occurrence; therefore no phenomena actually recur in their concrete wholeness. The meaning of identity is always "identical for the purposes at hand." To introduce *order* with its various scientific implications, including prediction, the scientist necessarily ignores the unique, the extraneous, and non-recurring, and thereby departs from perceptual experience. This departure is the necessary price he must pay for the achievement of abstract generality. To conceptualize means to generalize to some degree. To generalize means to reduce the number of objects by conceiving of some of them as being identical. The reduction of the number of objects reduces the number of relations to be examined. Since these relations are between conceptual elements they always remain hypothetical relations.

Scientific concepts never exhaust perceptual experience, for they always involve selection. Concepts do not reflect the totality of raw experience in all its diversity and complexity, and are therefore, in a sense, unreal. To repeat, all concepts are generalizations and all generalization implies abstraction. The nature of this abstractive process is often ignored. Abstraction may take place in two closely related ways, both of which contribute to the general character of the concept.

First, there is abstraction of the common quality from the differing particulars. Thus we ignore the ways in which spruce, pine, fir, palm, and apple differ from each other and grasp their generic resemblance via the concept of tree. Tree is the conceptual unity by means of which we grasp a multiplicity of unique aspects and comprehend them within an order. The concept is abstract in the sense that the specific differences are lost in the abstractive process. Second, there is abstraction in the form of selection based upon the particular theoretical interest of the scientist. Resemblance is usually complex and involves a plurality of simpler qualities. Consequently, the scientist is presented with a group of associated resemblances from which he can select to the extent that it pertains to a particular problem. Those qualities that are abstracted from the total complex become a part of the content of the concept, whereas those that are neglected are excluded. In this process the concept has again become artificial because of its imposed limitations, omissions, and exclusions. It is this aspect of abstraction, however, that enables the scientist to distinguish between essential and nonessential attributes with respect to a particular problem.[1]

To avoid vagueness, indistinctness, and complete elasticity, a

[1] "Social scientists are not completely frustrated, however, by their inability directly to subdivide man as a social totality. They can, in effect, partly achieve this objective by indirect means. They can resort to the use of fiction and imagine that men as a social totality embodies an economic man, an ethical man, a political man, a reasonable man, and whatever other type of man is called for. They can do this by subdividing man's interpersonal behavior into categories (within each of which a comparatively homogeneous collection of activities is assembled) and assigning custody of each category to the specialists presumably most suited to deal with it. In short, by analytical and mental means social scientists can accomplish in part that which they cannot achieve physically by any means. This they have been doing for several centuries, an outcome being the differentiation and specialization so characteristic of contemporary social science." J. J. Spengler, "Generalists Versus Specialists in Social Science: An Economist's View," *The American Political Science Review*, 44 (June, 1950), pp. 359-360.

concept must be *given* precision. Precision can only be given negatively, by setting up limits beyond which the concept has no meaning.[2] Consequently the very limits that give a concept precision are
responsible for some necessary degree of separation of the concept
from perceptual experience. No concept is ever a perfect symbol
of that which it symbolizes—for inevitably its content will be less.

It is clear, then, that concepts are constructs even when they
closely reflect perceptual experience. Concepts define what is to be
observed, and they are the variables between which empirical relations are to be sought. It is the function of the concept to make explicit the character of the data subsumed under it and, conversely,
to function as a bench mark for determining that which is omitted.

When all concepts are seen as constructs, and when it is granted
that all constructs are in one sense selectively developed due to their
abstractive genesis, then the way is open to move one step further
and develop the constructed type. Ordinary concepts are given
precision as constructs through selection and limitation; constructed
types are given precision through selection, limitation, combination,
and accentuation. The constructed type organizes experience in a
somewhat different fashion than does the ordinary concept in that
it forms a series of attributes into a configuration that is not necessarily directly experienced and accentuates one or more of the attributes for theoretical purposes. In contrast to the concept, a constructed type is determined to a greater degree by the selective and
creative activity of the scientist. The primary distinction, however,
is that its value as a component of knowledge is not to be measured
by the accuracy of its correspondence to perceptual experience (although some degree of correspondence is essential), but *in terms of
its capacity to explain,* however tentative and preliminary that explanation may be. A scientific function of the constructed type is to
order the concrete data so that they may be described in terms that
make them *comparable,* so that the experience had in one case,
despite its uniqueness, *may be made to reveal with some degree of*

[2] For an excellent discussion of the limited applicability of concepts in
the context of an analysis of comparative studies, see Reinhard Bendix, "Concepts and Generalizations in Comparative Sociological Studies," *American
Sociological Review,* 28 (August, 1963), pp. 532-539.

probability what may be expected in others.[3] The constructed type is a special kind of concept especially developed for descriptive, comparative, and predictive purposes.

The constructed type is a heuristic device. It is a devised system of attributes (criteria, traits, elements, aspects, etc.) not experienced directly in this form, but *useful* as a *basis* for comparing and understanding the empirical world. It is a construct made up of abstracted elements and formed into a unified conceptual pattern wherein there may be an intensification of one or more aspects of concrete experience. The elements of the type have discoverable empirical referents, or at least can be legitimately inferred from existent evidence. The constructed type is a pragmatic expedient and does not purport to be empirically valid in the sense of retaining all the unique aspects of the empirical world. The main purpose it serves is to furnish a means by which concrete occurrences can be compared, potentially measured, and comprehended within a system of general categories that may be developed to comprise the types.

The comparison and measurement of empirical approximations reveals nothing but deviations from the construct. At some level, depending on the construction, nothing but exceptions to the constructed types exist. This is not only to be expected, but is to be sought after, for it is the basis of the value of the typological method. These deviations will be relative—to each other and to the constructed type. This procedure, then, can lead to quantification in terms of *degree* of deviation. If degree of deviation is to be deter-

---

[3] Implicit reference here is to a statistical probability. "It seems wise to stress the point that 'statistical probability' means just that, and *not* 'degree of belief probability.' The actuary uses the term in *our* sense when he says, 'There is a greater probability that a man of age thirty will attain his fortieth birthday than there is that he will attain his fiftieth.' Contrasting with this usage, we have historical statements such as, 'There is a great "probability" (i.e., plausibility) that Caesar visited the site of the present city of London than that he visited the site of the present city of Edinburgh.' In the latter case, the word is used by the historian as an indication of his 'degree of belief' in the statement. This belief is based on the information available about Caesar's travels. . . . Not this 'degree of belief' *plausibility,* but 'actuarial' *probability,* is the kind that concerns us. . . ." Howard Becker, *Through Values to Social Interpretation* (Durham: Duke University Press, 1950), p. 97n.

mined repetitively and comparatively, then the base of measurement (the type) must be held constant. The relations between the elements (criteria) of the type are postulated relations; therefore they may legitimately be held constant. These relations *may* also be empirical if the type always has a probable empirical approximation. The type will logically contain within its structure all the essential properties or elements of a concrete structure or course of action, but not necessarily in the exact proportion or relationship pattern of any given empirical occurrence. These properties or elements constitute the variables within the type, and they remain in a fixed invariant relationship with each other for the purposes at hand. The removal of one or more of the variables, or the alteration of the relations between them, involves the development of a new type. Such removal or alteration may of course be necessary in the light of empirical requirements.

Although examination of empirical cases never reveals anything more than approximation to or deviation from the constructed type, it is essential that the type should be formulated as being objectively probable. The criteria are purposively selected on the basis of empirical evidence, and put into a pattern that the researcher hopes will serve as a significant base of comparison. A type implies a predictive schema. For instance, the concept of rational man implies the adaptation of means to ends. Granted certain ends and norms as being "given," then the test of rationality is the adequacy of selection of available means and their adaptation to the attainment of ends. Obviously no actual man is rational in all aspects of his behavior; yet his behavior can be comprehended in terms of the rational schema. There is an *expectancy* of man when he is viewed as rational man that is only partially met by any given man, although some men may meet the expectancy in very high degree. A comparison of the extent to which actual men meet the expectancy serves as the basis for explaining difference in their behavior.

To illustrate further, any type such as the feudal system, scientific man, charismatic leader, perfect vacuum, or perfect surface will imply a predictive schema on the basis of its criteria. Feudal behavior will vary from one concrete situation to another; yet despite these variations there is a feudal expectancy, different from any other expectancy, that enables one to comprehend the variations

within the pattern. Likewise, the expectancies one has of the course
of action of the charismatic leader are different than those of any
other kind of leader. The scientist behaves differently than other
people when he is operating as a scientist, despite the fact that there
is immense variation in the behavior of scientists. One does not find
perfect vacuums in nature; nevertheless it is the predictive schema
of the vacuum that makes empirical approximations comprehensible.
The perfect surface is also a fiction, but the expectancy of perfec-
tion is what enables us to compare degrees of roughness as found
in actual surfaces. Although it is possible to construct types that
are merely objectively possible in the sense of being logical fictions,
such types must have a limited utility. It must be remembered that
the primary function of the type is to throw actual structures or
courses of action into comparative light; hence a type possessing
mere theoretic possibility, and for which no empirical approximation
can be found, will be a questionable comparative standard. A type
lacking an empirical carrying context cannot be related to empirical
problems in the same significant way as can a type woven out of empirical regularities and possessing a unity that is itself subject to
empirical approximation. A type hewed and carefully built out of
the particularities of experience simply gives one a different focus
than does a type possessing mere logical consistency. The type
focuses on *uniformity*, and it is only through the notion of uniformity
that we have comprehension of variations or deviations. Obviously
any variation or deviation must be a variation or deviation from
something. To answer the question as to what that something is,
is necessarily to answer: a uniformity. If that uniformity has empirical substance, the predictive function of the type will unquestionably be enhanced.

To further clarify the concept of the constructed type it is
necessary to approach it from the negative point of view. Max
Weber very concisely stated what an ideal type *was not*. His following remarks are also relevant to the constructed type:

> "(1) It is not a hypothesis, in the sense that it is a proposition about
> concrete reality which is concretely verifiable, and to be accepted
> in this sense as true if verified. In contrast to this sense of concrete-
> ness, it is abstract. (2) It is not a description of reality if by this
> is meant a concretely existing thing or process to which it corre-

sponds. In this sense also it is abstract. (3) It is not an average . . . in the sense that we can say the average man weighs 150 pounds. This average man is not an ideal type. (4) Nor, finally, is it a formulation of the concrete things *common* to a class of concrete things, for instance in the sense that having beards is a trait common to men as distinct from women." [4]

As previously indicated, the ideal type is merely a special case of the generic constructed type.[5] Consequently, it is possible to add the following negative limits to the constructed type.

(1) The constructed type is not a homogeneous universe as that concept is ordinarily understood. The type certainly has classificatory significance, but it cannot be equated with class because it has a configurational significance totally lacking in the class as a homogeneous universe.

(2) The constructed type does not necessarily refer to the most common form of a phenomenon, but usually to the most significantly representative form. For instance, it makes sense to talk about the economic man despite the fact that it is doubtful that the rationality imputed to him is the most *common* form of economic behavior. It is through the notion of rationality as the outstandingly representative form that the nonrational forms of economic behavior are then apprehended.

[4] Talcott Parsons, *The Structure of Social Action* (Glencoe: The Free Press, 1949), pp. 603-604.

[5] See Chapter II of this volume for an analysis of the relationship of the ideal type to the constructed type. For an earlier attack upon this problem, see Howard Becker, "Constructive Typology in the Social Sciences," *American Sociological Review*, 5 (February, 1940), pp. 40-55. The following comment by Becker is noteworthy here: " 'Constructed type' has none of the epistemological and other ambiguities or unacceptable commitments that 'ideal' drags with it. . . . The time when 'ideal type' was first coined is now about fifty years in the past, and advances in epistemology, the logic of science, probability theory, and configurational psychology make its denotations and connotations liabilities far too great to be willingly borne today. 'Constructed type' has NONE of these liabilities, is bound up with a much more explicit method, has many more possibilities for quantitative formulation while at the same time doing full justice to qualitative demands, . . ." Howard Becker, "1951 Commentary on Value-System Terminology," in Howard Becker and Harry Elmer Barnes, *Social Thought From Lore to Science* (2nd ed., Washington, D.C.: Harren Press, 1952), p. ii.

(3) The constructed type is not a stereotype, in that the stereotype often lacks an empirical referent and is an unplanned, affectual exaggeration that is not empirically useful because of a lack of explicit criteria that make it comparable to concrete cases. Also, there is never any compulsion to make empirical comparisons because the stereotype not only has an emotional base but serves as an emotional weapon. In contrast, the constructed type is a purposive, planned selection, abstraction, combination, and (sometimes) accentuation of a set of criteria with empirical referents that serves as a basis for comparison of empirical cases.

Now that the constructed type has been described both positively and negatively, it is perhaps appropriate to examine its relationship to other constructs and to comment on the prevalence and indispensability of the type. The aspect of unreality of the type seems to be of greatest concern to those who are dubious of the typological technique. Unreality is a characteristic of all concepts, even of those with the closest perceptual counterparts. On examining such empirically legitimate terms as the median, mean, and mode, one finds that they are all conceptual creations that exaggerate the empirical referent that they supposedly represent. These averages are merely central tendencies of a distribution, and hence their representation of the extreme items is necessarily quite unreal. In contrast, the constructed type is representative of a distribution in a different fashion in that it is deliberately formulated as *a limiting case* from which degree of deviancy is potentially measurable. The tasks that the average and the constructed type perform are simply different ones, and their relative research status cannot be decided on the basis of the assertion of unreality.

No concept is ever a copy of anything real. This is most strikingly evident in the realm of physical science. No scientific concept deals directly with perceptual experience, but only with the limits as constructively formulated. In theory, for instance, a sphere and plane can touch each other in only one place. In the empirical world, however, allowances have to be made for roughness of surface and the pressure of a real sphere on a plane. There are irregularities that are not a part of the limiting constructed case. Consequently they must be qualified as empirical deviations from the construct which made them comprehensible.

As Cassirer once put it:

> "We investigate the impact of bodies by regarding the masses, which affect each other, as perfectly elastic or inelastic; we establish the law of the propagation of pressure in fluids by grasping the concept of a condition of perfect fluidity; we investigate the relations between the pressure, temperature and volume of gas by proceeding from an 'ideal' gas and comparing a hypothetically evolved model to the direct data of sensation." Or, as Wilhelm Ostwald put it more tersely: "We thus stand before the fact that many and among them the most important laws of nature are asserted and hold of conditions, *which in reality in general are never found.*" [6]

In the light of the foregoing, is it an unreasonable and invalid procedure on the part of the social scientist to construct units with which to work? Is he flouting the scientific canons when he utilizes such concepts as secular society, instrumental relationship, and bureaucratic system even when he knows that seldom, if ever, will any concrete plurality pattern have the pure characteristics of any one of those structures? Is the social scientist antiempirical when he looks for imperfect concrete versions of the constructed processes of urbanization, accommodation, and assimilation? The answer is an unequivocal "no." It is scientifically advantageous and necessary to utilize theoretical constructs which are only approximated in the empirical world.

The failure on the part of many social scientists to recognize the indispensability of the constructed type may be partially attributed to the current casual use of typology, as well as to a lack of codification and routinization of the typological method. The most widespread misuse of typology involves the unjustifiable reification of the types. When a set of characteristics has been abstracted out and formulated into a type, the users of that type frequently tend to forget that it is merely a tool for the ordering of concrete phenomena.[7] The "orthodox" economists have been especially guilty of this and have thereby caused considerable unnecessary disillusionment with economic theory. Even such skilled typologists as Parsons,

[6] W. H. Werkmeister, *A Philosophy of Science* (New York: Harper and Brothers, 1940), pp. 102-103. (Italics his.)

[7] For an analysis of this problem, see Hans Zetterberg, *On Theory and Verification in Sociology* (New York: Tressler Press, 1954), pp. 16-28.

Sorokin, and Durkheim tend to reify their types and thereby to obscure their scientific utility. The "as if" aspect of typology can never be lost sight of in interpretive use.

The failure to recognize the conditional character of predictive generalizations based upon typological abstractions is another problem area in typological interpretation.[8] All that the constructive typologist can ever say is "if and when" certain factors recur under certain conditions there will be a probable result. The typologist merely creates the type, not the actual behavior that conforms to it in varying degrees. The continuing observation of actual behavior in terms of the type cannot be done away with; it is a necessary task, and indeed the primary justification for constructing the type in the first place.

Another kind of misunderstanding frequently arising in typological use is the notion that all constructed types are of equal generality. This is a gross error in view of the fact that types vary tremendously in their degree of generality—necessarily so, for the form of the type, if it is to function scientifically, has to be related to a problem area, hypothesis or battery of hypotheses, observational techniques, data, and predictive range.

It is the *use* of the constructed type that determines its scientific value. There are certain things that it can and cannot do, and clear recognition of its functions and limitations is essential to the fulfilment of its potential. A manifest function of all types, statistically derived empirical types as well as those that are more impressionistically constructed, is to identify and simplify.[9] The constructed type performs the task of guiding the intial selection of data in terms of the schema of a given science. The construct may be used as a means of interpreting particular situations; in other words, the type functions as the general standard by which a concrete occurrence is

[8] For an analysis of this problem within a theoretical and substantive context, see Howard Becker, "Current Sacred-Secular Theory and Its Development," in Howard Becker and Alvin Boskoff (eds.), *Modern Sociological Theory* (New York: Dryden Press, 1957), pp. 133-185.

[9] W. J. Goode, "A Note on the Ideal Type," *American Sociological Review,* 12 (August, 1947), p. 473. Also see R. F. Winch, "Heuristic and Empirical Typologies," *American Sociological Review,* 12 (February, 1947), pp. 68-75.

comprehended. The type can also be used as a generalizing concept by means of which one can extract its empirical versions from different cultural contexts. This is implicit in any search for universals. The constructive type as such has classificatory significance, although it is not merely a class, and thereby differentiates phenomena and sets the stage for prediction.

The constructed type serves as a point of reference for the analysis of the social order in that it serves as basis for comparison and potential measurement of concrete occurrences. First of all, the comparison of the actual processes or situation with the typical construct will indicate the degree of prevalence of the typical factors and thereby indicate the degree of probability of occurrence of the typical consequences. Secondly, through the indication of degree of prevalence of the typical factors, the comparison will indicate the possible need for further constructed types on a different level of generalization so as to include more of the apparently unique in a generalized scheme. Thirdly, the comparison of the construct with the empirical data should serve as a fruitful source of more specific hypotheses, which in turn may be examined on a less general level by a more rigorous methodology. And, finally, when the constructed type is used in conjunction with an appropriate hypothesis it may have predictive value. Using the conditional terms demanded by the degree of probability involved, the social scientist can say, "if and when" these typical factors occur in the typical relationship pattern, these will be the typical consequences.

These varied aspects of the utility of the constructed type seemingly give ample justification for concern with the development, codification, and refinement of the typological method.

——2

The Polar Variables of Type Construction

A great many varieties of types have been described in the literature. Reference is frequently made to ideal, pure, extreme, heuristic, polar, empirical, real, classificatory, and constructed types. Unfortunately, the emphasis has largely been upon the assumed or actual differences between these types and the accompanying assertion of superiority of one version of typing over others. As a result, the common qualities of *all* types and typing have been largely ignored, and the basic fact that all types are constructed has not often been considered.[1]

The writer has no quarrel with the above type labels, and feels that their delineation and usage has made some contribution to the clarification of typological procedure. Many ambiguities and obscurities remain. As descriptive labels, some of the above reflect purpose (the heuristic type), serial order (the polar type), character of attributes (the pure type), function (the classificatory type), or developmental procedure (the constructed type). Such contrasting bases for labeling have tended to obscure the fundamental qualities of similarity shared by all types. From a methodological point of view these qualities center around *how types are conceptually de-*

[1] The single major exception lies in the work of Howard Becker. See in particular, *Through Values to Social Interpretation* (Durham: Duke University Press, 1950), *passim;* and "Interpretative Sociology and Constructive Typology," in George Gurvitch and W. E. Moore (eds.), *Twentieth Century Sociology* (New York: Philosophical Library, 1945), pp. 70-95.

veloped. When one looks closely at the variety of types extant in any substantive field, it is impossible to avoid the central fact that the development of each of them involved a task of *construction.* This is not to assert that all types are alike in their construction; it is merely a way of saying that all types are constructed around certain persistent variables. In surveying a broad range of major typologies it would appear that the major variables are (1) the relation of type to perceptual experience, (2) the degree of abstraction involved in the types, (3) the purpose of the type, (4) the temporal scope of the type, (5) the spatial scope of the type, and (6) the function required of the type.

When these variables, which are either explicitly or implicitly present in any type, are viewed as the *axes* around which types are constructed, they appear as the main *dimensions* of types in general. They are seen as a series of continua which serve to delineate the *structure* of types. For purposes of analytic convenience and description we will label the polar points of these continua and thereafter treat them as the *polar variables of type construction.* We then have the following variables: (1) ideal–extracted; (2) general–specific; (3) scientific–historical; (4) timeless–time-bound; (5) universal–local; and (6) generalizing–individualizing.

It is possible to analyze any given type in terms of its tendency to conform to the requirements of one pole or another on each of the above continua. It is important to note, however, that these continua are not mutually exclusive and do not reflect the same level of abstraction. On the contrary, they are mutually implicated, overlap to a certain unavoidable extent, and are reflective of methodological relevance rather than logical purity. In other words, these continua represent the empirically persistent points of methodological concern in the development of substantive types. We will utilize these continua to construct a *typology of types* in this chapter. It should be carefully noted that this is not meant to be an exhaustive classification system; it is designed merely as a rough cognitive map of the structure of typology. As such, it tentatively delineates the attribute space within which any substantive type or typology will fall.

Ideal–Extracted. The name invariably linked with the ideal type is that of Max Weber, its most famous proponent.[2] Ideal types are, of course, common in all the sciences as well as the discipline of history, but it was Weber who made us most conscious of this kind of type.

In Weber's generalizing procedure[3] he was looking for order in behavior, and his approach led him to the formulation of the typical in its ideal or pure form. To Weber these conceptual formulations were merely expedient heuristic devices that were useful in understanding the phenomena under consideration. Weber's conceptual system was essentially elastic and readily modifiable in terms of empirical necessity and interest.

Weber conceived of the ideal type as being both abstract and general. For instance, his types did not describe or directly represent concrete courses of action, but instead were representative of objectively possible modes of action. This would be a course of conduct assuming certain ends and means to be in consistent usage by the individuals involved. Further, this would be a typical course of action not necessarily duplicated in concrete situations by individual modes of behavior, but would be normative in character. The ideal type would logically contain within its structure all the essential

[2] A comment made by Paul Lazarsfeld should be called to attention here since, in effect, it constitutes a serious methodological challenge in social research. "Max Weber did spectacular work in historical sociology, a field badly neglected in recent years. But he also wrote a few pages on what he thought he did, calling his procedure the construction of ideal types. These self-declaratory statements contradict each other at many points; they have no visible relation to the actual content of his studies, and they have led to endless and confused literature which is concerned mostly with terminology and, as far as I can see, has resulted in no new investigations. No one has explicated what he did in his actual studies, which has contributed to the difficulty of emulating his skill." See "Philosophy of Science and Empirical Social Research," in Ernest Nagel, Patrick Suppes, and Alfred Tarski (eds.), *Logic, Methodology and Philosophy of Science* (Stanford: Stanford University Press, 1962), p. 464.

[3] As Schelting pointed out many years ago, Weber actually used two different kinds of ideal types—the generalizing and the individualizing. Our concern for the moment is the generalizing type which is the one of direct scientific relevance. See Alexander von Schelting, *Max Weber's Wissenschaftslehre* (Tubingen: J. C. B. Mohr, 1934), final chapter; and Talcott Parsons, *The Structure of Social Action* (Glencoe: The Free Press, 1949), pp. 601-610.

properties or elements of a concrete course of action, but not necessarily in the proportion or relationship pattern of any given empirical occurrence. These properties or elements constituted the variables within his type and were held in fixed relationship with each other for theoretical purposes.

As abstractions, Weber's ideal types were conscious deviations from concrete experience. They were structured in such a way as to accentuate some attribute or group of attributes relevant to his research purpose or interest. In a sense, they were a distortion of the concrete in that all empirical occurrences appeared as deviations from the theoretically conceived ideal type. This is the real core and basic significance of the ideal type. The observations of empirical occurrences yielded nothing but deviations when compared to the ideal type, but these deviations were relative (a) to each other, and (b) to the ideal type. Hence the ideal type served as the model or basic comparative unit. In the light of this, it is obvious that Weber conceived of ideal types as being merely necessary logical expedients. They were not in themselves empirically valid, and were theoretically not subject to reification. They did not directly represent any concrete reality or constitute an essence of actuality. They merely served as consciously devised and delimited conceptual tools in the analysis of the empirical world. In Weber's view, typologies were subordinate to the aims of sociohistorical research, namely the causal analysis of historical events.

At the opposite end of the continuum and from the pole represented by the ideal type, we have the extracted type, which is often called the empirical type.[4] These types are definitely not exclusive of one another; on the contrary, they graduate into each other. It must be pointed out that, even though the ideal type is theoretically derived, it must still have empirical referents in that it is based upon

[4] For example, Winch refers to this type as the "empirical type." This is quite justifiable, but for substantial reason this writer prefers the label "extracted type." Part of the negative attitude extant toward ideal types is based upon the mistaken notion that they are antiempirical types. Consequently it seems inadvisable to contribute in any way to the perpetuation of the impression that there is an ideal–empirical dichotomy. See R. F. Winch, "Heuristic and Empirical Typologies: A Job for Factor Analysis," *American Sociological Review,* 12 (February, 1947), pp. 68-75.

the particularities of actual occurrence. Weber made this very clear in terms of what he did rather than in terms of what he said about the ideal type. Conversely, no matter how empirical its base, the extracted type involves a certain amount of problem or theory-oriented selection and hence construction. Both types serve the purpose of simplifying and identifying the object world. Their differences lie primarily in their formulations and the way in which they represent the object world; this, of course, has implications for what they can "do" in research.

Kretschmer's description of how he arrived at his two general biotypes, the *cyclothymic* and *schizothymic,* is a classic example of the extractive method:

> The types are no "ideal types" which have emerged, consciously created in accordance with any given guiding principle or collection of pre-established values. They are, on the contrary, obtained from empirical sources in the following way: when a fairly large number of morphological similarities can be followed through a correspondingly large number of individuals, then we begin measuring. When we compute averages the outstanding common characteristics come out clearly, while those peculiar marks which only occur in isolated cases disappear in the average value. In exactly the same way we treat the remainder of the characteristics which can only be described from mere optical observation. So we proceed as if we were copying at the same time the picture of one hundred individuals of a type on the same picture-surface, one on top of the other, in such a way that those characteristics which cover one another become sharply outlined, while those which do not fit over one another disappear. Only those characteristics which become strongly marked in the average values are described as "typical." [5]

The types arrived at by Kretschmer throw the average and common traits into bold relief, not necessarily the crucial or significant. The role of interpretation is much greater in the method of ideal typing. The ideal type involves comparison from the ideal limits of the case, whereas the extracted type involves comparison from central tendencies. The extracted type is based upon the notions of average, common, and concrete rather than upon those of

[5] Ernst Kretschmer, *Physique and Character* (New York: Harcourt, Brace, 1925), pp. 18-19.

accentuation and abstractness. Nevertheless, a certain amount of essential ideation is involved in the establishment of extracted types, as for instance in the delineation of the traits involved (a case of abstraction), and the treatment of a combination of traits as a composite whole (a case of simplification based upon elimination of the seemingly irrelevant and hence, again a matter of abstraction). As one views the various typologies extant, it is easily recognized that none of them are either ideally or empirically pure, but in actuality are representative of tendencies to emphasize one pole or the other. In this connection it might be mentioned that the Becker–McKinney model of type construction is a conscious and purposive attempt to combine aspects of ideal and extracted types in order to capitalize on what they both have to offer and to avoid their limitations.[6]

The constructed type as conceptually developed by Becker and defined by McKinney is a *purposive, planned selection, abstraction, combination, and (sometimes) accentuation of a set of criteria with empirical referents that serves as a basis for the comparison of empirical cases.* Although all types are constructed, Becker and McKinney adhered to this particular model of construction because they found it to be useful with regard to the kinds of problems they were interested in. This model obviously is a close relative to the ideal type, and the Weber type version is admittedly the primary source of its development. There is a significant difference, however, which can be pointed out by saying that the Becker–McKinney model has been drawn *away from* the ideal pole of the continuum and *toward* the extracted pole. This has been accomplished by placing the emphasis on the *objective probability* of the empirical occurrence of the type rather than on its mere *objective possibility.* The latter can mean mere logical possibility; it can refer to a plausible fiction that

[6] Much of the work of Howard Becker over a period of approximately thirty years was oriented toward this problem. One gets a sense of development and considerable change in contrasting his approach in *Systematic Sociology on the Basis of Beziehungslehre and Gebildelehre* with Leopold von Wiese (New York: John Wiley, 1932), with that in *Through Values to Social Interpretation.* The first analysis relevant to this problem by McKinney was in "The Role of Constructive Typology in Scientific Sociological Analysis," *Social Forces,* 28 (March, 1950), pp. 235-240. The first published reference to the Becker–McKinney model was contained in J. C. McKinney, "The Polar Variables of Type Construction," *Social Forces,* 35 (May, 1957), pp. 300-306.

can never be even remotely approximated in real life. In contrast, Becker remarks that

> The accentuation or stressing of salient features of the constructed type, and its "closure," is fictional only in the sense of empirically "limited fiction." Examination of the empirical evidence must always enable the researcher to say, "The probability that this type will ever be matched in reality is *very* slight, but the probability is not inherently nil." [7]

For a concrete example of what this distinction means, let us use the familiar pattern-variables of orientation developed by Talcott Parsons.[8] Because of the process of their derivation, the pattern-variables can theoretically occur in *any* combination in the subject–object relation. Consequently, any combination of the variables could presumably be labeled as a *type* of subject–object orientation. Empirically, however, some combinations simply never occur; they are merely objectively possible "empty cells" in a formal system. In actuality there are empirical clusters of certain variables, and it is these that we would conceive of as objectively probable types. It would be these combinations that we would concentrate upon in type construction and investigation in the research process. We would feel justified in eliminating the former combinations as being inherently unstable or fictional, and consequently would draw in the limits of type construction to fit the empirical context. In summary, the Becker–McKinney model of constructed type is an ideal type shorn of any purely fictional qualities, firmly grounded in the particularities of actual situations, and constituted by attributes that are empirically discoverable.

General–Specific. Types can also be distinguished by their relative generality or specificity. Cognizance must be taken of the levels of abstraction involved in the formulation of types. The more general a type is, the greater the simplification of the empirical attributes; the more specific a type is, the greater the number of general characteristics obscured by the mass of ideographic detail. Empirical generalization made through the use of the more general

---

[7] Howard Becker, *Through Values to Social Interpretation*, p. 261.
[8] See *The Social System* (Glencoe: The Free Press, 1951), *passim,* for the delineation and use of the pattern-variables.

constructed types must necessarily remain relatively indefinite in the sense of being highly general. Generalization means omission and simplification of particularities. Consequently, as a type effects wide coverage, its adequacy in accounting for specific variations is lessened. This is not to say that general types are not useful; it is merely to take account of the fact that more specific types must be used in conjunction with them for many explanatory purposes.

Such types as *Gemeinschaft, Gesellschaft,* sacred, secular, communal, associational, rural, urban, folk, state, familistic, contractual, primitive, and civilized are obviously "sponge types" as they stand; nevertheless, they have been extremely useful. Numerous subtypes are necessarily involved in their extensive application, but it is the general type which makes the subtypes possible and furthermore gives them an interpretive context or coherence within a schema.[9] The degree of generality–specificity involved in the construction of a type is unalterably related to the purpose at hand and the predictive task it must perform. An extracted type can be general, but tends to be specific due to the nature of its distillation. On the other hand, an ideal type can fall freely at various points on the general–specific continuum.

Scientific–Historical. Construction of types may proceed in terms of the purposes of the scientist or in terms of the purposes of the historian. It must be recognized that they can and do use the same data, for all data are in a sense historical. The scientist, however, is in search of the general and recurrent, and the historian is primarily interested in the actual sequence of unique events. Both use constructed types to achieve their objectives.

Max Weber used the two different kinds of constructs in his historical and sociological work. His construct of modern capitalism, for instance, is a unique, or historical, conception. It is an ideal type construct of behavior, but it is not generally applicable. Its sole referent as a type is to a particular time and place. It does not make

---

[9] For illustrations of the use of subtypes, see Howard Becker, "Sacred-Secular Societies," in *op. cit.,* pp. 248-280; C. P. Loomis, "The Nature of Rural Social Systems—A Typological Analysis," *Rural Sociology,* 15 (June, 1950), pp. 167-174; and C. P. Loomis and J. C. McKinney, "Systematic Differences Between Latin American Communities of Family Farms and Large Estates," *American Journal of Sociology,* 61 (March, 1956), pp. 404-412.

empirical sense to speak of modern capitalism as being existent prior to the seventeenth century. Further, it cannot be appropriately applied anywhere outside of the western world. Nevertheless, it is a construct in that it does not contain within it all the behavioral minutiae of the epoch. The reference of modern capitalism is individual and historical, not analytical and general.

Max Weber's sociological usage of typology was in line with scientific purposes. His second kind of type dealt with recurrent and prevalent phenomena which typically appeared as constituent elements in repetitive social occurrences. Among his concepts that had general application in a variety of historical contexts are those such as his four types of action: purposive rationality, valuational rationality, affectual, and traditional. The concepts of legitimacy, routinization, charisma, sect, and numerous others ought also to be included here.[10]

Georg Simmel, the primary initiator of "formal sociology," is another example of the user of generally applicable, nonhistorical types. He detached such concepts as leadership–obedience and superordination–subordination from their historical or concrete settings, and maintained that they were applicable in even the most diverse groups, regardless of their social setting. The form of the types made them universally applicable. Hence, they were scientific rather than historical tools.[11]

Constructed types of historical value tend to be highly complex, time-bound, and localized, whereas those of scientific value tend to be *relatively* timeless and universal, relatively simple, contain a limited number of criteria, and include so limited a content that they are applicable in many diverse historical situations. The historical construct is general in the sense that it does not depict the full concrete reality in all of its concrete manifestation, and the scientific construct is historical in the sense that the behavior it symbolizes

[10] See Max Weber, *The Theory of Social and Economic Organization*, translated by A. M. Henderson and Talcott Parsons (New York: Oxford University Press, 1947); and *From Max Weber: Essays in Sociology*, translated and edited by H. H. Gerth and C. W. Mills (New York: Oxford University Press, 1946).

[11] Georg Simmel, *The Sociology of Georg Simmel*, translated and edited by K. H. Wolff (Glencoe: The Free Press, 1950); and N. J. Spykman, *The Social Theory of Georg Simmel* (Chicago: University of Chicago Press, 1925).

necessarily bears a resemblance to that which has historically occurred. The differences in the constructs answer to the purposes for which they are formulated.

Timeless–Time-bound. This axis is very closely related to the one just treated in that the scientific universal is the closest approximation to the timeless pole of the continuum and the historical construct is the closest approximation to the time-bound pole. Nevertheless, it is important to treat it separately to get at the *relative* timelessness of the scientific construct. It must be recognized that scientifically useful constructs vary enormously in the extent to which they are "timeless." They stand in different relative positions on the timeless–time-bound continuum.

The concept *Gemeinschaft* as Tönnies used it is unquestionably as timeless as the sociologist can make a concept.[12] Tönnies regarded all social relationships as the creations of human will. He designated two types of will, *Wesenwille* (essential will) and *Kurwille* (arbitrary will). *Wesenwille* refers to any process of willing originating in the traditional adherence to beliefs and sentiments common to the group. *Wesenwille* is responsible for the *Gemeinschaft* relationship and makes it as timeless as the natural behavior of man. On the other hand, *Gesellschaft,* the presumed antithesis of *Gemeinschaft,* is not timeless to the same extent. Being the product of *Kurwille,* the arbitrary will, and involving the expedient adaptation of means to ends, it necessarily is restricted to a more *particularized* behavioral development, and hence in point of time must be a development out of *Gemeinschaft.* Consequently, it is timeless to a lesser degree.

To use another illustration, the concept of superordination–subordination appears to be quite timeless in view of the fact that some type of hierarchical relationship can be found even in the most primitive of contemporary societies. It is not necessarily entirely timeless, for if there were ever such things as hordes or conditions of completely mechanical solidarity it would not have been applicable. As a principle, however, it seems to be a close approxima-

---

[12] Ferdinand Tönnies, *Community and Society* (*Gemeinschaft und Gesellschaft*), translated and edited by C. P. Loomis (East Lansing: Michigan State University Press, 1957).

tion to the timeless pole. In contrast, the sociologically significant concept of class appears closer to the time-bound pole of the continuum than the concept of superordination–subordination does.

It is important to note that scientifically useful constructs are only *relatively* timeless. It is the task of the scientific researcher to remove the time-markings from the phenomena under analysis in order to get at the general and recurrent, but his success is always a relative one. Time will still leave discernible markings on many of the most useful scientific social types.

Universal–Local. The spatial counterpart of the timeless–time-bound continuum is that which we call universal–local. Just as the former deals with the temporal scope of the type, the latter is concerned with its spatial scope, and together the two axes determine the area of applicability of any given type. Constructs vary as to where they fall on the spatial continuum. When a type is applicable anywhere that the particular class of phenomena it deals with is available, then it may be said to be universal. If a type is applicable only to a very limited and specific locale and is not approximated anywhere else, it may be called localized.

The sacred type of relations may be cited as an example of the universal type. Sacred relations are discernible in any society. Although the objects and content will vary, the attitude of sacredness with resultant behavior can be found among all peoples. In contrast, the sacred type of society tends to be considerably more localized. There are many societies that must be characterized as secular rather than sacred even though they have some sacred relations within them. The prevalence of secular societies obviously limits the scope of the sacred societal type, although the sacred type relation remains a universal. Additional spatial limitations are imposed when one starts to derive sub-types from the generic types. When Becker speaks of a "prescribed sacred" society, for example, he is sharply delimiting the locale of applicability of the type because there simply are not many actual societies that approximate it; hence it is a much more localized type than its generic parent.

To illustrate further, a German peasant type is localized by deliberately restricting it to German culture. This is accomplished by using criteria (attributes) within the type that are supposedly idiosyncratic to German social structure. A "Russian peasant" type could also be constructed that would differ from the former in that it would contain within it certain traits peculiar to the Russian locale. If one wishes to speak of a "peasant" type that accounts for the relevant behavior in the two areas, or indeed if he wants to broaden the type to account for similar behavior in France, England, Latin America, China, and elsewhere, he must focus upon what they have in common as the basis for the type. This can only be accomplished by deleting the type criteria localized within a given area and retaining those criteria common to all the cases dealt with. Thus it is possible to legitimately speak of the peasant type. But when one wants to be more specific he has to localize the type, which means again including behavioral attributes relevant only to a given area.

In his scientific orientation, the sociologist is driven to search for universal types—those that are applicable "across the board" in society and culture. In actual practice and as a function of the research process, however, most of his types tend to be localized, in that spatial markings are difficult to remove from sociocultural types. Indeed, for purposes of most research, it is not even desirable to extend the applicability of the type beyond a given area. In the long run, however, our normative orientation toward science demands that we universalize as many types as possible.

Generalizing–Individualizing. Constructed types may be conceived of as being primarily either generalizing or individualizing. They are not unrelated. Indeed, numerous generalizing constructs are usually required to support an individualizing concept and, conversely, through modification an individualizing construct can frequently be adapted to more general use.

Max Weber used the individualizing construct as a means of delineating what he called the "historical individual," the thing to be explained. The impossibility of handling all the data and determining its relevance made it necessary to construct the individual unit to be examined. The construct of "modern capitalism," for instance, was woven out of the particularities of an historical epoch, but it was obviously simplified, selective, and limited.[13] It contained what appeared to be the crucial characteristics of the capitalistic form that distinguished it from other economic configurations. To describe this complex historical individual, however, it was necessary for Weber to imply numerous *generalizing* constructs such as "rationality" and "bureaucracy," which have a range of applicability far beyond the particular case of "modern capitalism." It is only through the use of such explanatory generalizing constructs that the historical individual is made comparable in any respect. The construction of the historical individual has the function of preparing and organizing the mass of concrete data for analysis in terms of general constructs and ultimate predictive statements of relationships.

The way in which an individualizing concept may be adapted to more general use can be illustrated by the construct of "caste." The Indian caste system is certainly an individualizing construct representing extraordinarily heterogeneous phenomena. There is only one Indian caste system, and even as an historical individual it has to be enormously simplified in order to be comprehended at all. It is possible, however, to extract from this heterogeneous pattern a number of essential elements whose presence justified the attachment of the label "system." When such elements are extracted out it is possible to drop the prefix "Indian" and talk about caste as a general phenomenon. These elements can be conceived of as constituting caste as a general construct: (1) rigidly endogamous groups, (2) arrangement of hereditary groups into a superiority–inferiority hierarchy, (3) group relationship to the division of labor in the form of hereditary occupations, and (4) the maintenance of ceremonial barriers. This abstracting process makes it possible to observe a caste relationship in parts of the world other than India.

---

[13] Weber followed Marx in believing that capitalism (or rational bourgeois capitalism at least, as he described it) as a system of profit-making enterprises based on rational capitalistic organization of formally free labor was an unprecedented system. Capitalism solely in the sense of pursuit of profit by the utilization of opportunities for exchange but without the market organization of free labor, however, was an ancient system. See Max Weber, *The Protestant Ethic and the Spirit of Capitalism,* translated by Talcott Parsons (London: Allen and Unwin, 1930), pp. 20-24.

For instance, only a procedure of this sort justifies the use of caste with regard to the Negro–white relationship in the American South. Through adaptation from the historical individual it becomes possible to conceive of a phenomenon that otherwise might be neglected.

The generalizing construct emerges out of the particularities of history but is applicable in many diverse situations. Its quality of abstract generality gives it the capacity to serve as a basis of measurement and comparison of various empirical structures and courses of action. Its hypothetical typicality enables it to function as a tool of analysis in an indefinite plurality of individual cases and enhances understanding of an indefinite number of concrete situations. It is the generalizing constructs of this sort that are of immediate scientific relevance in the predictive context.

In the preceding analysis, emphasis has been placed upon the point that all types are constructed and that there are recognizable dimensions of the basis of construction. It should be made quite clear that no attempt has been made to create a logical classification of types. The endeavor here is confined to pointing out the features of substantive typing that have been empirically persistent. No assertion is made, nor should it be implied, that the six polar variables listed above exhaust all the elements that might go into a formal classification. The variables dealt with here have been arrived at on the basis of an intensive review of the great bulk of modern sociological literature cast in the typological form. All the variables are found to be analytically applicable to all substantive types; hence any formal system of classification of the construction of types would have to provide categories that would account for the phenomena dealt with here under our essentially empirical rubrics. In brief, we have constructed a *typology of types*. As such it constitutes a crude cognitive map of the structure of typology.

However crude or limited this particular typology may in the future be demonstrated to be, it is clear that construction in typological procedure varies with respect to at least six different dimensions. Consequently, types can vary greatly in terms of their structure, depending upon where they fall on the series of continua considered here to be the major dimensions. It is suggested that the user of types in social analysis and research could attain a greater understanding and hence control of those types by taking cognizance of these dimensions. In all likelihood, this understanding and control would enable him to use types with greater precision, and would caution him to require of them only the function they can legitimately perform on the basis of their structural attributes.

——3

Types in Relation
to the Methodology
of the Social Sciences

One of the major objectives of this volume is to analyze the methodological character of constructive typology and thereby clarify the place that it may take in the battery of approaches available in the social sciences. There appear to be four strategic points on which this analysis must focus if the role of typology within the total social research process is to be made more explicit. (1) The essential relationship of the constructed type to systematic theory must be demonstrated if the type is to claim major scientific significance. (2) The relation of typology to experimental procedure is crucial with respect to the logic of its explanatory use. (3) The relationship of constructive typology to quantitative procedure is worthy of examination because of the potentially important contribution they can make to each other. (4) The constructed type and historical procedure are mutually implicated because types must be developed out of the particularities of history if they are to have genuine scientific relevance; comparative history requires a conceptual structuring for which types are admirably suited. The relationship of constructive typology to the case study is an important aspect of this problem area since description of "unitary" cases constitutes the raw material from which types are developed. The analysis will proceed by taking up these points of salient relationship in the order listed here. Our first concern is with systematic theory.

Systematic Theory

It is generally accepted that an ideal of science is to achieve a systematic interconnection of propositions. This implies a systematic interconnection of observations made of some aspect of the universe. Isolated propositions do not constitute a science. Such propositions merely create the opportunity to find the connection between them and other propositions. Such an arrangement of propositions attains coherence "as a whole." [1] It is permissible, then, to speak of a system of propositions. However, it is not merely the propositions that are responsible for system; indeed, they presuppose the existence of a body of logically interdependent generalized concepts of empirical reference. These concepts are the *categories* within the system that give rise to empirical propositions.

A theoretical system is a conceptual scheme which may be taken to mean a set of concepts standing in relation to one another, wherein each individual concept assumes meaning relative to the others. Integration of such a scheme is a matter of degree, and reflects the extent to which each concept is a function of the relationship pattern. According to Parsons, such a scheme performs two functions. [2] One consists in furnishing the *frame of reference*. This is the most general framework of categories within which empirical work takes shape and "makes sense." The second function of a conceptual scheme is to provide structural categories. This implies that in empirical reality phenomena are interrelated and thus constitute systems. Structure is then the static aspect of the descriptive treatment

[1] "The word 'system' commonly connotes an orderly arrangement or union of diverse but interrelated parts, all of which move in accordance with some form of controlling principle. The conceptual language through which the controlling principle is anchored and articulated can usually be phrased in terms of the logic of universal laws and generalizations . . . the logic of universal law including, as it must, definitions of necessary and sufficient conditions. On the basis of these definitions, we can describe the most familiar relation in a system of sociological generalizations, that of correlation or association among variables." Llewellyn Gross, "System-Construction in Sociology," *Behavioral Science*, 5 (October, 1960), p. 281.

[2] Talcott Parsons, *Essays in Sociological Theory: Pure and Applied* (Glencoe: The Free Press, 1949), pp. 18-19.

of a system. The conceptual scheme enables one to view a system "structurally" as it is composed of units and their interrelations.

Conceptual schemes as scientific systems may vary in terms of a number of different characteristics.[3] All such systems are abstract, and therefore they vary in terms of their *construction*. The characteristic of *generality* means the inclusion of many particulars or specifics under a common rubric. The question of "how general" refers to the relative number of particulars that have been subsumed under a given category. *Complexity* as a characteristic refers to the intricacy of the system in terms of the stated relations of its parts. The use of broad, general categories would mean simplicity, in contrast to the use of numerous specific categories which would make the interrelationship of the parts more complicated. The characteristic of *integration* refers to the internal unity of the system. This is manifest in the degree to which relations within it are derivable from the logical presuppositions of the system. This refers to the extent to which an alteration in relationships can be consequent upon the manipulation of a part. *Coherence* refers to the internal consistency of the system: the extent to which its elements sustain the system. *Closure* as a characteristic of a system refers to the exclusion of all concepts not definable within the framework and through the principles of the system itself. It is based upon the act of closure, which means to encompass, or shut off, and thereby establish the boundaries of the system. This is the terminal phase of the construction of the system.

Taking the above variables into consideration, one can regard a theoretical system as a body of interrelated generalized concepts based upon a coherent series of premises and assumptions that are noncontradictory in nature. The development of such theory is best exemplified by the physical sciences; this development in the social sciences is relatively primitive by comparison. Among the social

---

[3] It should be noted that within the context of this discussion we are using the term "system" to indicate the interrelation between concepts. The characteristics or attributes under discussion are those of the system as a conceptual construction. In later chapters we consistently use the term "system" to refer to the connection between the parts of substantive social systems. The present remarks are confined to the conceptual unity definable as a system.

sciences, the extension of a theoretical system in classical economics is the closest approximation. In general it may be stated that the social sciences are in what has been referred to as a "categorical system" phase of development. This means that the fields have only a fragmentary knowledge of the laws or principles of behavior that they are concerned with, but they do have a rough grasp of the general patterns of that behavior. This results in a delineation of structural categories that are not merely *ad hoc,* but are bound together in a state of interdependence that roughly fits the interdependence of the subject matter. There is an articulation of the categories commonly used that reflects the state of the phenomenon as it is empirically observed. These relations are not specified to any great degree as propositions, however, and certainly they cannot be classed as laws within the normal use of that term.

Conceptual systems seemingly can perform two major functions in addition to those pointed out above. First, they aid in the codification of our accumulating concrete knowledge. Discrete hypotheses and observations can be unified under general categories. They can be tentatively "placed" in a larger context, and consequently their "meaning" can be assessed or interpreted in the light of more general implications. Second, theory of this order can serve as a guide to research. It enables us to locate and define the areas of our knowledge and ignorance by pointing up problematic areas. In the light of a system one can "see" problems of interest and significance relative to presumed interconnections or relationships. In a sense, problems are a function of ways of looking at things, and to look at behavior from the point of view of a system of categories gives the possibility of establishing a set of hypotheses that are also interrelated. Consequently, this can increase the possibility of correlating empirical observation with theoretical systems possessing general applicability.

The importance of the theoretical system, even in its highly imperfect versions, is generally conceded in the social sciences. The development of a theoretical system is another matter, and the difficulties involved are pernicious and challenging. The constructed type is of potential utility in this area. *The constructed type can* *perform the important service of functioning as a bridge between systematic substantive theory and relatively unstructured empirical data*. As a conceptual device, the constructed type represents an attempt to advance concept formation in the social sciences from the stage of description and "empirical generalization" to the construction of theoretical systems.

It has been noted that a constructed type is not an ordinary concept, but is a *special* kind of concept. It is special in the sense that it *may* deliberately emphasize and state the ideal limits of the case. Moreover, it is special in the sense that it consists of a set of characteristics wherein the *relations between the characteristics* are held constant for the purposes at hand. Hence, the constructed type is a *system* in itself. It has the character of a descriptive model. Conceivably it can function as an analytic element in a more comprehensive theory. Thus, in a highly developed theoretical system, the constructed type can be absorbed and articulated within the more comprehensive scheme.

There is no contradiction between the formulation of systematic theory and the formulation of constructed types. Type concepts can be readily formulated *ad hoc* for innumerable empirical purposes; given the diversity of the empirical situation, the primary development and utilization of types will probably remain on this basis. To realize their full potential, however, types have to be placed in a larger context and arranged in a definite order of relationships. This is not to propose the premature imposition of classical mechanics in a situation where we need good carpenters. It is merely to suggest that types gain in both theoretical and empirical significance as they are placed in a more general scheme. The experience of Weber indicated that this cannot take place on an *ad hoc* empirical basis, but on the contrary involves the use of more general categories.[4] Weber, implicitly at least, had a generalized scheme underlying his type constructs. Social action was conceived of in terms of structural categories of social relationships and groups. Typological variation could then be stated within the structural categories. It was this implicit Weberian system that served as the primary point of departure for Parsons in his development of the structure of social action. This development indicates that although systematizing on the

---

[4] Max Weber, *The Theory of Social and Economic Organization*, translated and edited by A. M. Henderson and Talcott Parsons (New York: Oxford University Press, 1947), pp. 28-29.

constructive typological level is difficult, it is inevitable. The explanatory use of the type involves reference to elements external to it. Explanation necessarily entails putting a type in context; hence types are either theoretically or impressionistically bound to more general categories. Their appearance within these categories forces the statement of propositions regarding their relationships. System to type and type to system is a two-way developmental relationship.[5] Parsons states this succinctly as follows:

> Indeed, it is impossible to work out a systematic classification of ideal types without developing at the same time, at least implicitly, a more general theoretical system. For the relations between the types in the classification can only be stated by employing the categories that comprise such a generalized system. Thus, by virtue of the fact that maximization of economic rationality is common to them, traditional and free enterprise belong, for certain purposes, in the same class.[6]

No matter how independent it might seem, the constructed type is an initial selection of data in terms of the orientation of a given science. It is theoretically constructed as a means of defining

[5] Attention here might be called to Parsons' "pattern variables." A rather considerable amount of analysis and research has focused upon or utilized the pattern variables, some combination of them (e.g., universalism–particularism), the dilemmas of action they indicate (e.g., role–conflict), or derivative orientations (e.g., instrumental–expressive). See Allen D. Grimshaw, "Boundaries of Constructed Types," *The Sociological Quarterly*, 3 (July, 1962), pp. 179-194, for a listing and description of some of this work. Also see Talcott Parsons, "Pattern Variables Revisited," *American Sociological Review*, 25 (October, 1960), pp. 467-483. Much of the importance of this partially accumulative work resides in the fact that the types constructed at the level of problem relevance, e.g., types of voluntary associations, leadership, role enactment or conflict, etc., relate to the pattern variables as *types of orientation;* these, in turn, are integrated into the Parsonian model of the social system. Indeed, it may be asserted that the pattern variables constitute a central theme around which action within the social system is organized in the Parsons explication. The linkage between types constructed for very special or limited purposes and a macro view of society is thus established and sustained to the mutual benefit of the types (as descriptive and explanatory devices) and the systematic theory (by establishment of empirical undergirding).

[6] Talcott Parsons, *The Structure of Social Action* (Glencoe: The Free Press, 1949), pp. 618-619.

and structuring the empirical situation. Therefore it is desirable that it be related to a generalized scheme. Since it lies in the context of a substantive theory based on a given class of data, it is not interchangeable with the constructed types of other sciences. Every science has its constructed types, but they are indigenous to those sciences and to the domains of problem relevance which they represent. Further, insofar as the constructed type is articulated to a generalized scheme it serves the important function of orienting empirical research to systematic theory. This is an important step in the reduction of two types of sterility: that of the trial and error of empirically random research, and the scholasticism of system building in the abstract. The constructed type aids in lending direction to research by pointing up problematic areas that are of theoretical significance.

Systematic theory is valued in terms of its explanatory utility. This explanatory utility is scientifically bound to the procedures of empirical verification and the framework of prediction.[7] Empirical procedures directly reflect the systematic frame of reference. It is here that the constructed type fits in as a legitimate scientific instrument in the theoretically directed examination of the empirical world. On the one hand, the type is related to a conceptual scheme and hence is implicated in a theoretical context more broadly conceived than any problem under immediate consideration. On the other hand, it serves as the unit for comparison and probability statement of empirical occurrence. When used in conjunction with a suitable hypothesis it serves as a device that can bridge the gap between the interrelated set of propositions emerging out of the system of categories and the empirically occurring events. The cogent comment of Hobson should suffice to terminate this phase of the discussion:

> [The development of the conceptual scheme] . . . has actual physical experience as its essential condition, but the *constructive* and generalizing work of thought is no less essential. The original function of such a scientific theory, or conceptual scheme, is to provide an *ideal* representation of some more or less restricted range of physical phe-

[7] C. G. Hempel, "Typological Methods in the Natural and Social Sciences," *Proceedings,* American Philosophical Association; Eastern Division, 1 (1952), pp. 65-86.

nomena as actually observed, that is of certain sequences and regularities in percepts. But the functions of a conceptual scheme are much wider than those of merely describing symbolically what has actually been observed. The scheme is applied hypothetically to predict what will be observed in circumstances which differ in some degree, or in some characteristics, from those in which the experiments or observations which led up to the theory were made. The value and the range of validity of the particular conceptual scheme have to be estimated by its actual success in the fulfillment of this function of prediction.[8]

The Logic of the Experiment

Systematic theory is commonly looked upon as being the base of the deductive aspect of science. The "experimental method" is accorded the same status with regard to the inductive aspect of science. The notion of experimental procedure, however, is rather loosely used in the social sciences. Optimistic expressions regarding the application of the procedure to social data have been made many times in the history of the development of the social sciences. The term has also been applied to empirical studies wherein it is an obvious misnomer with reference to the actual procedure. One of the difficult facts that social scientists must face and live with is that the great bulk of human behavior is not susceptible to the sort of control that is the distinctive characteristic of the experimental procedure. This is not to say that the logic of the experiment is not just as important in the social as in the natural sciences; it is merely to indicate that the manipulatory control which accompanies that logic to a high degree in the latter is largely lacking in the former.

Briefly, the methodological core of the experiment is represented in the ability to isolate a set of factors or immunize them to external influence. These factors are the potential variables within the defined "boundaries" of the experiment. Next, a singly determinate change is effected with reference to one variable with all the other potential variables being held simultaneously constant. Deter-

8 E. W. Hobson, *Domain of Natural Science* (New York: Macmillan, 1923), p. 31. [Italics mine.]

minate differences in the end result are then noted. Scientific custom accordingly decrees that the variation in results was produced by the change induced in the variable. *Manipulatory* control is evident throughout in this, the prototype of the experimental procedure.

With numerous exceptions which should not be discounted, such manipulation is impossible in the realm of human behavior.[9] The social scientist frequently settles for the use of the *logic* of the experiment in his search for uniformities.[10] It is this limitation to the logic of the procedure that dictates the adherence here to Becker's definition of science, wherein the phrase "prediction of the *hypothetical* or actual recurrence of social phenomena" is used.[11] It is necessary to use the term hypothetical along with actual for the reason that much of the recurrence with which the social scientist deals is hypothetical rather than actual. The use of the *if* and *when* proviso means that certain types of results occur when certain factors combine under certain conditions. These conditions are *usually* not producible at will. The social scientist usually cannot actualize them, and if they do become actual they usually do so independently of the scientist. The social scientist is primarily a controlled *observer*, not a controlled manipulator.

As Weber and Becker have suggested, the social scientist can use the constructed type as a tool to engage in a "mental experiment" in the attempt to fulfill the *if* and *when* proviso. Weber remarks that in the absence of experimental control "there is available only the dangerous and uncertain procedure of the 'imaginary experiment' which consists in thinking away certain elements of a chain of motivation and working out the course of action which would then

---

[9] For a concise treatment of the logic of the experiment, see R. G. Francis, "Principles of Experimentation," in J. T. Doby *et al., An Introduction to Social Research* (Harrisburg: Stackpole, 1954), pp. 101-122. For excellent examples of experiments under natural conditions, see K. W. Back, Reuben Hill, and J. M. Stycos, "The Puerto Rican Experiment in Population Control," *Human Relations,* 10 (November, 1957), pp. 315-334; and Reuben Hill, J. M. Stycos, and K. W. Back, *The Family and Population Control* (Chapel Hill: University of North Carolina Press, 1959).

[10] Howard Becker points out why this is necessary, in *Through Values to Social Interpretation* (Durham: Duke University Press, 1950), pp. 102-103.

[11] See Howard Becker, "Constructive Typology in the Social Sciences," *American Sociological Review,* 5 (February, 1940), pp. 40-55.

probably ensue, thus arriving at a causal judgment."[12] Weber reached his judgment of "objective possibility" by establishing what *would* have happened *if* certain factors in the situation had operated differently. The *if* and *when* proviso is only hypothetically fulfilled.

Schelting gives a convenient summary of the steps involved in this type of causal imputation. The construction of the historical individual (the individualizing type—the thing to be explained) is presupposed. The procedure is then outlined as follows:

> (1) Analysis of this complex phenomenon (or process) in such a way that it is broken down into elements of such a character that each of them may be subsumed under a general law. . . . (2) There is presupposed previous knowledge of such general laws. (3) Hypothetical elimination or alteration of one or more factors of the process, concerning which it is wished to raise the question of its (or their) causal significance for the result. (4) Hypothetical construction of what would *then* (after the elimination or alteration) be the expected course of events (application of the category of objective possibility). (5) Comparison of the hypothetical conception of a possible development (really that which would *have been* possible had certain things happened differently) with the actual course of events. (6) On the basis of this comparison, the drawing of causal conclusions. The general principle is that, insofar as the two, the actual and the possible, courses of events differ, the difference may be causally imputed to the factor "thought away" or considered as changed. If, on the other hand, this hypothetical change fails to make a difference, the judgment is justified that the factors in question were not causally important.[13]

Briefly, the researcher, on the basis of evidence, constructs a type. This may be a type of process, structure, social organization, personality, or the like. It is then hypothesized that under given circumstances this type would probably behave in a particular fashion. The researcher next looks for the "setup" that approximates the ideal circumstances in order to effect a comparison between the construct and the empirical approximation. The differences are imputed to the factors thought away in view of the fact that they were not a part of the objectively possible pattern.

12 Weber, *op. cit.,* p. 97.

13 Alexander von Schelting as interpreted by Parsons, in *The Structure of Social Action,* pp. 610-611.

There are numerous implications in the Schelting formulation, and it is necessary to examine some of them. As the series of steps stand, they are in the tradition of some of the fundamental work in physical science, for of course the "mental" or "imaginary" experiment is quite common in all of the sciences. On the basis of points (1) and (2) it is possible to distinguish between two kinds of imaginary experiment: the *experiential* and the *derivative*.[14] The experiential type prevails in the social sciences and the derivative type prevails in the physical sciences. The diversity accounts for significant differences in validity of the results.

The derivative type of imaginary experiment presupposes a set of explicitly stated general laws. The outcome of the experiment is anticipated in terms of deductions made from those principles in combination with a set of conditions constituting the experimental situation. The experiment is imaginary in the sense that the situation it refers to cannot be technically produced. Ideal gases or pendulums or perfectly elastic impacts cannot be created for manipulatory purposes. The question of what would happen *if* an ideal pendulum were at work is not answered by thinking away the physical aspects of a pendulum at variance with the ideal, and then attempting to envisage the difference in outcome. On the contrary, the question is answered by rigorous deduction from available theoretical principles or laws.

Obviously the type of imaginary experiment envisaged by Weber and Becker cannot employ this type of deduction because the general laws are not there. The type of imaginary experiment they are concerned with is of the experiential variety. Imaginary experiments of this kind do not have deductive access to general laws that serve as the base for systematic prediction. Prediction here is guided by experience with empirical "regularities," assumed general "principles," and often in terms of assumptions and data that are not made explicit in the predictive process at all. Even the most ingenious experiential mental experiments, such as those of Weber,

[14] These two types of experiment correspond with those called *intuitive* and *theoretical* by Carl Hempel. This would seem to be an unfortunate terminology in view of the many nonscientific connotations of the word "intuitive." The terms *experiential* and *derivative* were suggested by Howard Becker. See Hempel, *op. cit.*, pp. 76-77.

cannot give results that may be considered to be compelling evidence in the strict scientific sense. The "prophecy" arrived at may be interesting, but it is of secondary importance. The method is fruitful, however, when it performs a recognizable, heuristic function. It can serve to suggest hypotheses and can give theoretical insights. It can also serve in the construction of a type that can be examined under other circumstances. Causal imputation based upon it must admittedly be extremely tentative. It must be emphasized that the difference between the experiential and derivative imaginary experiments is the relative absence or presence of theoretical laws that have independent verification. An experiential experiment may attain the status of a derivative experiment when general theory can be developed adequately accounting for the experiential experimental results. To date, of course, it has been demonstrably easier to construct types than to develop general theory in the social sciences.

Returning to the Schelting formulation, it is necessary to examine further the explanatory significance of the constructed type. Note that the final steps listed by Schelting involve a comparison of the construct and the actuality with a resultant causal imputation. Explanation is thus given on the basis of a comparison; but it must be noted that here again a significant difference exists between contemporary physical and social scientific procedure.

Typical social scientific procedure imputes cause to the factors thought away insofar as they are held accountable for the difference obtained between the hypothetical and actual. This procedure assumes that the constructed type contains within it all the relevant criteria and that the area to which the type is applicable has been clearly delineated. Although both assumptions are currently pragmatically necessary, they must be recognized as assumptions that are reached impressionistically.

It must be remembered that any constructed type is really an explanatory schema. The "structure" of the type consists in a postulated relationship between a set of criteria. This structure is an implicit theory developed on the basis of hypotheses about a problematic area. The drawing out of this theory results in the explicit statement of hypotheses about the type. What these hypotheses will be, however, is determined by the structure of the type. The type is really a hypothetical or "model" course of action, process, structure, entity, etc. What one is saying when one uses a constructed type is that this is the *expected* behavior of the sect, the ecclesia, the bureaucracy, the profession, the union man, the entrepreneur, or whatever it might be. But something different has actually happened. What factors have interfered with the expectancy? That is the question which must be answered before empirical explanation can be said to exist.

In any science, to explain an actual occurrence amounts to showing that it had to be expected in view of the presence of certain factors prior to and/or contemporaneous with it. It is here that the physical and social sciences frequently part company at the present time. In the physical sciences such explanation frequently consists in the deduction of the occurrence from general principles and limiting conditions describing the relevant antecedent and contemporaneous occurrences. The "logic" of the social scientist is the same. The difference lies in the fact that he does not have general principles to draw upon as freely, but must depend upon particular empirical uniformities. Also, he is usually not in a position to state accurately the explicit limits of the applicability of the construct he has used. The "ideal" use of the constructed type as part of a predictive schema involves a statement specifying its area of application. An empirical interpretation must be given the type, thus linking it to observable phenomena. It is not enough to say that the perfect gas exists under perfect conditions—that is a tautology. Hypotheses about the perfect gas must be stated in terms of its characteristics which can be found to be existent to varying degrees in actual gases. Similarly, statements about economically rational behavior must be stated in terms of the economic variables it is specifically concerned with, such as money, profit, utility, etc. It is only when the theoretical parameters are made explicit that the hypotheses about the construct attain full empirical import. It is then that they become susceptible to disconfirmation as well as confirmation and thus satisfy the canons of scientific explanation.

In the light of the foregoing analysis it is evident that the *logic* of the experimental procedure is as important to the social scientist as it is to those scientists possessing manipulatory control over their data. The logic of experimental procedure is the logic of the explanatory use of the constructed type. The use of the constructed type as a predictive schema demands that it be testable under empirical conditions. This means the making of *comparisons* in the sense of experimental logic. The fact that most of these comparisons must be made with reference to "naturally" occurring data, and cannot be produced at will, is a handicap to the social scientist, but it does not deny him explanation in the scientific sense.

When a constructed type is conceived of as an explanatory schema, it embodies certain empirical propositions which function as a theoretical system. Any constructed type is thus a system in its own right. Its full potential as a system has only been partially realized in the social sciences. Hempel lists the following objectives as being essential to a full realization of that potential.

> [The constructed type can serve as a theoretical system by] (a) specifying a list of characteristics with which the theory is to deal, (b) formulating a set of hypotheses in terms of those characteristics, (c) giving those characteristics an empirical interpretation, which assigns to the theory a specific domain of application, and (d), as a long-range objective, incorporating the theoretical system, as a "special case," into a more comprehensive theory.[15]

The attainment of these objectives would mean the absorption of *some* constructed types into a systematic theory where they would have the status of analytic elements. This would not mean the disappearance of constructed types, however. It would merely mean that more of them, with varying bases of abstraction, could either be profitably deduced from or inductively incorporated into the system itself, after suitable empirical construction.

Quantitative Techniques

The experiment has been identified as the prototype procedure of the inductive aspect of science. Obviously there are severe limitations involved in experimentation in the realm of social behavior. On a pragmatic basis statistical procedures are used in the social sciences in order to attain some of the advantages of

15 Hempel, *op. cit.*, p. 84.

experimental design. Consequently the relationship of quantitative technology to constructive typology is worthy of examination.

It may be asserted that *there is nothing antiquantitative in the method of constructive typology*. It has been the historical case, however, that researchers skilled in the use of the constructed type have not been strongly interested themselves in statistically validating their findings. Conversely, researchers possessing considerable statistical skill have not felt it worthwhile to inquire carefully into the presuppositions and working techniques of constructive typology. An unfortunate limitation has been placed upon the fruitfulness of social research as a result of the failure to capitalize on the complementary relationship of quantitative and typological procedures. The emergence of a number of social scientists who are procedurally competent in both typology and statistical techniques would quite probably enrich the contemporary research perspective.

One primary value of the constructed type is that it serves as a basis for *comparison* and potential *measurement* of concrete occurrences. The constructed type serves as a point of reference for the analysis of the empirically occurrent. The analysis can only proceed in terms of the *comparison* effected between the empirically occurrent and the heuristic construct. Both quantification and measurement are implicit aspects of comparison even with respect to constructs. Consequently, the adaptation of quantifying and measuring techniques to typological procedure represents its *natural* line of development. It must be noted that this has reference only to the generalizing constructed type, not to the individualizing type.

Scientific observation is concerned with qualitative distinctions and with quantitative discernments between those distinctions. The reason for this is accuracy of statement with regard to comparison. Empirical accuracy requires that one say not merely that *A* is heavier, warmer, larger, taller, more secular, more sacred, or more solidary than *B,* but that *A* is *so and so much* heavier, is *so and so much* more secular, is *so and so much* more solidary, etc., than *B.* Statements of this kind involve that aspect of quantification called measurement which is the procedure for the assignment of quantitative values to certain qualities of objects or events.

Empirical accuracy can also require that one say not merely that *A* occurs more frequently than *B*, but that *A* occurs *so and so much* more frequently than *B*. Statements of this sort entail counting, and objects or events can be counted. The process of counting culminates in "statistical" surveys. Counting and statistical surveys involve an *enumeration* of objects or events. Statements of relative frequency can then be made. Measurement and enumeration are companionate features of the *comparative* statements involving constructed types and their empirical approximations.

With respect to measurement, it must be recalled that the abstract type deviates from "reality" in that it accentuates to a pragmatic extreme some attribute or group of attributes relevant to a system of analysis. In a sense it is a simplification of the concrete, in that all occurrences will be individually different in some way from the constructed types. At some level of analysis, one will get nothing but deviations when empirical courses of action are observed. But these deviations will be relative—to each other and to the constructed type. Logically, then, the typologist is led to the problem of measurement in terms of *degree* of deviation. This is not an end in itself, for it facilitates further scientific activity. First of all, the comparison of the actual actions or structures with the typical construct will indicate the relative degree of prevalence of the typical factors and thereby indicate a degree of probability of occurrence of the typical consequences of those actions or structures. Secondly, the comparison will, through the indication of degree of prevalence of the typical factors, indicate the possible need for further constructed types on a different level of generalization so as to include more of the apparently unique in a generalized scheme. Third, the comparison of the construct with the empirical approximations should serve as a fruitful source of more specific hypotheses, which in turn will be applicable on a less generalized level.

With reference to enumeration, it must be recalled that the generalizing constructed type is applicable to varied historical and cultural contexts. The *extent* of prevalence of a given type within a given universe can often be of problematic significance to the researcher. For example, the relative *frequency* of occurrences of democratic as opposed to autocratic orientations within a concrete group can assist the typologist in interpreting the behavior of that group. Similarly the relative number of constructive, routine, impulsive and subversive followers within a movement indicates relative possibilities to the researcher with regard to the realization of the aims of the movement. Likewise, the relative frequency of manifestations of rational behavior as contrasted to valuational, traditional, or affectual behavior within various concrete groups gives the analyst the ability to make significant comparative statements about the value and action systems of those groups.

Whatever may be said about the constructed type it must be clearly understood that it is not antiquantitative in nature; indeed, the realization of its scientific potential seemingly binds it to quantitative procedures. The reduction of the role of "impression" in the approach of the constructive typologist would seem to be related to the development of his ability to harness and utilize quantitative techniques. The constructed type is a theoretically plausible course of action or structure which has been *constructed* on the basis of observed empirical occurrences. It is the concept of statistical probability that enables the typologist to avoid the false reification of his construct. It is the concept of probability that puts an empirical interpretation upon the constructed type and bridges the gap between the heuristic device and the empirical occurrence.[16] The generalizations based upon the constructed type are always probability statements. For example, Weber cast his statements in the form of "typical changes for the expectation of a certain course of action under the presence of certain conditions."[17] Both enumeration and measurement are implicit in such a formulation.

Statistical control is a desirable adjunct of the constructed type, for it enhances the predictive power of the theoretical device. The constructed type isolates the behavior that is theoretically significant. It does not in itself say anything about the frequency of that behavior; that is a function of enumeration. Any numerical

---

[16] Attention is directed to the scheme propounded by Howard Becker for empirically examining hypotheses about types. It takes the form: "If P, then Q, and if Q', then P'." See *Through Values to Social Interpretation,* pp. 262-275.

[17] Theodore Abel, *Systematic Sociology in Germany* (New York: Columbia University Press, 1929), p. 146.

statement about degree of deviation is a function of measurement. Whatever statistical controls are used, however, are put on the empirical data that the type has reference to, not on the type itself, although the attributes composing the type may be reached quantitatively. The criteria of the constructed type are assumed to be structurally interrelated. The relations that obtain between the elements of the type are postulated, and hence the type is a system that need not be manipulated. The way in which it can be held accountable for empirical variation is through the extraction of subtypes that isolate lesser universes for statistical manipulation. Quantitative methods can be applied in the empirical validation of the predictions based on the type, but not to the type itself.

From the foregoing exposition it should be evident that the constructive typologist and the statistician stand on the threshold of an important research relationship. At base both adhere to experimental and probability logic; hence there is apparently nothing except time and effort that stands between them and a fruitful cooperative procedural relationship. It must be frankly admitted, however, that such a relationship has been slow in developing. Constructive typology is still largely in a prequantitative state. In certain phases of typological procedure this must always be so, since one of the prime values of the approach is that it enables the scholar to work in areas of limited and fragmentary knowledge and accomplish an initial cognitive mapping of the area. On the other hand, it is clearly desirable that scholarly work in these areas be refined through the utilization of all available and appropriate techniques. Historically there have been several cases where typological and quantitative techniques have been used in successful conjunction. For illustrative purposes two such contributions will be cited here. These are relatively "old" studies but they are deliberately chosen, since a vast and important literature has grown up around each work.

One of the pioneer usages of social statistics was that of Durkheim in his study of suicide.[18] His enumeration in that study had

---

[18] Emile Durkheim, *Suicide*, translated and edited by George Simpson (Glencoe: The Free Press, 1950).

reference to constructed types.[19] He distinguishes four types of suicide which spring from peculiarities in the relations between the individual and society. "Altruistic," "egoistic," "anomic," and "fatalistic" are constructed sociological types. The altruistic type of suicide refers to the case wherein the individual is so immersed in his social relationships that his own life counts for little. This is a self-sacrificing type of suicide. On the other hand, egoistic suicide springs out of the opposite situation. It is a self-asserting type of suicide emergent out of a social system stressing individuality. Fatalistic suicide derives from excessive regulation in the form of oppressive discipline. Aspirations and passions are so blocked and choked off by an inflexible order that life has no holding power.[20] Standing opposite the fatalistic is the sociologically intriguing anomic type. This is a type reflecting the "normlessness" of a society. There is confusion with regard to the standards of behavior and the equilibrium is upset. The stability of the individual is seen as reflecting his ability to preserve his customary standards and thus his social role.

Utilizing these types it was then possible for Durkheim quantitatively to check their rate in various concrete groups. For instance he shows the suicide rate is higher among Protestants than among Catholics and interprets this as being due to the fact that Protestantism stresses individuality more and puts more responsibility on individuals than some of them can bear. Mother Church encompasses the Catholic, whereas the Protestant faces God alone. The result is a higher incidence of egoistic suicide among Protestants.

Durkheim's verification of the anomic suicide is largely based upon the correlation between suicide and the business cycle. Peaks

[19] The following is an *interpretive* explication rather than a literal exposition of the work of Durkheim on suicide. Durkheim primarily presents correlations of suicide rates with outside factors. Some of them are interpreted as "anomic," "egoistic," etc., but his data are always of the same correlational nature. His focus of attention was not explicitly or primarily on the types of suicide, as is the case in the following commentary.

[20] The fatalistic type is not a part of the main scheme. See Durkheim, *op. cit.*, p. 276, for a brief treatment.

as well as troughs indicate an absolute increase in suicides. Loss of money is obviously disturbing and makes life intolerable for some people. Durkheim points out that the opposite can also be true. Sudden access to fortune can cause as much stress as the loss of fortune. This can only be interpreted as meaning that people are closely fitted into their social niches and the drastic alteration of a style of life is in itself intolerable for some people. Anomic suicide as a societal current thus reflects the relative normlessness or flux of standards in society.

This brief treatment of Durkheim's suicidal currents should merely serve to illustrate the possibility of enumerating concrete cases in concrete groups and relating them to heuristic types. This amounts to saying that certain suicides may be considered to be empirical approximations of a given type, and hence may be considered to be "identical for the purpose in hand." [21] When variation of type incidence in various groups can be detected, then the analyst is in a position to make certain general statements about those groups. The heuristic type has been given an empirical interpretation through enumeration of relative frequency.

With reference to measurement, certain things have been done that show promise for users of the constructed type. It is the peculiar advantage of the constructed type that it readily lends itself to statement in the form of polar antitheses. Types may be, and frequently are, constructed so as to constitute the outer limits of a conceptual continuum. In such a case the problem of measurement of the constructed type is the familiar problem of the continuum. When a continuum is assumed its character must be demonstrably probable. The *scaling* of the continuum is the most efficient way of demonstrating the "continuum character" of the construction.[22] Scaling consequently offers considerable promise to

[21] The constructed type is obviously not a "class"; nevertheless it can serve a classificatory function.

[22] There are a number of significant efforts which have been made in relation to this matter; two examples will be cited here. Daniel Lerner utilized latent structure analysis to determine the soundness of his original typology of societies as presented in *The Passing of Traditional Society* (Glencoe: The Free Press, 1958). See the Appendix of his volume for this post-analysis. He comments that "LSA did verify the existence of the latent attribute which we call 'style of life'; and it permitted the identification of three rank orders—

the constructive typologist in the matter of enabling him to make statements of *degree* of deviance from the ideal limits of a case. Much of the work done by scholars interested in scaling involves the implicit usage of constructed types. Such well-known distinctions as liberal–conservative, progressive–traditionalist, democratic–autocratic, introvert–extrovert, and numerous others are of this character. A continuum is comprehensible only in terms of its limits; hence the necessity for the constructed type.

The following scaling adaptation of the constructed type clearly indicates the potential in this area. The Allport–Vernon *Study of Values* aims to measure the relative prominence of six basic interests or motives in personality: the *theoretical, economic, aesthetic, social, political,* and *religious*.[23] These types are recognizable as being Spranger's types of men.[24] Spranger defends the view that the personalities of men are best known through a study of their values or evaluative attitudes. These types are then ideal value perspectives and the problem becomes one of determining

Traditional, Transitional, Modern—along a single basic scale composed of all five factors in our typology" (p. 439).

Another notable scaling venture regarding typology was undertaken by Linton Freeman and Robert Winch, in "Societal Complexity: An Empirical Test of a Typology of Societies," *American Journal of Sociology*, 62 (March, 1957), pp. 461-466. They examined the very basic question as to whether or not societal complexity constitutes a single dimension that falls along a continuum as implied by all the major polar typologies of society, e.g., *Gemeinschaft und Gesellschaft* (Tönnies), mechanical and organic (Durkheim). Their procedure involved drawing data on forty-eight societies from the Human Relations Area Files and scoring according to Guttman's scalogram analysis. Six of the eight variables they subjected to test varied along a continuum and constituted a technically acceptable scale. Their conclusion was that, "Since these qualities [the six scalable items] are all subsumable under folk–urbanism, *Gemeinschaft-Gesellschaft,* and other polar constructs of that order, the conclusion is that Redfield, Tönnies, *et al.* have indeed been describing a unidimensional phenomenon—societal complexity. Furthermore, this analysis has established a series of scale types or positions of societal complexity . . . which may be used to describe or arrange societies, as well as merely to sensitize observers, as some have claimed" (p. 464).

23 G. W. Allport, P. E. Vernon, and Gardner Lindzey, *Study of Values* (rev. ed.; New York: Houghton Mifflin, 1951).

24 Edward Spranger, *Types of Men*, translated by Paul Pigors (New York: Stechert-Hafner, 1928).

degree of deviance from them on the part of individuals identified with different concrete groups.

The Allport–Vernon test consists of a number of questions based upon a variety of familiar controversial situations wherein either two of four alternative answers are provided. An equal number of questions on the test refer to each of the value perspectives. The subject records his preferences numerically by the side of each alternative answer. His score is then determined. Norms are established for different concrete groups, and significant differences are demonstrated with regard to their value perspectives. Table 1 indi-

TABLE 1

Illustrative Occupational Differences	Theoretical	Economic	Aesthetic	Social	Political	Religious
53 Students of Engineering (male)	46.62* 6.97**	45.79 7.66	37.25 8.43	34.70 7.37	43.08 8.12	32.59 10.13
173 Students of Business Administration (male)	42.09* 6.36**	49.25 7.69	32.58 7.34	35.16 5.96	45.68 5.96	35.24 8.42
93 Students of Medicine (male)	50.68* 7.52**	33.90 9.18	44.83 9.85	38.12 8.45	38.86 6.80	33.48 11.70
68 Graduate Students of Education (male)	44.31* 8.30**	37.14 8.29	43.76 9.34	41.98 7.27	39.17 6.22	33.64 10.63
24 Clergymen	37.07* 6.44**	27.12 5.93	35.54 7.01	43.67 4.95	38.57 4.17	58.07 3.84
15 Theological Students	35.67* 5.82**	27.40 7.16	40.73 7.97	45.20 5.79	36.80 4.74	54.20 5.97

Source of table: Allport, Vernon, and Lindzey, *op. cit.,* p. 9.

* The means on the above table are horizontally in line with the single asterisks.

** The standard deviations on the above table are horizontally in line with the double asterisks.

cates the various value norms (means and standard deviations) with reference to different groups of college students. A glance will indicate that students of engineering and medicine are more theoretically oriented than theological students. Students of engineering and business administration are more economically oriented than students of medicine, education, and theology. Theological students are more socially oriented than students of engineering and business administration, and so on. One can state a different value expectancy with reference to each concrete group on the basis of the scaling of the deviance from the constructed value types.

The preceding examples of enumeration and measurement are given merely to illustrate the possibility of eventually quantifying predictions made from constructed types. The utility and predictive value of the generalizing constructed type would unquestionably be enhanced if quantifying procedures were followed *whenever it was feasible*.

Historiography and Case Study

The relationship between typological and statistical procedures shows promise of becoming increasingly fruitful. It has been repeatedly noted, however, that quantification is always quantification of *something*. Statements as to what that something is involve description of the empirically occurrent and qualitatively distinguishable. It is here that the data of the historian are of importance to the typologist, and where a common basis of the generalizing typological and historical procedures constitutes an important convergence of social scientific and historical methodology.[25]

There is a distinction, however obscure and ambiguous at times, between social-scientific and historical procedure, for their procedures answer to their respective research purposes. All data are historical; consequently the data of history and science are the

[25] See Geoffrey Barraclough, "Scientific Method and the Work of the Historian," in Ernest Nagel *et al.* (editors), *Logic, Methodology and Philosophy of Science* (Stanford: Stanford University Press, 1962), pp. 584-594, for a recent examination of the relations between history, "scientific history," the social sciences, and scientific thought generally.

same. The difference between the disciplines lies in what they do with the data.[26] In typological terms, the research task of the scientist is to generalize and that of the historian is to individualize. Both are legitimate enterprises and play important roles in the accumulation and interpretation of knowledge. No confusion need exist between them at the level of typification of their procedural styles, although it seems inevitable that there should be considerable "overlap" at the level of addressing particular problems.

No serious quarrel can be made with the proposition that all objects or events are unique in time and space. Such a thesis need not involve the argument that objects or events are *merely* temporal and that they can be known only in their uniqueness, with their time and space markings clearly evident.[27] On the contrary it is possible through the use of conceptual constructs to conceive of the identical, recurrent, and the typical. History is "even-structured" for both the historian and the social scientist; events not only can be viewed chronologically and individually, but also as relationship series involving necessary and sufficient antecedents of consequents. Such conditions and consequents can be categorized, and types and the relations involved can be abstractly stated as general relations. It is thus the perspectives of the historian and the social scientist which differ.

The field of the historian is the whole range of human activi-

[26] The following comment by Barraclough is intended to represent the prevailing attitude of the historical profession: ". . . I share the horror felt by the historical profession as a whole at what seems to us to be the attitude of social scientists to history. It seems to us that, for them, history is only material to be processed, and that they regard historians as purveyors of material for them to process; which, if true, reveals in our view a total misunderstanding of the abstruse and complex nature of historical 'fact.' Social scientists, we believe, are prepared to manipulate historical data in ways which historians regard as illegitimate; they seek results which we do not consider the material, of its nature, is capable of giving." *Ibid.*, p. 585.

[27] There is, of course, a long-standing tradition, based primarily in German historicism stemming from the idealistic mode of thought, which resists any "generalizing" due to the "uniqueness" and "individuality" of "actual history." For modern expressions of this perspective, see K. R. Popper, *The Poverty of Historicism* (London: Routledge and Kegan Paul, 1957), and Isaiah Berlin, *Historical Inevitability* (London: Oxford University Press, 1954).

ties. The social sciences in their division of labor cover the same range. But whereas the historian is concerned with processes and structures that are singular in their space–time occurrence and does not conceive of them as being repeatable, the social scientist adopts the opposite perspective.[28] The social scientist is concerned with the repetitive and constant factors, or tendencies of regularity of human society. For example, a sociologist may try to determine and state the recurrent aspects involved in the process of urbanization; the historian, on the other hand, will try to state the specific course which urbanization has taken in a given place over a given period of time. This is another way of saying that the sociologist attempts to extract whatever is "universal" from the phenomenon, whereas the historian attempts to expose the relevant "particulars" on one case of the phenomena. Relative to this point Rickert writes: " 'that the most comprehensive generalizing concept of natural science would represent its objects in the simplest possible form, whereas the most comprehensive individualizing concept of history would have to comprise the greatest possible heterogeneity of historically significant elements.' " [29]

To approach the problem from a different perspective, it is possible to assert that there is no such thing as a "knife-edge present," for the present can be comprehended only in terms of events, and any event has a temporal spread. Any given event has its antecedent conditions and thus has a past that it is bound to, and is implicated in a future that is in part responsible for the course of action. The delineation of a present from the historical continuity of which it is a part is accomplished only through the conceptualization of events. What is then *called* the past is "history" and what is *called* the present is "contemporary," but there is no intrinsic difference between them. They are constituted of the same "stuff."

From the foregoing it is evident that historical and scientific data are identical; for instance, each science has its own historical

[28] See Hans Meyerhoff, *The Philosophy of History in Our Time* (New York: Anchor Books, 1959), p. 203 *passim*.

[29] Quoted in Alexander Goldenweiser, "Relationship of Natural Science to Social Science," in H. E. Barnes, Howard Becker, and F. B. Becker (editors), *Contemporary Social Theory* (New York: Appleton Century, 1940), p. 101.

development, and each body of scientific knowledge has emerged historically. The difference in the disciplines lies not in the data, but in their *perspectives, problems, procedures,* and *techniques.*[30] Granted this, it is entirely justifiable, and indeed necessary, that the social scientist concern himself with data which are unquestionably historical. History is not merely the business of the historian, but is also of crucial concern to the social scientist, for it offers him a wealth of material that must be accounted for in his "general" formulations.

It is neither appropriate nor legitimate for the social scientist to refuse to consult data merely because it is considered to be "historical." If his formulations are truly general they must stand the test of time. Their generality lies not only in the removal of spatial markings, but in the removal of temporal markings. The society of today is intimately related to the society of yesterday and the days and years preceding. To get at processes and structures that are not merely unique, it is necessary to examine them in the light of the data of history. It must be remembered that social phenomena cannot in most cases be experimentally produced by the observer. Social phenomena usually cannot be deliberately created for purposes of further examination and manipulation. The social scientist must by and large accept his data as they naturally occur.[31] Consequently it is essential that he utilize whatever data fits the "if and when" setup of his predictive schema, regardless of when it occurred.

As Becker has pointed out, prediction can be either *retrospective* or *prospective.*[32] In other words, the typical conditions, factors, and emergent phenomena may be searched for in the data of his-

---

[30] "Historians as a body have done little to clarify the position of their work in relation to science and to scientific method. Their attitude for the most part is that of craftsmen who are suspicious of theory and are perfectly satisfied with the product of their trade." Barraclough, *op. cit.,* p. 584.

[31] See William Dray, "The Historian's Problem of Selection," in Ernest Nagel, *et al., op. cit.,* pp. 595-603, for an examination of the differences involved in the selection of both data and problems by the historian and the generalizing social scientist. See also Ernest Nagel, "The Logic of Historical Analysis," in Herbert Feigl and May Brodbeck (editors), *The Philosophy of Science* (New York: Appleton-Century-Crofts, 1953), pp. 688-700.

[32] See Howard Becker, *Through Values to Social Interpretation,* pp. 285-290.

tory as well as in that of the contemporary or future scene. For example, on the basis of a hypothesis a type of leadership can be constructed. One can then look for the situations in history that meet the "if and when" requirements, and check for verification or refutation of the initial hypothesis. If charismatic leadership is to be a genuine sociological construct, then it must have applicability to leaders outside of a given epoch. It explains the position of a Jesus or a Mohammed as well as that of a Hitler or a Mussolini. The prediction involved is based upon events that have already occurred, but all events that are comprehensible have already occurred. Retrospective prediction is entirely legitimate in that it involves relatively timeless processes and structures. This type of prediction also serves to illustrate the fact that a social scientist cannot prophesy the occurrence of a given phenomenon at a given time, because the factors and conditions essential to the occurrence of the phenomenon are beyond the control of the social scientist. He can merely state conditional occurrence in terms of typical action. The constructed type makes a contribution here in that it serves warning to the social scientist to abide by the limitations of his "if and when" proviso. This demands the avoidance of the unjustifiable habit of prophesying on the empirical level and requires greater expenditure of effort toward statement of prediction in probability terms on the typical level.

Merton makes the following critical remarks about the validity of retrospective prediction:

> *Post factum* explanations remain at the level of *plausibility* (low evidential value) rather than leading to "compelling evidence" (a high degree of confirmation). . . .

> The logical fallacy underlying the *post factum* explanation rests in the fact that there is available a variety of crude hypotheses, each with some measure of confirmation but designed to account for quite contradictory sets of affairs. The method of *post factum* explanation does not lend itself to nullifiability, if only because it is so completely flexible. . . . The analysis is fitted to the facts, and there is no indication of just which data would be taken to contravene the interpretations. As a consequence, the documentary evidence merely illustrates rather than tests the theory.[33]

[33] R. K. Merton, "Sociological Theory," *American Journal of Sociology*, 50 (May, 1945), pp. 468-469.

The preceding statement applies to explanation based upon the use of individualizing types. It is a statement that also has reference to what can happen to the generalizing constructed type when its area of applicability is not clearly stated. With regard to the individualizing type it is seemingly impossible to overcome the problem of nullifiability. That is why it would be so difficult to negate such a hypothesis as Max Weber's connection of Protestant and capitalistic ethics. Alternative hypotheses cannot be readily dispensed with; hence any hypothesis based upon individualizing types has low evidential value.

With regard to the generalizing construct, however, the situation is different. When the parameters of the constructed type are clearly stated, the internal criteria of the type made explicit, and the hypothesis properly qualified, explanation based upon the generalizing construct can constitute compelling evidence. One does not look explicitly for the *type* in history, although admittedly as short-cut procedure one frequently looks for approximations when a type has already been formulated. Ideally, however, one looks for the "if and when" setup. If a setup satisfying the requirements of a given constructed type is found and the consequent behavior is not in some degree of accordance with that which is hypothesized on the basis of the type, then the hypothesis may be considered to be inadequate if not nullified. Because the behavior cannot be in *exact* accordance with the behavior of the construct there is a necessity for statements involving relative degree of accordance. Since several empirical cases can be examined and compared, due to the general character of the construct, it is possible to demand a high degree of consistent and general accordance with the expected behavior. If it is not found, one is forced to reformulate the hypothesis and devise a substitute type or types that will expose consistent regularities in the empirical behavior.

Neither a type nor a hypothetical course of action based upon it can be sacred to the scientist. The justification for the existence of a constructed type is that it can serve to expose empirical regularities; if it does not do so, it can have no real utility. The ultimate test of the constructed type is that of the instrument. It has to pass the pragmatic test of being useful as an instrument.

Returning again to the distinction between historical and scientific objectives, it is legitimate to say that the historical approach is concerned ideally with a description of the particular and unique aspects of a given phenomenon. On the other hand, the scientific approach is concerned ideally with the *comparable, repetitive,* and *typical* aspects of phenomena. The type constructs that enable the social scientist to conceive of phenomena in this light are *necessarily* woven out of the particularities of the historian. The historian has much to offer the social scientist in view of the fact that the scientific constructs presuppose a knowledge of the particulars from which they are drawn.

It must be noted that a generalizing constructed type can be drawn legitimately from only two different places. It can be *derived* from theory or more general types that have already received substantial empirical verification, or it can be *constructed* directly from the particulars of a historical situation. In view of the limited character of theory available in the social sciences, the latter case is most frequent and most desirable. The "derivation" of the "principal types of social structure" by Parsons is an excellent example of the inadequacy of type derivation too far removed from the empirical world.[34] Constructed types are at their working best when they can be *articulated* with a substantial theoretical scheme; but whether or not such a scheme exists it is essential laboriously to proceed from the particularities. In such cases, the construct cannot be deliberately designed with generality as the primary aim. The construction of the individualizing type—the historical individual or thing to be examined—is the necessary first step. The logic of induction requires this.

Once the type has been constructed it is then possible and advisable to check its applicability to other epochs and cultures. The

[34] Talcott Parsons, *The Social System* (Glencoe: The Free Press, 1951), pp. 180-200. The material presented in this chapter seriously mars what in most other respects has to be considered one of the major works in the history of sociological development. The "derivation" process adhered to by Parsons left us with a very dubious and artificial typology of social structure that adds little if anything to our knowledge of or capacity to explore society. Contrast this with the laborious and increasingly fruitful efforts of such scholars as Merton, Blau, Gouldner, Stinchcomb, and Udy to explicate, modify, and qualify the original Weberian formulation of bureaucracy as a basic type of social structure.

original Troeltsch church–sect formulation which has achieved increasingly general significance through its application to diverse phenomena in various studies is an example of this kind of application.[35] Likewise, it is possible to construct devices such as economic, scientific, or academic man, but their areas of applicability cannot be determined ahead of time. Obviously there are numerous *time* and *place* restrictions on their applicability. Most of recorded history as well as many contemporary cultures are immune to analyses based upon these types. It is nonsense to talk of economic man (and the presumptions entailed) with reference to typical behavior prior to the emergence of capitalism. It is likewise nonsense to speak of scientific man with reference to primitive societies, or of academic man prior to the emergence of the occupational role upon which it is based. Constructs cannot ignore facts; on the contrary, they must account for facts. Clearly, then, the historian with his facts has much to offer the social scientist in the way of data and preliminary formulations.[36] Among the formulations, the "case

[35] Such a concept as the "sect," for instance, has been applied in the study of such diverse phenomena as religious orientation, religion and power, acculturation, secularization, and social movements. See C. Y. Glock, "The Sociology of Religion," in R. K. Merton *et al., Sociology Today* (New York: Basic Books, 1959), pp. 153-177, for an extensive review of the church-sect typology in its various forms and usages.

[36] The following comment by Spengler is not only relevant to the economist, but to social scientists generally: "The contributions of the historian to the economist's understanding of economic behavior are thus at least three in number. (a) He can supply particularized information respecting the past functioning and the natural and evolutionary history of man's culture and institutions from the point of view of their influence upon man's economic behavior. (b) He can alert the economist to the frequent importance of those very *particularities* which his methods of analysis often cause him to gloss over or to ignore. (c) Economists frequently have attempted to formulate laws of growth and change. They have pretended to discover invariant cultural lags, the allegedly overwhelming influence of technological change, interclass relations, etc. Marx and Veblen were but two among many. The historian is well-equipped to make the economist aware of the empirical limitations, or factual invalidity, of the propositions out of which such theories of economic change tend to be constructed." J. J. Spengler, "Generalists Versus Specialists in Social Science: An Economist's View," *American Political Science Review,* 44 (June, 1950), p. 373.

study" is perhaps the single most important area of historical and
social scientific convergence.

The relationship of the constructed type to the case study is
essentially the same as to the historical approach in general. It is
doubtful that the study of cases should be called a method at all.
The study of cases is an essential aspect of science and is preliminary to the formulation of types and generalizations.[37] The case
study is a way of ordering social data with the view of preserving
the unitary character of whatever is being studied. It merely selects
out and treats some socially defined object or act as a *whole*. This
whole constitutes the case unit, and the case unit may involve any
level or base of abstraction. The case may be a person, an episode
in a person's life, a group, a concrete set of relationships, a specific
process, a culture; it includes any aspect of the empirical world
reacted to as a unit. The function of the case study is to describe
the case in terms of the particularities that are observable. This
means the intensive examination of the specific factors implicated
in the case.

The wholeness or unitary character ascribed to this concrete
case is a constructed wholeness. There are no concrete limits to
any object or act. The limits imposed reflect the perspective and
theoretical interest of the observer. The limits defining an individual may be "dissolved" when one is observing from the perspective
of the group. In turn, the limits defining the group may be dissolved
when one is conceptualizing in terms of a social order. All units
are thus constructs, delineated for pragmatic purposes within the
limits of empirical occurrence. Whatever unit has been abstracted
out may be examined and described in its uniqueness. This is what
the historian and the ethnographer do, and the descriptive work
that they produce constitutes important data to the social scientist
interested in generalizing.

Whatever unit has been abstracted out is temporally and spatially bound. It has a particular historical development and is a
unique configuration. This unit may be described as a case by an
indefinite number of facts. These facts may be obtained from many

[37] See Howard Becker, "Culture Case Study and Ideal-Typical Method,"
Social Forces, 12 (March, 1934), pp. 399-405.

diverse sources, depending upon what the case is. They may be obtained from documents, life histories, from the individual, from informants in a group, from participant observation—from all the avenues open to the historian and the ethnographer. The imputation of these facts to the case merely describe; they do not have explanatory value in the comparative sense.

It is here that the social scientist with his procedure of constructive typology can make his special contribution. For instance, the sociologist may be interested in the repetitive characteristics and uniform relations involved in revolutions. He desires theoretically to predict revolutions by use of the "if and when" proviso. This involves statements of uniformity and regularity with respect to revolutions. Such statements are based upon answering questions with regard to typical elements and sequences occurrent in revolutions in general. The ability of the sociologist to make such statements and answer such questions is based upon his ability to construct types on the basis of intensive examination of specific revolutions as empirical cases.

On the basis of his familiarity with empirical uniformities appearing in a thoroughly described case or several cases pragmatically classified as being similar, the constructive typologist erects a model revolution, which in effect is a type. Initially this type will be dated and localized as an historic individual and closely resembles the empirical case or type. The collection of such dated and localized types is representative of the first step toward generalization. Types of revolution that are relatively free from time and space markings can only be developed by accumulating these dated and localized types and modifying them to make them applicable to more and more empirical cases on a comparative basis. This means that the type becomes increasingly generalized and can consequently explain an increasingly wider range of cases of revolution.

In brief, the case is an abstraction. The case study preserves the unity of that abstraction and involves the accumulation of facts describing it in its particularity. The individualizing constructed type marks a first step away from the uniqueness of the case, in that it selectively pulls out what seem to be significant uniformities. This type is temporally and spatially bound. The attempt to free it from these bonds involves the examination of other empirical cases with the view of modifying the type or types to represent ideal manifestations of a variety of cases. The constructed type is thus inductively established as a model and basis for comparing and generalizing empirical cases.

The preceding analysis has attempted the task of making explicit the relations, actual and potential, between constructive typology, systematic theory, and experimental, quantitative, and historical procedures. As an *exploratory* analysis it has obviously included considerable speculation and utilized interpretive leeway. It has perhaps made the fundamental point, however, that it is essential that we continually concern ourselves with these relations if greater methodological order is to be achieved in the social research process. This analysis is put forward, therefore, as another minimal bench mark that presumably can function as a point of departure for future, more refined analyses of intrarelations in the social research process. Despite its exploratory character, the present analysis should suffice to establish the point that constructive typology has a vital role in the total research process that has been only partially exploited. A fuller exploitation of that role would seemingly be of genuine benefit, both substantively and methodologically, to the social sciences.

—4

Constructive Typology Within the Context of Modern Sociology

As indicated earlier, the process of typification, involving the utilization of some form of typological procedure, is virtually universal. The social sciences in general rely very heavily on types and typological procedures in their endeavors. Nevertheless, it is the discipline of sociology which has devoted the most effort in attempting to clarify the nature of the typing process. Formal consideration of the problems related to the derivation, construction, and utilization of typologies has been heavily concentrated in sociology ever since the turn of the century. Originally this was a focal point of interest and analysis on the part of the German sociologists and was an aspect of their flourishing work in the first quarter of this century. The transfer of German intellectual interests to the United States in the period starting approximately after World War I gradually transferred primary concern with the methodological issues surrounding typological procedure to American sociology. The transfer involved an input from the American scholars trained in Germany during that period, an increased utilization of the German literature expedited considerably by the translations of the "great works" in the thirties and forties, and by the increased importation of German scholars to America during the Hitlerian period. These factors, coupled with the rapid growth and development, and more importantly with the evolution of a particular style in American sociology since World War I, established a new "home" for the consideration of typological problems.

It is asserted here that typological procedure can be most ef- fectively understood, developed and refined if approached as an aspect of a pragmatic research methodology. This pragmatic orien- tation has been visibly characteristic of American sociology for many years. American sociology, of course, has many other characteristics since it has increasingly become a very complex enterprise. An understanding of the status and potential development of typologi- cal procedure will perhaps be facilitated by an examination of the context within which it has persisted as *one among many* method- ological devices. In 1919 Bushnell made the following comment on the state of sociology:

> The working equipment of sociology up to this date often looks more like a museum full of curios than a workshop full of tools; and such is necessarily largely the fact: for as a new science, sociol- ogy has been engaged extensively in raking together things that might prove useful in constructing a better social order, rather than accurately adapting the materials assembled.[1]

To the layman and people in other disciplines this might seem to be the case today, but the professional sociologist knows that his discipline has come a long way in the intervening period. The so- ciologist not only has a workshop full of tools to perform tasks which were impossible in 1919, but there also is emerging an organizational pattern, or methodology, that is less fragmentary and *ad hoc* than formerly.

The growth of substantive disciplines has always been closely related to the development of *methodology,* refinement of *procedure,* and proliferation of *techniques.* A plenitude of research techniques does not in itself guarantee substantive expansion, but it does repre- sent an indispensable prerequisite of that expansion. The increased emphasis on methodology, procedure, and technique in sociology in recent decades is an unmistakable sign of maturation. It is obvious that sociology has accumulated an enormous amount of substantive material during these years, but more important from the long-

[1] C. J. Bushnell, "Scientific Method in Sociology," *American Journal of Sociology,* 25 (July, 1919), pp. 45-46.

range perspective of becoming an eminent scholarly field, it has made significant methodological progress.

Methodology may be viewed as consisting of the principles of investigative procedure: the norms by means of which procedures and techniques are selected and articulated.[2] Methodology must be distinguished from sociological theory, which has as its subject matter certain aspects of the interaction of people and hence is substantive in character. Methodological and substantive theory are closely associated but not identical. Since methodology in most respects is not bound up with peculiarly sociological problems, it therefore transcends any body of substantive theory. The problems of methodology are usually common to a group of disciplines, those of a more general character being common to all scientific procedure. Sociologists must be methodologically competent in that they have to have an understanding of the design of investigation, the norms of procedure, the nature of inference, or the nature of appropriate use of theoretic systems, but these skills do not determine the *content* of any theory or study. Methodology essentially answers the question of "how"; substantive theory answers the question of "what." It is in the area of "how" that the sociologists have made their most salient gains in the modern epoch.

The development of methodology has not occurred in a unitary fashion; on the contrary, broad frontal movements have been made that are radically divergent. Several distinctive trends are discernible, but their theoretical opposites are also represented. Developments have come from very different positions; hence methodology has many ambivalent characteristics. These differences constitute "polarities" or typifications in the overall approach of sociologists to their subject matter, and consequently can be conceived as a series of continua along which methodological convergence develops between the opposing or polar types.

The continua representing the major methodological trends

2 A careful distinction must be made here between what a social scientist is doing when he is acting as a *methodologist* and when he is adhering to a methodology while pursuing a substantive inquiry. In the former case he is explicating a procedure, while in the latter case he is explicating a substantive problem by means of adherence to the prescriptions and proscriptions implied in the established norms of social research. See Julius Gould and William L. Kolb (editors), *A Dictionary of the Social Sciences* (New York: The Free Press of Glencoe, 1964), entry entitled "Methodology," pp. 425-426.

are those of empiricism–rationalism, neopositivism–anti-positivism, induction–deduction, quantitative–qualitative, and idiographic–nomothetic. On the basis of analysis, it is concluded that the strong tendency toward the empirical, positivistic, inductive, quantitative, and idiographic poles has produced a complex responsible for the convergence of several subsidiary trends that are treated here as unitary subtypes of that complex. They are behaviorism, operationism, and pragmatism.

Rampant and Modified Empiricism

Some of the methodological issues that have troubled sociology have become obsolescent, whereas others have been more persistent. One of the persistent polarities is evident in the relative roles of empiricism and rationalism as approaches to sociological knowledge. Empiricism became dominant soon after World War I, and during the twenties and thirties rationalism almost completely capitulated. It was the University of Chicago which was dominant in sociological circles during the twenties. The "Chicago school" played a tremendous part in encouraging the development of empiricism. Robert E. Park, probably the most influential figure in the Department in the development of its famous style, made the following comment to a group of students.

> You have been told to go grubbing in the library, thereby accumulating a mass of notes and a liberal coating of grime. You have been told to choose problems wherever you can find musty stacks of routine records based on trivial schedules prepared by tired bureaucrats and filled out by reluctant applicants for aid or fussy do-gooders or indifferent clerks. That is called "getting your hands dirty in real research." Those who thus counsel you are wise and honorable; the reasons they offer are of great value. But one thing more is needful: first-hand observation. Go and sit in the lounges of the luxury hotels and on the doorsteps of the flophouses; sit on the Gold Coast settees and on the slum shakedowns; sit in Orchestra Hall and in the Star and Garter Burlesk. In short, gentlemen, go get the seat of your pants dirty in *real* research.[3]

[3] Unpublished statement made by Robert E. Park and recorded by Howard Becker while a graduate student at Chicago in the twenties.

The advice seems effectively to express the rising sentiment of the era. The mid-forties, however, witnessed something of a rationalistic revival that at the present time can be interpreted as a distinct modification of radical empiricism, and a re-equilibration in a modified empiricism.

Empiricism is a label for a way of thinking and working with data. It indicates an attitude complex characterized by an utmost faith in the senses, a firm belief in the power of observation, a willingness to be ruled by observable evidence, a belief that scientific conclusions should never get beyond the realm of extrapolation, and a feeling that the rational universe of science is nothing more than the habitual association of certain ideas of a perceiver.

Rationalism represents the opposite way of thinking and working with facts. In rationalistic method the criterion of truth is not sensory but intellectual and deductive. It assumes the universality of natural laws, and hence its appeal to sense perception is in pursuit of particulars. There is a direct preoccupation with conceptual schemes, constructions, and logical manipulations. The supreme embodiment of rationalism is in pure mathematics.

Prior to World War I it was rationalism, as exemplified in crude nonmathematical form by the classical systematists, that dominated sociology. And although, after a decline, rationalism has recouped considerably in recent years, there is still no more honorific word in all of American sociology than the adjective "empirical." Evidence of this appears in the situation wherein the modern representatives of sociological rationalism, as for instance the constructors of mathematical models and formal deductive systems, consistently lay claim to doing empirical work.[4]

The spread of empiricism in American sociology has been responsible for several important emphases. There has been a sincere striving for objectivity and a direct concern with modesty of conclusion. The aim has been precision in statement with respect to

----

[4] Bierstedt makes the following comment with regard to empiricism: ". . . the word, and all its congenors, has become so sacrosanct in current sociological literature that the radical positivism of Lundberg, the 'quantic' formalism of Dodd, and the critical exegesis of Parsons all contend for the label." See Robert Bierstedt, "A Critique of Empiricism in Sociology," *American Sociological Review,* 14 (October, 1949), p. 588.

the evidence that has been collected by the most trustworthy of instruments. Emphasis has been upon quantitative methods and standardized modes of inquiry, by virtue of their promise of objectivity and precision. An extended array of basically descriptive and concrete studies has appeared. There has been an astonishing number of studies of particular populations, communities, areas, structures, processes, and roles. Gangs, families, jack-rollers, plumbers, taxi-dance halls, villages, ethnic groups, cults, sects, cliques, unions, fads, and many other phenomena have been extensively examined—but usually without benefit of explicit hypotheses or unifying theory.

The consequences are varied with respect to methodology. First, the refreshing contrast of empirical research with the *a priori*sm of the classical encyclopedists discredited the completely speculative approach and thus delivered the sociologist from the armchair. Second, empiricism established the necessity of controlled observation and research design as components of scientific investigation. Third, the necessity of keeping theory in touch with evidence and relating it to the bedrock of accumulative fact is an empirical contribution. Fourth, empiricism made an outstanding contribution to the procedural rules of research, for the empirically oriented have been to a great extent the ones who have codified the research rules and practices. Fifth, the empiricists have accomplished an enormous amount of investigation.

On the other side of the ledger, empiricism has had several limiting consequences for methodology.[5] First, it has contributed to a particular form of methodological naiveté. Although empiricism has eliminated certain surface forms of subjectivism, it certainly has not eliminated some more subtle and tenacious forms of *implicit* subjectivity. Second, a great many of the sociological investigations of the recent past have closely resembled a collection of facts and hence have not closely approximated the scientific model subscribed to by the empiricists. Third, the roles of theory and research have been reversed as compared to standard scientific practice; rather than evaluating research in terms of its contribution to theory, there is a powerful tendency to evaluate theory solely in terms of its cur-

[5] See Bierstedt, *op. cit.*, pp. 584-592, for a penetrating critique of empiricism in sociology.

rent research utility. Fourth, radical empiricism has led to random, helter-skelter, uncodified, and frequently trivial research. It has placed emphasis on immediacy rather than the long view because it distrusts theory as a guideline. Fifth, the de-emphasis of systematic theory at the expense of empirical enterprise has increased the difficulty of extracting sociological principles and generalizations from the mass of idiographic data.

The tendency of American sociology to proceed almost purely along empirical lines has not hastened its arrival as an accepted science. Viewing American sociology from the perspective of the several converging European traditions, Karl Mannheim declared:

> American sociology is characterized by its peculiar delight in a form of empiricism which I should be inclined to call an "isolating empiricism"; for, whilst the enumeration and description of facts becomes always more exact and refined, the constructive bases of social life are completely veiled behind the mass of secondary details. This, it seems, can only be attributed to the fact that the most urgent impulses to the growth of sociological investigation in the United States arose from the immediate problems of everyday life which present themselves in any colonizing society that spreads itself over an expansive territory and has to develop its social institutions in a relatively short span of time. In such a society the most difficult and vital problems crop up one by one, and social study concentrates on the solution of these isolated problems. Here we have one reason for the prevalence in American sociology of questions such as those of gangs, of delinquency, of the conflict of different races living in the same territorial region, of the psychic adjustment of immigrants, all of which are problems that arise from particular needs at particular moments. But, as has been pointed out above, the phenomena that do not become apparent are: the totality of society, the dynamic forces operating throughout society and the class problems that exist in society. The totality of society is veiled because of the general belief that if the difficulties of single institutions and particular institutions are solved in the right way, the entirety of society will reveal itself through a process of integrating the solutions of individual social difficulties.[6]

[6] Karl Mannheim, *Essays on Sociology and Social Psychology* (New York: Oxford University Press, 1953), pp. 224-225.

The preceding statements are generally applicable to the period of rampant empiricism of the twenties and thirties, and to a lesser extent applicable to the modified empiricism of the present. However, rationalism has never been entirely squeezed out as an avenue of approach to knowledge, and since World War II several developments have taken place that are in the rational tradition.

Rational resistance to radical empiricism has taken several different lines, but in general they can be reduced to three. First, there has been the emphasis on *system* in the work of several leading theoreticians. The delineation of "action theory" by Znaniecki in the late twenties, followed later by Sorokin and then by Parsons,[7] the transformation of "formal" sociology into the structural-functionalism manifest in such diverse approaches as those of Wiese–Becker, Parsons, Davis, and Homans,[8] and the current concern with the properties of and comparative study of social systems, largely by the neo-Parsonians, are just a few examples of this tradition.[9] In each instance these efforts represent a striving for explanation in the sense of providing a conceptual context within which individual elements were ascribed meaning.

Second, there has been the emphasis on conceptual apparatus, primarily in the form of constructed types, empirical and mathematical models, and conceptual schemes. There have persistently been a few sociologists who have felt compelled to emphasize the fact that there can be no coherent body of fact without conceptualization, and no system of knowledge without theory.

[7] Florian Znaniecki, *Social Actions* (New York: Farrar and Rinehart, 1936); P. A. Sorokin, *Social and Cultural Dynamics,* 4 vols. (New York: American Book Co., 1937-1941); Talcott Parsons, *The Structure of Social Action* (New York: McGraw-Hill, 1937).

[8] Howard Becker, *Systematic Sociology on the Basis of the Beziehungslehre and Gebildelehre of Leopold von Wiese* (New York: John Wiley, 1932); Talcott Parsons, *The Social System* (Glencoe: The Free Press, 1951); Kingsley Davis, *Human Society* (New York: Macmillan, 1949); G. C. Homans, *The Human Group* (New York: Harcourt Brace, 1950).

[9] C. P. Loomis, *Social Systems* (New York: D. Van Nostrand, 1960); M. J. Levy, *The Structure of Society* (Princeton: Princeton University Press, 1952); N. J. Smelser, *Social Change in the Industrial Revolution* (Chicago: University of Chicago Press, 1959); Max Black (editor), *The Social Theories of Talcott Parsons* (Englewood Cliffs: Prentice-Hall, 1961).

Finally, there has been the emphasis on research design within the *logic* of the experimental method. The experimental method is normally classed as an aspect of empirical science. Upon closer observation, however, one cannot overlook the tremendous role of reason in experimental design. The vastly improved design of sociological research undertaken in recent years attests to the rational modification of extreme empiricism.

Although there has recently been some tendency for sociologists to avoid the extreme poles of either empiricism or rationalism, and although there has been some important convergence of the two methodologies, it would be entirely misleading to leave the impression that either the "collectionists" or "closed-system logicians" are extinct. Both, however, are subject to tremendous pressure to come into the crucial area of convergence. For instance, Parsons and associates obviously feel under strong compulsion to demonstrate the utility of their "structural–functional" theory. Conversely, more sociologists today tend to seek more than a purely descriptive study of some particular phenomenon.

The speciousness of attempting to separate theory and research in sociology is gradually being recognized. Theory in many respects has been monopolized by verbal specialists who have demonstrated little interest in formulating verifiable propositions and in the process of verification. On the other hand, research in sociology was under the monopoly of those who were technically equipped and "fact-oriented," but who through theoretical indifference or incompetence were not attuned to either theoretical extrapolation or generalizability. There is a growing recognition that some bridges have to be built before the scientific situation improves. This recognition seems to indicate that American sociology has learned the lesson of fact and research that empiricism had to teach, but now feels the need of improved conceptual equipment in the rational tradition in order to comprehend its facts and intelligently conduct its research. An early bridge of the historical gap between empiricism and rationalism may be seen in such a work as that of Samuel Stouffer and associates in their research on military personnel.[10]

---

[10] See S. A. Stouffer *et al., The American Soldier: Studies in Social Psychology in World War II* (Princeton: Princeton University Press, 1949).

These volumes provide a record of the attitudes of the American soldier in World War II, and of the techniques developed to study these attitudes. As a record it is unique in many respects. Never before had modern techniques of social science been employed on so large a scale by so many competent technicians. Its value to the social scientist is unquestionably greater than its value to the military for whom the original research was done.[11] In this work one sees a modest kind of theory standing in juxtaposition to an enormous amount of data. It is the kind of work that could not have been done by either "collectors of minutiae" or "theory-spinners of the grand tradition."

The following comment by Merton can perhaps be taken as an optimistic representation of the current relationship between theory and research.

> The stereotype of the social theorist high in the empyrean of pure ideas uncontaminated by mundane facts is fast becoming no less outmoded than the stereotype of the social researcher equipped with questionnaire and pencil and hot on the chase of the isolated and meaningless statistic. For in building the mansion of sociology during the last decades, theorist and empiricist have learned to work together. What is more, they have learned to talk to one another in the process. At times, this means only that a sociologist has learned to talk to himself since increasingly the same man has taken up both theory and research. Specialization and integration have developed hand in hand.[12]

Neopositivism and Its Opponents

Positivism in modern trappings has had a distinct vogue in American sociology. Although evidence of it has been discernible for many years, the classic statement of neopositivism was not made

---

[11] R. K. Merton and P. F. Lazarsfeld, in *Continuities in Research* (Glencoe: The Free Press, 1950), consolidate the theoretical gain made in *The American Soldier* and thereby set the stage for less *ad hoc* efforts in the future.

[12] R. K. Merton, *Social Theory and Social Structure* (Glencoe: The Free Press, 1949), p. 97.

in sociology until 1939.[13] The neopositive approach is double-barreled in nature. Primarily it is a metasociology oriented to the methodological assumptions of physical science. In this respect it develops a hardheaded ascetic methodology based upon the premises that (1) societal phenomena are subject to natural laws, (2) there is no distinction between sciences that deal with human beings and those that deal with other phenomena, and (3) the subjective aspects of societal phenomena can only be studied scientifically on the basis of their objective, overt manifestation. This methodology is undeniably clear-cut; equally certain is that it has been subject to a great deal of criticism.[14]

The second aspect consists of the typical pattern of moral and practical considerations stressed by positivists in their desire for a scientifically articulated world. Lundberg makes this comment: "Positivists do not admit the assumed dichotomy between the pursuit of science on the one hand and social action on the other. We contend, on the contrary, that *the pursuit of science is the most fundamental of all social action.*"[15] The fusion of science and action has not necessarily made it any easier to attain the ideal of a natural science of society. This is due to the fact that the methodological rigor of the physical sciences, aspired to by the neopositivists, becomes subjugated to the problems of society rather than to the problems of theoretic significance in the discipline. This has resulted in an emphasis on practical and immediate research that is *useful* from the point of view of its sponsors in society, and has reinforced the moralistic, reform, and policy-oriented position of early American sociology. The early interest of sociologists in such phe-

[13] G. A. Lundberg, *Foundations of Sociology* (New York: Macmillan, 1939).

[14] The critics of neopositivism have not been silent. See Sorokin's review of Lundberg's *Foundations of Sociology,* in *American Journal of Sociology,* 45 (March, 1940), pp. 795-798; Ethel Shanas, "A Critique of Dodd's Dimensions of Society," *American Journal of Sociology,* 48 (September, 1942), pp. 214-230; Florian Znaniecki, "The Proximate Future of Sociology: Controversies in Doctrine and Method," *American Journal of Sociology,* 50 (May, 1945), pp. 514-521; and Parsons, *The Structure of Social Action,* *passim.*

[15] G. A. Lundberg, "Contemporary Positivism in Sociology," *American Sociological Review,* 4 (February, 1939), p. 54. (His italics.)

nomena as crime, delinquency, prostitution, poverty, divorce, racial discrimination, and alcoholism has persisted, in part at least, due to this reinforcement. As a consequence, many modern sociologists are not merely interested in understanding aspects of society but are also carriers of the faith that their kind of knowledge can instigate change in "the right direction." The existence of such a dynamic organization as the Society for the Study of Social Problems as an affiliate of the American Sociological Association is evidence that the social-problems orientation is still a vital tradition in American sociology.

The opposition to neopositivism in American sociology has been powerful and effective, although it has been so diversified that it is difficult to label. Unquestionably, however, the strongest single source of opposition lies in that composite orientation known as *structural-functionalism*.[16] This perspective encompasses several subsidiary or "feeder" traditions, including the German tradition of *verstehende* (understanding or interpretive sociology),[17] *action* theory with its emphasis on the subjective categories of action (action as it is viewed from the perspective of the actor),[18] and *symbolic-interactionism* with its emphasis on the meaning of behavior as it originates and is conducted in terms of social relations.[19]

The structural-functional style of thought has assumed an increasingly dominant role in American sociology in the past two decades. Resting on different premises than neopositivism, this methodological position has performed the task of emphasizing (1) the value of theory in research, (2) the significance of the concept of system and the potential of "systems analysis", (3) the necessity of the comparative study of social systems, (4) the need of motivational theory and the instruments by means of which it can be

[16] Note works previously cited with respect to structural-functionalism. See also Talcott Parsons *et al.* (editors), *Theories of Society,* 2 vols. (Glencoe: The Free Press, 1961).

[17] In particular, see Howard Becker, *Through Values to Social Interpretation* (Durham: Duke University Press, 1950).

[18] Note works previously cited with respect to action theory. In addition, see Florian Znaniecki, *The Method of Sociology* (New York: Farrar and Rinehart, 1934).

[19] G. H. Mead, *Mind, Self and Society* (Chicago: University of Chicago Press, 1934).

tested, and (5) the necessity of giving attention to the qualitative aspects of research.

At the present writing the conflict has died down rather considerably. No decisive victory has been registered by any position, but methodology has benefited from the fact that proponents of the different positions have had to give intensive consideration to the problems involved.[20] The metaphysical assumptions remain, for neopositivism as well as its opponents, but on the procedural level distinct modifications of the extreme positions have taken place.

Inductive Supremacy

One of the basic methodological polarities in sociology revolves around the emphasis on inductive and deductive procedures. In the most general sense, induction may be defined as the process of inferring a general assertion from the observation of a number of particular facts. Conversely, deduction is the process of analytical reasoning from general to particular or less general, involving logical inference of a conclusion from one or more given premises. These two procedures are not mutually exclusive; indeed, in some situations it is possible to interpret either one as a special case of the other. The interplay between deduction and induction is an observable feature in the conduct of any research project, and it is difficult to conceive of either one as being purely adhered to. Nevertheless, it is possible to say that sociology has become increasingly inductive since the days of its break with the classical systematists.

There are still sociologists who tend to start with purely abstract rules, premises, or systems, which they develop rationally and correct in varied ways so that empirical incongruities are reduced. The discipline, however, is no longer crowded with such scholastics. On the other hand, there is a preponderance of sociologists who begin with ordinary and restricted notions and try to refine them more and more by making them more definitive, removing contra-

[20] See Reinhard Bendix, "The Image of Man in the Social Sciences: The Basic Assumptions of Present Day Research," *Commentary*, 11 (February, 1951), pp. 187-192, for an insightful review of some of the problems of viewpoint posed by the assumptions underlying social science research.

dictions, and delimiting their area of applicability. Such investiga-
tors are content if they can make a modest generalization that applies to a limited universe of particulars. Thus the modern sociologist is primarily inductive, and his approach takes two major forms:
analytic and enumerative induction.

As a procedure, analytic induction begins with an explanatory
hypothesis and a provisional definition of something to be explained.
The hypothesis is then examined in the light of the facts, and
modifications are made in one or both of two ways: the hypothesis
itself is modified so that all facts will fall under it, and/or the
phenomenon under examination is redefined to exclude the cases
not explained by the hypothesis. In either case it is a *complete* induction. Analytic induction finds only rare application in sociology,
as in such instances as that of Lindesmith's study of opiate addiction
and Cressey's study of the causes of embezzlement.[21]

Enumerative induction is the dominant mode in sociology and

[21] A. R. Lindesmith, *Opiate Addiction* (Bloomington: Principia Press,
1947); D. R. Cressey, *Other People's Money* (Glencoe: The Free Press,
1953). See also W. S. Robinson, "The Logical Structure of Analytic Induction," *American Sociological Review,* 16 (December, 1951, pp. 812-818.
Despite the vigorous advocacy of analytic induction and polemic against
enumerative induction by Florian Znaniecki and the subsequent controversy
in the thirties, analytic induction has not flourished as a mode of approach
in sociology. See his *The Method of Sociology* (New York: Farrar and Rinehart, 1934). Logically there is no basis for assuming that these two modes
of approach should be in conflict; on the contrary they are complementary.
As Znaniecki indicates: "While in enumerative induction . . . a certain
logical class is defined, and the problem is to find characters common to and
distinctive of the particular objects belonging within this class which were
not explicitly or implicitly included in the definition, in analytic induction
certain particular objects are determined by intensive study, and the problem
is to define the logical classes which they represent" (*ibid.,* p. 249). The
relative lack of use of analytic induction in sociology cannot be explained
on the basis of any inadequacy of the method, since it has been demonstrated
to be useful. The explanation apparently lies in the dominance of a *style* in
sociology that does not encourage, in training or practice, proponents of
analytic induction. As the discipline becomes more "pluralistic," as it clearly
is in many respects, one can assume that analytic induction will experience
some revival as a mode of inquiry. The powerful thrust of the developing
computer technology will almost unquestionably, however, insure the continued dominance of enumerative induction.

is a characteristic of all studies using generalizing statistical procedures. An obvious example would be the case of public opinion
polling where statements about the political universe are attempted
on the basis of very limited sampling. Enumerative induction takes
the form of a statistical generalization based upon the examination
of cases within a defined universe. If *all* the individual instances
that come under the generalization are examined, it is said to be a
complete induction. Since the subject matter does not lend itself
readily to complete induction, *incomplete* inductions are typically
made that are based upon a sample of the universe. It is here that
statistical procedures become a substitute for induction in the classical analytic sense.

Although induction reigns in American sociology, deduction
still plays a key role and probably will be more important in the
future. The radical inductive myth of the true scientist starting by
observing the facts without any conceptual anticipations has been
responsible for the unnecessary discrediting of deduction. This
myth, the *tabula rasa* fallacy, has had a strong foothold in American
sociology. It is unusual to find other scientists who feel that they
can or should want to approach their subject matter with a blank
mind. On the other hand, the traditional "methods books" in sociology have on occasion encouraged sociologists to approach their
material without any preconceptions, theories, concepts, or evaluative judgments. Realization that this is logically impossible and contrary to actual history has spread rapidly in recent years. Without
anticipatory ideas and conceptual directions one can neither know
what facts to look for nor recognize what is relevant to the inquiry.
It would be difficult to start by observing the facts, for to determine
what are the facts is a primary object of scientific inquiry. Deduction is thus a necessary part or instrument of research.

Deduction has been best exemplified in American methodology
by conceptual schemes in the form of systematic theory, by constructed types, and by mathematical and empirical models. Such
conceptual frameworks as that of the social system can perform at
least two scientific functions. First, they can aid in the codification
of our accumulating concrete knowledge. This means that discrete
hypotheses and observations can be unified under general categories.
They can be tentatively placed in a larger context; consequently

their meaning can be assessed in the light of more general implications. Second, theory of this order can serve as a guide to research.
It enables us to locate and define the areas of our knowledge and
ignorance by pointing up problematic areas. In the light of system
one can see problems of interest and significance relative to hypothetical interconnections or relationships.[22]

Constructed types represent a bridge between systematic theory
and empirical observation, and thus have some of the same functions as systematic theory. The constructed type as a conceptual device represents an attempt to advance concept formation in sociology
from the state of description and strictly empirical generalization to
the construction of theoretical systems.

Although models have actually been used by sociologists for
years (types and systems can be models, for example), interest in
the explicit construction and interpretation of models has increased
recently.[23] Tiryakian has defined the model as follows:

> In a technical sense, a model is a set of assumptions, axioms, or fun-
> damental premises which focuses the direction of subsequent research
> by pointing to the immediately relevant aspects of the phenomena
> under scrutiny. The model itself is not a composite of statements
> of fact, hence cannot be directly validated or invalidated; from the
> model one deduces propositions regarding existing conditions and it
> is these that are subject to empirical verification.[24]

[22] For a recent extensive examination of the current major theoretical
approaches in sociology, see C. P. Loomis and Z. K. Loomis, *Modern Social
Theories* (New York: D. Van Nostrand, 1961).

[23] See P. F. Lazarsfeld (editor), *Mathematical Thinking in the Social
Sciences* (Glencoe: The Free Press, 1954), for an extensive treatment of
model usage in the social sciences. Also, K. J. Arrow, "Mathematical Models
in the Social Sciences," in Daniel Lerner and H. D. Lasswell (editors), *The
Policy Sciences* (Stanford: Stanford University Press, 1951); Svend Riemer,
"Premises in Sociological Inquiry," *American Journal of Sociology,* 59 (May,
1954), pp. 551-555; Paul Meadows, "Models, Systems and Sciences,"
American Sociological Review, 22 (February, 1957), pp. 3-9; James Beshers,
"Models and Theory Construction," *American Sociological Review,* 22 (Feb-
ruary, 1957), pp. 32-38; and May Brodbeck, "Models, Meaning, and Theories,"
in Llewellyn Gross (editor), *Symposium on Sociological Theory* (Evanston:
Row, Peterson, 1959).

[24] E. A. Tiryakian, "Methodology and Research," in J. S. Roucek
(editor), *Contemporary Sociology* (New York: Philosophical Library, 1958),
pp. 163-164n.

In general terms, analysis by means of a model involves both a definition of the model and a test to determine how well a sample of data approximates the model. The model as a deductive device is given an empiric interpretation by means of comparison with data. If the discrepancy between the model and the sample data can be reasonably ascribed to chance rather than to factors not contained in the model, then it can be assumed that the data have a structure akin to the model. A preeminently inductive statistical sociologist is really following this procedure when he fits a frequency distribution to a "normal" curve and then tests the goodness of fit by chi square. The various analytic statistical devices all involve this element of deduction.

Lately several mathematical models have been developed in sociology that are indicative of a trend toward measurement of social phenomena. The area of attitude study has been particularly productive in this respect, especially in view of the fact that the models apparently are applicable to many elements of behavior besides attitudes. For example, the currently popular Guttman scale belongs in this category. The Guttman technique, as the successor to earlier ranking scales, received extensive application in the area of attitude study during and since World War II. In addition, it is gradually being adapted to more general sociological problems. For instance, scale-analysis has already been used in research dealing with such diverse matters as women's neighborliness, ecological patterns, concept development in children, status, consensus, and interpersonal communication. These are areas that formerly would have been adjudged susceptible only to qualitative analysis. Thus the use of the Guttman model has extended the zone of quantification in the study of social behavior.

The sociologists' concern with models has increased since World War II. This is not only indicative of the strength and persistence of deductivism as a component of methodology; it is also a sign of the increased quantitative sophistication of the American sociologist. However, it is interesting to note that, despite the prevailing belief that typologies are imprecise and "sloppy" and that models are precise and technically refined, many ambiguities remain with respect to what models are and do. At the 1960 International Congress for Logic, Methodology and Philosophy of Science, a meeting of world leaders in these fields of the natural and social sciences, a considerable amount of attention was devoted to models. In reviewing the proceedings, Yuen Ren Chao listed no less than *thirty* different synonyms and characterizations of model used by the participants. Ironically this did not include the use of "type" as one of the synonyms.[25]

The Drive for Quantification

There has been a great deal of controversy as to the role and value of quantifying techniques in sociology. Extreme positions with respect to quantification were common during the twenties and thirties. Recently, however, the polemic fervor has died down. The tendency now is to look upon quantifying techniques as an essential part of the conceptual equipment of the sociologist rather than to view quantification as an end in itself.

Conspicuous in the methodological thought of the twenties and thirties was the belief that sociology could become a natural science through statistical procedure. The neopositivistic orientation at the basis of the belief is clear-cut. The reasoning went as follows: The success of natural science may be attributed to the objective handling of its data and the quantitative expression of its results; hence if sociology is to emulate that success, it must change its ways of obtaining and processing data. In short, sociology must develop techniques which secure objective social data suitable for quantitative treatment by statistical means. There were numerous proponents of this thesis, but perhaps its earliest definitive statement was by Lundberg in 1929. The formulation was succinct enough to delineate the issue and facilitate the taking of sides in the controversy.

The opposition to this view was stated in most extreme form by those who were positive that human behavior was different enough from other phenomena to make it insusceptible to statistical treatment. The assertion was that the portion of sociological data that could be transmitted into quantitative form was by its nature the

[25] Y. R. Chao, "Models in Linguistics and Models in General," in Ernest Nagel *et al.* (editors), *Logic Methodology and Philosophy of Science* (Stanford: Stanford University Press, 1962), pp. 558-566.

least important of behavioral data, and moreover it was so insignificant as to hardly be worth the effort of getting it. This view was characteristic of many of the older or "pioneer" generation of sociologists. More important, it was advocated capably by such champions of qualitative research as Sorokin, MacIver, Waller, and Znaniecki.[26]

Although the issues were sharply drawn in terms of the extreme formulations, and although the polemical fervor was great, many first-rate sociologists were made very uncomfortable by what they considered to be a false dichotomy. As competent researchers they had technical leanings toward one or the other of the poles, but could not sympathize with either the oversimplification of or the formulation of the argument. This middle-range group of sociologists recognized and pointed out with increasing clarity that both positions rested on an assumption that was demonstrably false. The assumption had been made that sociology could be carried on only in terms of one particular approach. It was increasingly recognized that a quantitative scale was no more *the* answer to sociology's problems than analytic induction, logico-experimentation, case history, or any other device then in the hands of the sociologist. Granted that certain devices might have greater instrumental value than others, it remained true that there was no master-key or royal road to scientific knowledge. There were many ways of conducting systematic study in sociology, and their richness lay not in the potential elevation of any one of them to supremacy but in their articulation as a complementary and integrated set of tools. These middle-range sociologists explicitly recognized that enumerative and measuring devices were valuable, but at the same time they admitted that there were many other valuable components of the research endeavor.

The rise to preeminence of such middle-range scholars as Stouffer, Lazarsfeld, Guttman, Suchman, Moore, Becker, Loomis, Merton, Davis, and Hawley has pretty well demonstrated that there is a direct line of logical continuity from systematic qualitative research to rigorous forms of measurement. There is a whole battery of in-

---

[26] For a continuation of the critique, see P. A. Sorokin, *Fads and Foibles in Modern Sociology and Related Sciences* (Chicago: Henry Regnery, 1956); C. W. Mills, *The Sociological Imagination* (New York: Oxford University Press, 1959).

termediate devices which fill the gap between the quantitative and qualitative poles and thus create a research *continuum* rather than a dichotomy. Despite vast differences in their theoretical interest and orientations, sociologists representing this approach have, through their leadership in the work with systematic ratings, classifications, ranking scales, constructed types, simple quantitative indices, codification, research design, logic of proof or demonstration, and continuities in research, all conspired to reject the idea that qualitative and quantitative endeavor are somehow separate research procedures. In sum, quantification is now accepted as a normal and indispensable aspect of sociological endeavor. The controversies which surround it no longer refer to whether or not it is possible in the behavioral sciences; they now are technical controversies concerning the proper applicability of given techniques, under stated circumstances, to particular kinds of phenomena.[27]

Idiographic and Nomothetic Tendencies

In principle, American sociologists are almost universally committed to a nomothetic ideal for their science—an ideal which stems from a modified version of the original Windelband formulation of the nomothetic–idiographic dichotomy. This formulation distinguishes two classes of sciences: those studying the general, and enunciating natural laws (nomothetic); and those studying particulars in their historically determined configurations (idiographic). The problem as to whether sociology enunciates natural laws is not a current issue. It is pragmatically agreed that sociology studies the general, regular, and recurrent aspects of phenomena, and hence

[27] H. C. Selvin, "A Critique of Tests of Significance in Survey Research," *American Sociological Review*, 22 (October, 1957), pp. 519-527. For a view of the provocative interchange between Selvin and others regarding the applicability of tests of significance, see letters from David Gold and Selvin, *American Sociological Review*, 23 (February, 1958), pp. 85-86; and letters from James Beshers and Selvin, *American Sociological Review*, 23 (April, 1958), pp. 199-200.

can generalize and predict within the limits of its substantiated theory. It must be noted, however, that we refer to prediction here in the sense of prediction at the theoretical level, framed in terms of the standard "if–then conditional," *not* to prophesying on the empirical level. In other words, sociology cannot prophesy and say what is going to happen in the indeterminate future. It can, however, assert that given certain factors operating under certain conditions there is the *likelihood* of a given result. This theoretical prediction makes sociology a nomothetic discipline, despite the modest substitution of empirical generalizations for notably lacking natural laws as the basis of that prediction.

Like all other generalizing disciplines, sociology has a necessarily idiographic aspect. It contains numerous particular statements as well as generalizations. The problem centers around the extent to which the search for these particulars dominates the attempt to generalize, insofar as the attainment of general knowledge is the admitted aim of the discipline. Sociology has amassed a tremendous amount of descriptive data about particular people, places and events. There are case-studies of particular delinquents, surveys of particular communities, ecological descriptions of particular cities, observations of particular strikes, etc. The value of these descriptive treatments goes unquestioned to the extent that they serve as the base from which empirical generalizations evolve. Their value is questioned, however, when they remain in the form of particulars and are not brought into the framework of substantive theory. A promising, if modest, body of empirical generalizations has been built up in the past few decades, and it is legitimate to assume that this process will continue in the future.[28] Nevertheless, most theoretically oriented sociologists are seriously concerned with the paucity of generalizations as compared with the mass of particulars. Stated briefly, their concern has its basis in the fact that most sociologists affirm the desirability of formulating the general and recurrent, but in actual practice settle for the gathering of data and amassing of descriptive particulars.[29]

[28] Bernard Berelson and Gary Steiner, *Human Behavior: An Inventory of Scientific Findings* (New York: Harcourt, Brace and World, 1964).

[29] An able defense of idiography is given by N. S. Timasheff, "On Methods in the Social Sciences," *American Catholic Social Review*, 6 (October, 1945), pp. 169-176.

There is actually a very strong idiographic trend in sociology, despite the aims explicitly agreed upon by most sociologists. There seem to be several different sources of this trend. First, interdisciplinary contact with representatives of closely related fields such as cultural anthropology, institutional economics, political science, and history, which traditionally place strong emphasis on idiography, is an increasingly important source. Another primary source of idiographic emphasis is in the use of the statistical method. This is not to be taken as an assertion that the statistical method is exclusively idiographic in character. Indeed, its nomothetic aspects have been consistently gaining ground, and at the present value put upon statistical correlation, variance, and probability statements is probably greater than that upon statistical description. The statistical method involves an essentially nomothetic element because statistical enumeration is seldom exhaustive of the universe it has reference to. The rapid growth of sampling theory is evidence of this. Nevertheless the early statistics were primarily descriptive, and this remains true of much current statistical work. There are still many sociologists who enjoy assembling arrays of statistical data presumably independent of hypotheses and general categories.

Finally, and most important of all methodologically, a source of idiographic-nomothetic confusion centers around the problem of abstraction. In one sense all phenomena are unique if considered on a low enough level of abstraction. It has always been a scientific task to conceptualize these phenomena in abstract terms in order to comprehend their general character. The fact that World War II was a unique war is no more a deterrent to the sociological study of wars than the fact that any given earthworm is unique is a deterrent to the study of the general structure of earthworms. Abstraction is a general and pervasive scientific problem. It is true, however, that the problem persists in sociology partly because the sociologist is often more interested either in unique events or in occurrences in a small number of cases. The interest is stimulated by the fact that the cases are exceptional and hence curious. Insofar as the sociologist continues to be attracted by the exceptional rather than the comparative, the nomothetic aim remains as an ideal. The answers here seemingly lie in the development of an increased usage of analytic induction, or, in the situation involving few cases, the adaptation of a developing small-sample theory.

The Behavioristic Impact

Immediately after World War I behaviorism emerged as a movement of considerable proportions. Although relatively few sociologists accepted the extremism of Watson, the movement nevertheless had a significant influence on sociological thinking, particularly in that sector of sociology dealing with social psychological problems. Behaviorism rejected the concepts of consciousness, sensation, perception, will, image, mental experience, and the significance of motives in determining behavior. Such concepts as it did retain from the older psychology, as for example, thinking and emotion, it redefined as forms of observable or directly inferred activities. The emphasis was on the stimulus-response bond, and it was overt behavior that was of central importance.

This approach was in keeping with the growing empirical and pragmatic tendencies of the twenties, and moreover it seemed to satisfy the demand for objectivity and mechanical certainty in the conduct of research. Because of its emphasis on the mechanical character of the stimulus-response relations, it seemed particularly amenable to quantification and thus gave promise of freeing sociology from its subjectivism and converting it into an exact science. A comment by Read Bain, writing in 1928, is an example of this line of thinking:

> The development of sociology as a natural science has been hindered by: (1) emphasis upon its normative rather than upon its descriptive aspects; (2) too much attention to subjective factors, such as ideas, ideals, motives, sentiments, wishes, and attitudes, and too little attention to objective, overt behavior; . . .[30]

Unfortunately, the promise of radical behaviorism did not "pay off" in research. Scarcely any contributions really based upon the principle were made, possibly because the very things it sought to explain (sociological phenomena) did not easily, if at all, reduce to the mechanical circulation of stimulus-response. It is to be noted

[30] Read Bain, "An Attitude on Attitude Research," *American Journal of Sociology*, 33 (May, 1928), p. 940.

that the area of attitude study has developed enormously in recent years, and is today a well-established, sophisticated, and fruitful research area. This despite the obvious contempt of the dyed-in-the-wool behaviorist for such enterprise, as expressed in the above comment by Bain.

Nothing approaching scientific knowledge in the radical-behavioristic sense has accumulated regarding such phenomena as fashions, fads, crazes, conventions, rumors, public opinion, customs, institutions, and social systems. As a consequence a much more modest type of behaviorism, an extremely modified version, quickly supplanted the older branch in the thirties and is still current and predominant. This is the "symbolic-interactionist" version of behaviorism, championed in particular by Mead.[31]

The positive significance of modified behaviorism lies primarily in its partial closing of the gap, which appeared larger than it was, between objectivism and subjectivism by stimulating a more rigorous development of the objective indices of subjective phenomena. In turn, this has led to the development of a sociology of communication, a reorientation of attitude study so that attitudes are now typically studied in relation to social structure, the incipient development of a peculiarly American sociology of knowledge, and a related promising approach to the study of mass society.

Operational Controversy

The doctrine of operationism, established in physics by Bridgman, was transported into sociology in the thirties by several of the more pragmatically inclined sociologists. It was involved in considerable controversy during the thirties and forties, but the issue has died down considerably at the present. The central notion is expressed by Bridgman as follows: "In general, we mean by any concept nothing more than a set of operations; the concept is synonymous with the corresponding set of operations. . . . The meaning of a proposition is its verifiability." [32] Lundberg in par-

[31] Mead, *op. cit.*

[32] P. W. Bridgman, *The Logic of Modern Physics* (New York: Macmillan, 1927), p. 5.

ticular took this as a cue to recast the conceptual framework of sociology. He asserted that the continued use of current sociological symbols would doom the discipline to subjectivity. He pointed out the lack of agreement as to the meaning of even common concepts, the typical use of them in a variety of senses, the fact that they mean not only many things to many people but even different things to the same people on different occasions. Such semantic ambiguity he considered fatal to the scientific approach, and consequently he also asserted that the "only way of defining anything objectively is in terms of the operations involved." [33]

The objections to operational sociology tended to center around the limitations this approach put upon the role of concepts and of systematic theory. If Bridgman's original statement is taken literally —as it has been by some sociologists—then it does entail a severe limitation on concepts rather than the constituting of an implementation. For example, the traditional meaning of magnitude as a concept cannot be made synonymous with the physical operations involved in measuring magnitude. The physical operation of measuring magnitude never determines more than the magnitude of some specific object. The meaning traditionally ascribed to magnitude as a concept determined the operation of measuring, for without knowing that meaning the physicist would have been incapable of selecting a relevant measuring device appropriate to the object. To have measured a plowed field with a thermometer and called it "size" would have been no more incongruous than to measure intelligence with an achievement test and call it "intelligence." The operationists ignored the fact that concepts are always general, and that an operation is always specific and hence subject to determination by the former. Radical operationism of this type discounted the role of synthesizing rational thought in concept construction, and consequently became a form of raw empiricism.

The second ramification of radical operationism was the reduction of the role of systematic theory. Such typical operational statements as "intelligence is what intelligence tests test" imply that there can be as many intelligences as there are tests. If so, we are driven to a nominalism and eclecticism so extreme that it denies the pos-

[33] G. A. Lundberg, *Foundations of Sociology*, p. 69.

sibility of establishing a system of interrelated concepts of general empirical reference.

Although operationism has not dominated the important research developments in sociology, it nevertheless has left its imprint. First, a certain amount of operationism is evident in much empirical research. Second, and more important methodologically, operationism has assisted in bringing about the development and general acceptance of a more moderate approach known as *instrumentalism*. Originally formulated by Dewey, it is now a prevailing orientation adhered to by both the theoretically and empirically inclined. Instrumentalism (often still traveling under the label of operationism) simply maintains that concepts should be made subject to inquiry and susceptible to hypothetical statement for purposes of examination. Moreover, instrumentalism asserts that theories, discrete or systematic, must be evaluated in terms of their research adaptability, verifiability, and fruitfulness.[34]

The Pragmatic Orientation

Pragmatic, although it is a philosophic label, stands more for an attitude of mind than a system of ideas and hence appears in many diverse approaches and systems. Pragmatism is reflected in the habit of interpreting ideas or events in terms of their consequences. This closely aligns the pragmatic habit with the logic of experiment lying at the base of modern research science. In general, pragmatism does not imply any final philosophical conclusions but merely manifests a tendency to accept whatever it is that works in the conduct of research. It is thus an amplified empiricism that has become aware of the relation of conceptualization and theory to research.

The practice of scientific research has been to continually approach new problems, and with these new problems to formulate new hypotheses. The test of these hypotheses lay in the experience

[34] This orientation is implicit in the work of Stouffer and his associates and of Merton and Lazarsfeld, and even in the comprehensive systematic theory of Parsons.

of man as researcher, with whatever instruments he had at hand. The test was found in the actual process of cognition as based in experience. From this standpoint, mathematics, substantive theory, instruments, observational techniques, etc., simply represented the apparatus for working out hypotheses with respect to experience. Pragmatism as a doctrine is nothing more than an expression of scientific method as it has worked in the past.

The influence of pragmatism on sociology is clearly all-pervasive. Aspects of its orientation may be detected in any of the methodological positions dealt with here. It shows itself in several different ways. It is manifest in the decline of sociological dogmatism and the growing tendency to refuse to accept as final or definitive any single approach (such as quantitative), theory (such as structural-functional), or instrument (such as a Guttman scale). The pragmatic attitude in sociology identifies itself firmly with the use of scientific method as that method entails the continuing analysis of problematic situations, the development and consideration of alternative hypotheses relative to the problems, and the verification of the alternatives by some test of experience. Ongoing experience itself is conceived of as furnishing the ultimate test; for this reason the pragmatically inclined sociologist tends to be skeptical with respect to any instrument (theory, concept, method, technique, etc.) and resists allowing its conversion from a tool into an idol.

This pragmatic tendency to view and evaluate any heuristic device from the standpoint of its instrumental value in continuing an experiential (research) process gives considerable flexibility and adaptability to methodology. Nevertheless there are certain dangers involved in it. The dangers are similar to those of empiricism, and can be briefly summed up as normlessness, lack of direction and continuity, vacillation between conflicting approaches, concern with immediacy of problems and hence a lack of long-run vision. The primary contributions of the pragmatic point of view to methodology seem to lie in its emphasis on instrumentalism, experimental design (controlled experience), and modest working theory. Insofar as the emphasis is on these latter features rather than the former, methodology with respect to sociology and the social sciences generally has attained a "hardheadedness" rather than succumbed to a "headlessness."

The Orientational Mode
and Typological Procedure

There is still a vast disorder in sociology. Cumulative growth has been slow and has involved many methodological twistings and turnings, as evidenced by the various competing trends. Sociology has no definitive answers to society's major problems; it frequently seems to be preoccupied with the idiosyncratic and even trivial, in contrast to the general and comparative. There are elements in modern sociology, however, that show distinct promise of development toward a reliable scholarship. The selection of problems, formulation of procedures, and creation and application of techniques in modern sociology indicate a significant growth in methodological maturity and technical sophistication.

In retrospect it would seem that one of the most significant symptoms of movement into the epoch of unparalleled growth was the post-World War I publication of *The Polish Peasant* in 1920.[35] The publication of this monumental work by W. I. Thomas and Florian Znaniecki certainly cannot be held as the cause of the later developments in sociology, but it does represent in significant fashion the break with the classical encyclopedists and their speculative sociology, and the entry into the period of empirical development with all of its methodical and technical improvements. Thomas and Znaniecki, writing with reference to their research, made the following comment:

> Our work does not pretend to give any definite and universally valid sociological truths, nor to constitute a permanent model of sociological research; it merely claims to be a monograph, as nearly complete as possible under the circumstances, of a limited group at a certain period of its evolution, which may suggest studies of other groups, more detailed and more perfect methodically, thus helping the investigation of modern living societies to rise above its present stage of journalistic impression and preparing the ground for the determination of . . . general laws of human behavior.[36]

[35] W. I. Thomas and Florian Znaniecki, *The Polish Peasant in Europe and America*, 2 vols. (2nd ed.; New York: Knopf, 1927).

[36] *Ibid.*, pp. 1822-1823.

The preceding comment effectively expresses the general socio-logical outlook emerging at the time. The point of view represented by that statement is still symbolically characteristic of modern sociology. Moreover, it represents a comfortable working environment for the development and utilization of typologies and the exploration of their potential contributions and limitations. The aims of type construction are compatible with, indeed, analogous to, those expressed in the comment. The typologies presented in *The Polish Peasant* are no longer relevant except as a part of the historical record. Nevertheless the research process on the basis of which the work was produced, and the impact of that work on the social research process generally, must be viewed as of great importance. Similarly, typologies are always subordinate to the aims of research. As such, they are at the service of the social research process and have no relevance except that of a problem relevance within that context. It is for this reason that typologies can be viewed as natural tools within a pragmatically oriented social research process, striving continuously for increments or limited advances in knowledge with respect to social behavior.

Type construction can perhaps be best understood as an aspect of a pragmatic research methodology.[37] It is apparent that if typological procedure is to be increasingly utilized as a scholarly tool, the standards of quality and scholarship require an improved mastery and refinement of the use of the procedure. Moreover, as matters now stand it is American sociology which is most directly faced with the problem of refining that procedure. Despite the compatibility of the research orientation and context, this responsibility has been accepted in only a minor way in contrast to the assumption of many other responsibilities within the field of sociology. Nevertheless, noteworthy efforts have been made with respect to the explication of typological procedure.

[37] The ubiquitous Max Weber has been called many things. His talent was of such an order that he has been many things to many people, and he has been claimed as "one of their own" by scholars of different disciplines and widely varied orientations. At the risk of offending his many admirers, it is claimed here that he was a pragmatist. Moreover, in his utilization and explication of "the ideal type" he was a radical pragmatist. This is undoubtedly one of the factors contributing to his compatibility with the Americans and to their interest in the type.

The clarification which typological procedure has attained to date, however unsatisfactory, must be attributed primarily to the persistent empirical and theoretical labors of a small but active aggregate of sociologists. All of these scholars are, of course, greatly indebted to Max Weber for his ambiguous but highly provocative explication of "the ideal type." It must be noted, however, that the *reduction* of the ideal type as a *special case* of the *generic* constructed type represents a peculiarly American contribution. In the United States, Becker has unquestionably played the major role in developing the logical character of the type as well as in demonstrating its empirical utility. Tracing his writings, beginning in 1932 with those parts of *Systematic Sociology* which came directly from his pen, gives one the best single insight into the gradual transfer of attention from the ubiquitous ideal type to the more fundamental process of type construction.[38] The theoretical work of Abel, Barton, Bendix, Goode, Grimshaw, Hempel, Kolb, Lazarsfeld, Loomis, Parsons, Redfield, Rose, Shuetz, Sorokin, and Winch must also be cited with reference to the development of typology in the past three decades.[39]

---

[38] See Howard Becker and Alvin Boskoff (editors), *Modern Sociological Theory* (New York: Dryden Press, 1957), pp. 308-332, for key Becker bibliographic references.

[39] Theodore Abel, *Systematic Sociology in Germany* (New York: Columbia University Press, 1929); Allen Barton, "The Concept of Property–Space in Social Research," in P. F. Lazarsfeld and Morris Rosenberg (editors), *The Language of Social Research* (Glencoe: The Free Press, 1955), pp. 40-53; Reinhard Bendix, "Concepts and Generalizations in Comparative Sociological Studies," *American Sociological Review*, 28 (August, 1963), pp. 532-538; Reinhard Bendix and Bennett Berger, "Images of Society and Concept Formation in Sociology," in Llewellyn Gross (editor), *Symposium on Sociological Theory* (Evanston: Row, Peterson, 1959), pp. 92-118; W. J. Goode, "A Note on the Ideal Type," *American Sociological Review*, 12 (August, 1947), pp. 473-474; A. D. Grimshaw, "Specification of Boundaries of Constructed Types Through Use of the Pattern Variables," *The Sociological Quarterly*, 3 (July, 1962), pp. 179-195; C. G. Hempel, "Typological Methods in the Natural and Social Sciences," *Proceedings,* American Philosophical Association: Eastern Division, 1 (1952), pp. 65-86; W. L. Kolb, "The Peasant in Revolution: A Study in Constructive Typology" (unpublished Ph.D. dissertation, University of Wisconsin, 1943); P. F. Lazarsfeld, "Some Remarks on

There has also been a gradual increase in competent empirical and analytic adaptation of typology. Hughes studied the relation of personality types to the sacred and secular aspects of the division of labor; Hiller examined the "strike cycle" as it appeared in distinctive "patterns"; Redfield introduced the folk-urban continuum as a basis for the comparative examination of empirical cultures; Schmid intensively examined the German youth movement; Becker analyzed this movement and traced its ultimate perversion to Hitlerism; Foreman reported on the Negro lifeways in the South; Yinger analyzed the sociological significance of religion in the struggle for power; Young studied the secularization accompanying the acculturation of a Russian peasant group in an urban setting; Eister investigated the factors inducing and supporting the movement for Moral Rearmament; Loomis began the work of typing and comparing "social systems"; Merton developed his typology of modes of individual adaptation in approaching the problem of formulating a general theory of deviancy; Goode undertook an analysis of religion from a functionalist viewpoint through the use of types; Fichter developed a typology of religious orientation in examining the involvement of individuals in the life of the church; Gouldner developed a typology of bureaucratic structure in the attempt to break away from the traditional Weberian model; Riesman developed his typology of societal and personality types in his analysis of American social and cultural life; and Landecker delineated a typology

Typological Procedure in Social Research," *Zeitschrift für Sozialforschung,* 6 (1937), pp. 119-139; P. F. Lazarsfeld and A. H. Barton, "Qualitative Measurement in the Social Sciences," in Daniel Lerner and H. D. Lasswell (editors), *The Policy Sciences,* pp. 155-192; C. P. Loomis, "The Nature of Rural Social Systems: A Typological Analysis," *Rural Sociology,* 15 (June, 1950), pp. 156-174; Talcott Parsons, *The Structure of Social Action,* especially Chapters 14-17; Robert Redfield, "The Folk Society," *American Journal of Sociology,* 52 (January, 1947), pp. 293-308; Arnold Rose, "A Deductive Ideal-Type Method," *American Journal of Sociology,* 56 (July, 1950), pp. 35-42; Alfred Shuetz, "Concept and Theory Formation in the Social Sciences," *Journal of Philosophy,* 51 (April, 1954), pp. 257-273; P. A. Sorokin, *Social and Cultural Dynamics, passim;* and R. F. Winch, "Heuristic and Empirical Typologies," *American Sociological Review,* 12 (February, 1947), pp. 68-75.

of social integration.[40] The preceding citations are in no sense meant to be exhaustive of the great amount of typological activity that has been and is being carried on. It represents a mere skimming off of some of the work as an indication of the range of typological activity. In a pragmatic sense, American sociology has extensively utilized typological procedures in its advance toward a greater knowledge of social behavior.

[40] E. C. Hughes, "Personality Types and the Division of Labor," *American Journal of Sociology,* 33 (March, 1928), pp. 754-768; E. T. Hiller, *The Strike Cycle* (Chicago: University of Chicago Press, 1928); Robert Redfield, *Tepoztlan: A Mexican Village* (Chicago: University of Chicago Press, 1930); and his *The Folk Culture of Yucatan* (Chicago: University of Chicago Press, 1941); Robert Schmid, "German Youth Movements: A Typological Study" (unpublished Ph.D. dissertation, University of Wisconsin, 1941); Howard Becker, *German Youth: Bond or Free* (New York: Grove Press, 1946); P. B. Foreman, "Negro Lifeways in the Rural South: A Typological Approach to Social Differentiation," *American Sociological Review,* 13 (August, 1948), pp. 409-418; J. M. Yinger, *Religion in the Struggle for Power* (Durham: Duke University Press, 1946); Pauline Young, *Pilgrims of Russian Town* (Chicago: University of Chicago Press, 1932); A. W. Eister, *Drawing-Room Conversion: A Sociological Account of the Oxford Group Movement* (Durham: Duke University Press, 1950); C. P. Loomis and J. A. Beegle, "A Typological Analysis of Social Systems," *Sociometry,* 9 (August, 1948), pp. 147-191; R. K. Merton, "Social Structure and Anomie," in his *Social Theory and Social Structure,* pp. 125-133; W. J. Goode, *Religion Among the Primitives* (Glencoe: The Free Press, 1948); Joseph Fichter, *Social Relations in the Urban Parish* (Chicago: University of Chicago Press, 1954); A. W. Gouldner, *Patterns of Industrial Bureaucracy* (Glencoe: The Free Press, 1954); David Riesman *et al., The Lonely Crowd* (New Haven: Yale University Press, 1950); Werner Landecker, "Types of Integration and Their Measurement," *American Journal of Sociology,* 56 (January, 1951), pp. 332-340.

———5

The Societal Continuum: Polar Types

Few concepts have had greater impact upon the social sciences than *Gemeinschaft* and *Gesellschaft*. These fundamental concepts are constructed types which attempt to describe the essence of motivations in human relationships when, on the one hand, natural or spontaneous will has primacy, or, on the other, when rational will has primacy. The creation of the concepts *Gemeinschaft* and *Gesellschaft* resulted from Tönnies' effort to understand the true meaning of both the rational school of natural law and the opposing historical and romantic theories. They permitted a synthesis of two opposing conceptions of social order. Moreover, they enabled social scientists to understand more adequately the essence of *Gesellschaft*-like logic, upon which classical economics is based and the standards of efficiency by which such organizations as bureaucracies function, in contrast to the essence of the *Gemeinschaft*-like motivation in which the relationships are ends in themselves, as in friendship groupings.

The concepts made it possible to synthesize rationalism and romanticism, idealism and materialism, realism and nominalism. In addition, they made it possible to comprehend the main course of history in terms of structural change from *Gemeinschaft* to *Gesellschaft*. Moreover, the concepts made it possible to understand better the functional interpretation of *Gemeinschaft* and *Gesellschaft* type relations in concrete social systems.

However important the Tönnies formulation has been historically, it is merely one example of the very old tradition of typing social entities antithetically. As Sorokin has pointed out, the tradition may be traced back to the philosophical speculation of the Classical Greeks and to the epoch of Confucius.[1] Despite the age of the tradition, it still has a marked vitality, and appears to be one of the fundamental approaches to sociological phenomena. Other examples of this tradition are such familiar conceptualizations as Maine's status society and contract society, Spencer's militant and industrial forms, Ratzenhofer's conquest state and culture state, Wundt's natural and cultural polarity, Durkheim's mechanical and organic solidarity, Cooley's primary and secondary (implicit) groups, MacIver's communal and associational relations, Zimmerman's localistic and cosmopolitan communities, Odum's folk–state pair, Redfield's folk–urban continuum, Sorokin's familistic vs. contractual relations, Becker's sacred and secular societies, as well as such nonpersonalized but common dichotomies as primitive–civilized, complex vs. simple, literate–nonliterate, developed vs. underdeveloped, advanced vs. backward, traditional vs. modern, and rural vs. urban.

Obviously these varied polarizations are not interchangeable and do not abstract the same things out of the social world, but they do have something in common. Not only do they frequently represent similar "content," but, perhaps more importantly, in common they exemplify the view that it is necessary to distinguish fundamentally different types of social organizations in order to establish a range within which transitional or intermediate forms can be comprehended. The polar extremes in point are clearly ideal, or constructed types, despite the fact that some of the aforementioned theorists tended to treat their types as ontological entities rather than as conceptual devices. The polar type formulations—at first, implicitly but in recent years with increasing explicitness—have firmly established the point that the continuum is a vital notion in the comparative analysis of social phenomena. The types establish the outer limits, or standards, by means of which the processes of change or intermediate structural forms can be comprehended from the perspective of the continuum. It is in this sense that general types,

---

[1] P. A. Sorokin in the "Preface" to Ferdinand Tönnies, *Community and Society: Gemeinschaft und Gesellschaft,* translated and introduced by C. P. Loomis (East Lansing: Michigan State University Press, 1957).

such as those we have mentioned, continue to play an important role in sociological analysis.

The programme of this chapter shall include three separate but interdependent analyses. First, a brief examination of the historical significance of some of the major and more persistent general type constructs will be undertaken. Second, the polar typology *Gemeinschaft* and *Gesellschaft* will be reformulated in terms of (a) the attributes of the family of polar typologies, and (b) a fusion of the typology with the structural-functional perspective and style of social systems analysis. This undertaking is not viewed as a mere exercise; on the contrary it is based upon the assumption that such a fusion is preliminary to the further development of genuinely comparative studies of empirical social systems. Third, and following this brief explication of a "modernized" polar typology, an examination of the nature and potential of the comparative study of social systems is undertaken. The thesis is advanced that the conception of *fundamental types of social systems* is not an obsolescent perspective when formulated in terms of the societal continuum, and that such types constitute the major outlines of the cognitive map within which the comparative study of diverse empirical social systems can be efficiently pursued.[2]

Tönnies: Gemeinschaft and Gesellschaft

Tönnies conceived of all social relations as products of human will. He states:

> The concept of human will . . . implies a twofold meaning. Since all mental action involves thinking, I distinguish between the will which includes the thinking and the thinking which encompasses the will. Each represents an inherent whole which unites in itself

[2] The exposition in this chapter is based to a considerable extent on earlier collaborations with C. P. Loomis. See in particular: J. C. McKinney and C. P. Loomis, "The Typological Tradition," in J. S. Roucek (ed.), *Contemporary Sociology* (New York: Philosophical Library, 1958), pp. 557-582; and the "Introduction" to Tönnies, *Community and Society: Gemeinschaft und Gesellschaft*, pp. 12-29.

a multiplicity of feelings, instincts, and desires. This unity should in the first case be understood as a real or natural one; in the second case as a conceptual or artificial one. The will of the human being in the first form I call natural will (*Wesenwille*); in the second form rational will (*Kürwille*).[3]

The three simple forms of natural will are (a) liking, (b) habit, and (c) memory. In contrast, the three simple forms of rational will are (a) deliberation, (b) discrimination, and (c) conception. Emanating out of these two different wills are the two fundamentally different forms of human bonds. Tönnies calls all associations in which natural will predominates *Gemeinschaft,* and he views all those which are formed and conditioned by rational will as being *Gesellschaft.*

A *Gemeinschaft*-like entity may be distinguished by virtue of its possession of the following attributes: unity; a division of labor based upon mutual aid and helpfulness; an equilibrium of individual wills in mutual interdependence; authority based upon age, wisdom, and benevolent force; common habitat; common action directed toward common goals understood as given; kinship; friendship; reciprocal and binding sentiment; diffuse or blanket obligations; common language, custom, and belief; mutual possession and enjoyment; sacred tradition; and the spirit of brotherhood. In sum, *Gemeinschaft* is a relationship of concord based upon bonds of (a) blood (kindship), (b) place (neighborhood), or (c) mind (friendship).

In contrast, a *Gesellschaft* may be distinguished in terms of the following characteristics: separation rather than unification; individualism; action in terms of self-interest; conventions or positive and specific definitions and regulations; delimited spheres of contact; money and credit relationships; dominance by merchants, capitalists, and a power elite; obligations limited and the feelings and strivings of others disregarded on the level of sentiment; and lack of mutual familiar relations. In sum, the *Gesellschaft*-like entity, based upon rational will, consists of contractual and functionally

[3] Ferdinand Tönnies, *Fundamental Concepts of Sociology* (*Gemeinschaft und Gesellschaft*), translated and introduced by C. P. Loomis (New York: American Book Co., 1940), p. 119.

specific relationships consciously established for the attainment of planned objectives. The *Gesellschaft* is articulated through (a) convention, (b) legislation, and (c) public opinion, and exists in city, national, and cosmopolitan life.

Tönnies utilized the concepts of *Gemeinschaft* and *Gesellschaft* first of all as "normal types," or what Weber later called "ideal types" in the analysis of social structure. In addition, however, he utilized them to analyze the data of history and discovered them to be transhistorical sociological categories. Tönnies found the main evolutionary path of history to be the transition from *Gemeinschaft* to *Gesellschaft,* and in so doing indicated that they may coexist and be intertwined in various empirical structures in different degrees at different times. In viewing *Gemeinschaft* and *Gesellschaft* as transhistorical simultaneously, Tönnies helped to free sociology from its entanglement with the historical viewpoint so common in Germany. Moreover, although his concepts are psychologically relevant and psychologically based, he helped begin a tradition of thinking which may eventually articulate the relationship between the social system and the personality system without psychologizing the former.[4] In brief, Tönnies not only aided significantly in the establishment of a *de facto* field of sociology, but also contributed sociological conceptual forms that are still useful.

Durkheim: Mechanical and Organic Solidarity

Describing not merely the range of human existence, but what to him appeared as an irreversible historical trend, Durkheim in his study of the division of labor polarized society into two types.[5]

---

[4] As Hans Freyer says: "His system was no geometry of social forms and also no psychology of social situations. Rather it is composed of true structural concepts with which the social structures of man may be ordered." See Hans Freyer, *Sociologie als Wirklichkeitswissenschaft* (Leipzig and Berlin: B. G. Teubner, 1930), p. 188.

[5] Emile Durkheim, *The Division of Labor in Society,* translated from the first French edition, 1893, by George Simpson (Glencoe: The Free Press, 1947).

The first type is the *mechanically solidary society,* wherein beliefs and conduct are alike. People are homogeneous mentally and morally, hence communities are uniform and nonatomized. It is in this type of society that a totality of beliefs and sentiments common to all men exists, and which Durkheim called the *conscience collective.* This conscience is characterized by the attributes of *exteriority* and *constraint.* Exteriority refers to the fact that the conscience as totality is never a product of the members of society at any one point in time; constraint has reference to the significant point that the membership of a mechanically solidary society cannot morally refute its collective conscience. Offense against the collective conscience is moral offense and is punishable by repressive law.

Durkheim's second polar type, defining the direction of historical development, is the *organically solidary society,* wherein society is held together by the interdependence of its parts. The division of labor is a result of the struggle for existence, and the specialization of labor stimulated individualism and differentiation. People in the society are heterogeneous; their mental and moral similarities have disappeared. Volume and material and moral density of people are the necessary conditions for the division, since they make it possible for more individuals to make sufficient contact, and thus be able to act and react upon one another. This, in turn, makes possible the contact and interconnection of formerly separate collectivities and breaks down the insulation between them, with resultant diversification. The primary consequence of this whole process is the weakening of the *conscience collective.* Crime ceases to be an offense against common moral sentiments and becomes an offense against personal rights. Spontaneous relations between individuals are replaced by contractual associations. Offensive acts then lose their sacrilegious character and repressive law is replaced by restitutive law.

Durkheim's investigation of suicide[6] brought about a fundamental change in his conception of the *conscience collective* as put forth in *The Division of Labor.* The emphasis on the strong predominance of the conscience in the mechanically solidary society

[6] Emile Durkheim, *Suicide,* translated from the 1930 French edition (first edition 1897) by J. A. Spaulding and George Simpson (Glencoe: The Free Press, 1951).

and the weakening of the conscience in the organically solidary society was supplanted by a recognition of the existence of the *conscience collective* in the differentiated, heterogeneous, organically solidary society as the basis of either egoistic or altruistic order. A more specific definition of its absence was arrived at—the anomic society, wherein the collective beliefs and sentiments no longer effectively regulate social action and society persists only on the basis of a shifting and precarious consensus. The change from mechanical solidarity to organic solidarity does not result in an automatic loss of *conscience collective,* but in an alteration in its forms. The "non-contractual basis of contract" is a moral, and hence collective, foundation for individualistic and secular association. Durkheim's recognition of this, based upon the research use of his types, has given an undeniable impetus to the specialized socio-logical study of law, religion, and knowledge due to the now obvious relation of these phenomena to social structure.

Cooley: The Primary Group

Cooley, an American contemporary of Durkheim, main-tained that neither the individual nor the group has primacy in social action. Contrary to Durkheim, who gave the group primacy over its individual members, and contrary to Spencer, who asserted that the individual is basic and the group only the sum total of its members, Cooley perceived the importance of interactive process of mutual influence between group and individual. For him the most important groups in the formation of individual human nature and the development of social behavior and organization are what he called *primary groups.*[7]

The chief characteristics imputed to the primary group by Cooley were face to face association, an unspecialized character of that association, relative permanence, involvement of a relatively small number of persons, and relative intimacy among the par-ticipants. As characteristic examples of the primary group, Cooley typically cited the family or household group, the old-fashioned neighborhood, and the spontaneous play-group of children. Cooley

[7] C. H. Cooley, *Social Organization* (New York: Scribners, 1909), pp. 23-31.

took the view that children everywhere, under the most diverse circumstances, participate in such groups and that the intimate association developed there works upon them in fairly uniform fashion. The development of sympathetic insight into the moods of other people, of both the flexible type of behavior and the common attitudes and sentiments characteristic of people, are imputed to this mode of association.

> (Such groups) . . . are primary in several senses, but chiefly in that they are fundamental in forming the social nature and ideals of the individual. The result of intimate association, psychologically, is a certain fusion of individualities in a common whole, so that one's very self, for many purposes at least, is the common life and purpose of the group. Perhaps the simplest way of describing this wholeness is by saying that it is a "we"; it involves the sort of sympathy and mutual identification for which "we" is the natural expression. One lives in the feeling of the whole and finds the chief aims of his will in that feeling.[8]

Cooley's combination of organic theory and psychological orientation which led him to the development of the concept of the "looking-glass" self, and to the idea that "self and society are twin born,"[9] resulted in the conceptualization of the primary group apparently independently of the other theorists discussed here. He did not use the term "secondary group," but permitted the implicit type, under which fall those groups with characteristics opposite to the primary groups, to go unnamed. Since the time of Cooley, the primary group, in one form or another, has been a focal point of attention in American sociology. From the mid-thirties to the present, a tremendous amount of research pertaining to this form of social structure has been conducted.[10]

[8] *Ibid.*, p. 23.

[9] C. H. Cooley, R. C. Angell, and L. J. Carr, *Introductory Sociology* (New York: Scribners, 1933), pp. 55-56.

[10] For a brief and yet comprehensive statement on the study of the primary group, with particular attention to the contributions of Mayo, Lewin and Moreno, see E. A. Shils, "The Study of the Primary Group," in Daniel Lerner and H. D. Lasswell (eds.), *The Policy Sciences* (Stanford: Stanford University Press, 1951), pp. 44-69. See also A. W. Eister, "Basic Continuities in the Study of Small Groups," in Howard Becker and Alvin Boskoff (eds.), *Modern Sociological Theory* (New York: Dryden Press, 1957), pp. 305-339.

Redfield: The Folk–Urban Continuum

The folk-urban typology of Redfield has been the best known and most controversial typological formulation in cultural anthropology for the past three decades. It has often been criticized, particularly by idiographically-minded field workers, but it nevertheless has been the stimulant for a great amount of research.[11]

Redfield has formulated a typological version of folk society by linking together a set of attributes. In the absence of explicit delineation, the urban type is simply composed of the opposite attributes, and hence becomes the polar antithesis.

To Redfield, the folk society is a small collectivity containing no more people within it than can know each other well. It is an isolated, nonliterate, homogeneous grouping with a strong sense of solidarity. Technology is simple, and aside from the division of function between the sexes there is little other division of labor; hence the group is economically independent of other groups. The ways in which problems are met by the society are conventionalized by long intercommunication within the group, and these ways have become interrelated with one another to constitute a coherent and self-consistent system: a culture. Behavior is spontaneous, traditional, personal, and there is no motivation toward reflection, criti-

---

[11] To cite some of the examples of the use of the continuum, see Horace Miner, *St. Denis: A French–Canadian Parish* (Chicago: University of Chicago Press, 1939); Herbert Passin and J. W. Bennett, "Changing Agricultural Magic in Southern Illinois: A Systematic Analysis of Folk-Urban Transitions," *Social Forces,* 22 (October, 1943), pp. 98-106; Edward Spicer, *Pasqua: A Yaqui Village in Arizona* (Chicago: University of Chicago Press, 1940). Some of the more significant criticisms are contained in the following: Neal Gross, "Cultural Variables in Rural Communities," *American Journal of Sociology,* 53 (March, 1948), pp. 344-350; Oscar Lewis, *Tepoztlan Revisited* (Urbana: University of Illinois Press, 1951); Julian Steward, *Area Research: Concepts and Methods* (New York: Social Science Research Council, 1950); Gideon Sjoberg, "The Preindustrial City," *American Journal of Sociology,* 60 (March, 1955), pp. 438-445; Howard Becker, "Sacred and Secular Societies: Considered with Reference to Folk-State and Similar Classifications," *Social Forces,* 28 (May, 1950), pp. 361-376; and Oscar Lewis, "Tepoztlan Restudied: A Critique of the Folk-Urban Conceptualization of Social Change," *Rural Sociology,* 18 (June, 1953), pp. 121-134.

cism, or experimentation. Kinship, with its relations and institutions, is central to all experience, and the family is the unit of action. The value of traditional acts and objects is not to be questioned; hence they are sacred. The sacredness of objects is apparent in the ways in which objects are hedged-in with restraints and taboos that keep them from being commonplace. All activities, even those of economic production, are ends in themselves. The more remote ends of living are taken as given. Thus the folk society exists not so much on the basis of exchange of useful functions as in common understanding as to what is to be done.

Redfield contends that understanding of society in general and of our own modern urbanized society in particular can be gained through consideration of the societies least like our own—folk societies. His scheme defines a type, the *folk society,* which is the polar opposite of urban society. The type is a construct and no known society precisely corresponds to it. It is "created only because through it we may hope to understand reality. Its function is to suggest aspects of real societies which deserve study, and especially to suggest hypotheses as to what, under certain defined conditions, may be generally true about society." [12] The fact that the typology has served this function to a significant degree is evidenced by the gratifying amount of research done in terms of it since the initial tentative type formulation in 1930 in the study of Tepoztlan.[13]

Redfield explicitly indicates his indebtedness to Maine, Durkheim, and Tönnies, and points out that his folk society type results from a restatement of the conceptions of these three men in the light coming from consideration of primitive societies.[14] It is less generalized and abstract than any of the sets of concepts formulated by Maine, Durkheim, and Tönnies, but it contains essentially the same attributes. As a consequence, Redfield has succeeded in transferring the central considerations of these concepts to a cross-cultural basis and facilitated the comparative study of societies.

[12] Robert Redfield, "The Folk Society," *American Journal of Sociology,* 52 (January, 1947), p. 295.

[13] Robert Redfield, *Tepoztlan, A Mexican Village* (Chicago: University of Chicago Press, 1930).

[14] Robert Redfield, "Rural Sociology and the Folk Society," *Rural Sociology,* 8 (March, 1943), pp. 68-71.

Becker: Sacred and Secular Societies

The sacred–secular antithesis has been utilized by many people, but it has its most elaborate construction in the work of Howard Becker.[15] Becker makes it very explicit that sacred and secular societies are constructed types. He has meticulously and skillfully preserved their conceptual character and in so doing has contributed significantly to the methodology of typing.

The *sacred society* is isolated vicinally, socially, and mentally. This isolation leads to fixation of habit and neophobia, relations of avoidance, and traditional in-group–out-group attitudes. The concrete is emphasized at the expense of abstraction. Social contacts are primary. Tradition and ritual play a large part in the life of the individual. There is the dominance of sacredness even in the economic sphere, which works toward the maintenance of self-sufficiency and against any development of the pecuniary attitude. The division of labor is simple. Kinship ties are strong and are manifest in "great family" relationships. All forms of activity are under sacred sanctions, and hence violent social control is at a minimum. The forces of gossip and tradition are powerful tools of control. Nonrational behavior is predominant, with an important element of supernaturalism present. Rationalism, particularly in the form of science, is largely absent. The value system is impermeable.

The *secular society* lies at the opposite pole of the continuum and is vicinally, socially, and mentally accessible. Habit fixation is rendered difficult by the accessibility of the social structure. There is an absence of social barriers. Social circulation is unimpeded. Ends are evaluated in terms of happiness and means according to the norm of efficiency. Tradition and ritual are minimal. Rationality is dominant, and science is pervasive and powerful. The kinship group is manifest in the conjugal family form. Innovation is fre-

[15] See in particular: Howard Becker, *Through Values to Social Interpretation* (Durham: Duke University Press, 1950), pp. 248-280; "1951 Commentary on Value-System Terminology," in Howard Becker and H. E. Barnes, *Social Thought from Lore to Science* (2nd ed.; Washington, D. C.: Harren Press, 1952), pp. i-xxii; and "Current Sacred–Secular Theory and Its Development," in Becker and Boskoff, *Modern Sociological Theory*, pp. 133-185.

quent; change is sought after and idealized as progress. Informal sanctions are weak and formal law prevails. Offense against the law invokes little social disapproval. Legal contracts are the rule. Individuation is prominent in society and the value system is permeable.

These two constructed types cannot be found except in empirical approximations to the major subtypes derived by Becker. The *folk–sacred* society is best exemplified by the old-fashioned and primitive groups in the world. The *prescribed–sacred* finds its closest approximation in the Geneva theocracy of Calvin, the Jesuit state of Paraguay, Fascist Italy, Nazi Germany, and Soviet Russia. The *principled–secular* is an equilibrating society wherein the extreme aspects of the sacred are lost, and yet a principle derived from the sacred value system puts a check on rampant change and reduces the potential of mental accessibility. The *normless–secular* is the anomic form of the secular society. Instances are most frequently found in centers of culture contact wherein the devices of communication generate social accessibility.

The primary value of the Becker polarity lies in its use in discovering the sacred or secular aspects of a group relationship conceived of as *system,* and exposing the process of secularization or sacrilization as an aspect of change that might be taking place. In contrast to the preceding typologies, there is no notion of irreversible process in the sacred–secular schema. Although the main historical trend has been toward secularization, it is equally permissible to speak of specific cases of sacrilization, as for instance in the Nazi movement.[16] Also in contrast to earlier typologists, Becker has recognized the fundamental limitations of the general types: their construction on a very general level makes them "sponge" types, and hence precludes their use for many specific research purposes. As a consequence, Becker has derived a large number of subtypes incorporating particular combinations of attributes for which empirical approximations can readily be found in quite specific research contexts.[17] Due to the fact that the subtypes are derivations, theoretic

[16] Becker describes a sacrilezation process in *German Youth: Bond or Free* (New York: Grove Press, 1946).

[17] See Becker, *Through Values to Social Interpretation,* pp. 264 and 276, for a schematic presentation of the subtypes.

articulation is retained and hence the comparative study of concrete groupings is facilitated. The sacred–secular polarity has been constructed along comprehensive lines, and yet remains versatile and flexible.

Sorokin: Familistic, Contractual and Compulsory Relations

As Sorokin states in the foreword to the English edition of *Gemeinschaft und Gesellschaft*, these types are reiterated up to, and presumable in, his own thinking. Sorokin's *familistic* and *contractual* relationships correspond respectively to *Gemeinschaft* and *Gesellschaft* and have been used as pairs to accompany these concepts, i.e., *familistic Gemeinschaft* and *contractual Gesellschaft*.[18] Sorokin has himself stated that his third type, *compulsory* relations, represents conceptualization on a different level. Either *familistic* relationships or *contractual* voluntary relationships may be more or less in opposition to compulsory relations. We shall here treat only the *familistic* and *contractual* relationships. For Sorokin *familistic* relationships are permeated by mutual love, sacrifice and devotion. They are most frequently found among members of a devoted family and among real friends. *Familistic* relations represent a fusion of the ego into "we." Both joys and sorrows are shared in common and those involved need one another, seek one another, sacrifice for one another and love one another. Norms of such relations require that the participation be all-embracing, all-forgiving, all-bestowing, and unlimited.

The *contractual* relationship is limited and specified, covering only one narrow sector of the lives of the parties involved. Typical contractual relationships are those of employer and employee, buyer and seller, plumber and householder. The rights and duties of each party are specified by contract. The unity of such groups is rooted in the sober calculation of advantage. It is self-centered and utilitarian. Typically one member of the relationship tries to get as much from

---

[18] C. P. Loomis and J. A. Beegle, *Rural Social Systems* (New York: Prentice-Hall, 1950).

the other as possible with the smallest possible contribution. They may remain strangers to each other, one party little interested in the well-being, activities and philosophy of the other. There is no fusion to produce a homogeneous "we." Such relations are usually of limited duration, voluntary, and stand in contrast to those which are compulsory. Relationships may develop from familistic to contractual or vice versa.[19]

Weber: Types of Action Orientation

Although not following properly in the tradition of dichotomously typing society, the types of action constructed by Weber are directly relevant to the Tönnies formulation, the Parsons formulation which is to follow, and the present context in general. All the relationships discussed here, indeed, all relations, are based upon a continuity of social action.[20] Weber starts by typing the action context, and then constructs his varied relationship types on the basis of the underlying typical lines of action. Action is typed:

> (1) in terms of rational orientation to a system of discrete individual ends (*zweckrational*), that is, through expectations as to the behavior of objects in the external situation and of other human individuals, making use of these expectations as "conditions" or "means" for the successful attainment of the actor's own rationally chosen ends; (2) in terms of rational orientation to an absolute value (*wertrational*), involving a conscious belief in the absolute value of some ethical, aesthetic, religious, or other form of behaviour, entirely for its own sake and independently of any prospects of external success, (3) in terms of affectual orientation, especially emotional, determined by the specific affects and states of feeling

[19] P. A. Sorokin, *Social and Cultural Dynamics*, Vol. 3 (New York: American Book Co., 1937), p. 40. See also his *Society, Culture, and Personality* (New York: Harper and Brothers, 1947), pp. 93-118.

[20] We define as "action" any concrete system maintained by a sequence of what Parsons calls "unit acts." "In a unit act there are identifiable as minimum characteristics the following: (1) an end, (2) a situation, analyzable in turn into (a) means and (b) conditions, and (3) at least one selective standard in terms of which the end is related to the situation." *The Structure of Social Action* (2nd ed.; Glencoe: The Free Press, 1949), p. 77.

of the actor; (4) traditionally oriented, through the habituation of long practice.[21]

It may be seen that *zweckrational* is essentially expedient rationality and denotes a system of action involving an actor's motives, conditions, means, and ends wherein the actor weighs the possible alternative ends and means available to him in terms of his purposes and selects the course of action most expedient to him. A system of discrete ends exists for the actor, and an orientation toward them involves such considerations as efficiency, cost, undesirable consequences, amount of return, and calculating the results which condition the otherwise unrestrained adaptation of means to the achievement of ends. This form of rationality plays a dominant role in Weber's overall sociological analysis.

Weber differentiates *wertrational* orientation from expedient rationality through the inclusion of an "absolute value" which eliminates the possibility of the actor's selection from alternative ends. Ultimately, this bars the possible selection of certain means. This is a sanctioned form of rationality wherein the actual adaptation of means toward the achievement of the absolute, or ultimate end (value), may comply with the criteria of expedience, but cannot in itself be *zweckrational* in view of the lack of a discrete system of ends and the possibility of weighing them in terms of available means and prevailing conditions. The sole important consideration of the actor is the realization of the value.

Affectual action is actually treated by Weber as a form of nonrationality (possibly even irrationality), wherein means and ends become fused and, therefore, insusceptible to delineation in behavior. This form of action is dominated by emotional states of feeling of the actor and involves an impulsive or uncontrolled reaction to some exceptional stimulus. It occurs as a release from tension, and therefore the later phases of an affectual act may become increasingly rational.

Traditional action is also treated by Weber as a deviation from rational orientation, in that the means involved become ends in

[21] Max Weber, *The Theory of Social and Economic Organization*, translated by A. M. Henderson and Talcott Parsons (New York: Oxford University Press, 1947), p. 115.

themselves or hold the same rank as ends. This type of action is an almost automatic reaction to habitual stimuli which guide behavior in repeatedly followed and prevailing courses. Typically this means a conformity with the accepted and prevalent ways of behavior with little evaluation or consideration of their expedience.

These four ideal–typical modes of social action were formulated by Weber for purposes of comparison with actual occurrences of behavior. Such behavior, of course, shades across the types in various degrees of approximation. It is important to note, however, that in Weber's actual analysis of empirical occurrences there is a marked tendency on his part to utilize the *zweckrational* orientation as the basis for understanding and interpreting behavior, thereby reducing the other forms to the status of residual categories. In effect, this produces an implicit rational–nonrational dichotomy underlying the action types, which in turn results in the conceptualization of relationships in these terms. Weber's *Vergemeinschaftung* and *Vergesellschaftung* are directly modeled upon Tönnies' formulations, although Weber does introduce a third category of *Kampf* (conflict) that is not provided for in Tönnies' system. *Zweckrational* may be compared with Tönnies' *Kurwille* and the resulting *Gesellschaft*, whereas *wertrational, affectual,* and *traditional* behavior may be identified with Tönnies' *Wesenwille* and the resulting *Gemeinschaft*.[22] It is easy to see how Weber reached his conclusion that the main trend of history was that of increased rationalization. This compares directly with Tönnies' conclusions regarding the trend toward *Gesellschaft,* and also with the related conclusion of Sorokin, Becker, Durkheim, and Redfield.

Parsons: The Pattern Variables of Action Orientation

The pattern variables of action orientation (or of value orientation or role definition, as they are variously called) constitute

---

[22] Four years before his death Tönnies discussed his own typology in relation to these ideal types of Max Weber. His analysis concurs with the view presented here. See Ferdinand Tönnies, *Einfuehrung in die Sociologie* (Stuttgart: Ferdinand Enke, 1931), pp. 6 and 8.

the most persistent link between personal, cultural, and social systems in Parsons' theory of social action.[23] As a consequence, they are of central importance in articulating the scheme. It is apparent that the pattern variables were born as a negative reaction to what Parsons conceived of as the inadequacies of Weber's types of action and Tönnies' polar types. Parsons ends his classic discussion of *Gemeinschaft* and *Gesellschaft* with the following comment:

> . . . this discussion of *Gemeinschaft* and *Gesellschaft* should not be taken to mean that these concepts are unreservedly acceptable as the basis for a general classification of social relationships or, indeed, that it is possible to start from *any* dichotomy of only two types. The basic types cannot be reduced to two, or even to the three that Weber used. To attempt to develop such a scheme of classification would be definitely outside the scope of the present study. Such an attempt would, however, have to make a critical examination of the schemes of Tönnies, Weber and some others one of its main tasks.

> However, the aspects of Tönnies' classification with which this discussion has been concerned do involve distinctions of basic importance for any such scheme and would hence have to be built into the wider scheme, which would probably involve considerable alteration in their form of statement.[24]

At base the attitude of Parsons indicated a recognition of the fact that general "sponge" types had inherent limitations with respect to the handling of many specific problems. Weber manifested some recognition of this; Becker has been acutely aware of it; and Loomis, in particular, in recent years has been directly concerned with the problem. Whereas Becker approached the problem by deriving a series of subtypes for empirical purposes, Parsons, in line with his propensity for systematic theory, chose the approach of deriving the components of action orientation directly from the structure of social action.

In starting his analysis with an actor in a situation, Parsons contends that any actor must make five separate choices before the action will have a determinate meaning for him. Meaning does not automatically emerge in a situation, but is based upon the actor's selections from the five sets of alternatives posed for him in any situation. These dichotomies are termed "the pattern variables of action orientation" and the problems of choice between them are termed "the dilemmas of action."

Affectivity vs. *affective neutrality* is the gratification–discipline dilemma and involves the problem of accepting an opportunity for gratification without regard for its consequences or, conversely, evaluating it with regard for its consequences. It is a matter of whether evaluation will take place or not in a given situation.

Particularism vs. *universalism* is the dilemma of choice between types of value standards. It involves evaluating an object of action either in terms of its relations to the actor and his specific object relationship situation or in terms of its relations to a generalized frame of reference. This dilemma is one concerning primacy of cathectic or cognitive standards.

Ascription vs. *achievement* is the dilemma of choice between modalities of the social object and involves the actor's seeing the social object either as a composite of ascribed qualities or, conversely, as a composite of performances. This dilemma concerns the conception of objects as attribute or action complexes.

Diffuseness vs. *specificity* is the dilemma of the definition of the scope of interest in the object. It involves the concession of an undefined set of rights to be delimited only by conflicting demands, to a social object as against the concession to a social object of a clearly specified and limited set of rights. This dilemma concerns the scope of significance of the object in action.

Collective orientation vs. *self-orientation* is the collective interest vs. private interest dilemma, and involves the problem of considering an act either with respect to its significance for a collectivity or a moral code, or with respect to its personal significance. This dilemma concerns the primacy of moral standards in a procedure of evaluation.[25]

[25] For an extensive development of the pattern-variables and their relation to social structure, see Talcott Parsons, *The Social System* (Glencoe: The Free Press, 1951), especially Chapters 2 and 3. For critical examination see Max Black (ed.), *The Social Theories of Talcott Parsons* (Englewood Cliffs: Prentice-Hall, 1961), especially pp. 38-44, 283-288, and 310-363.

Parsons contends that these pattern-variables are the single most important thread of continuity in the action frame of reference, and that they enter in at four different levels. On the concrete level of empirical action, they exist as five discrete choices an actor must explicitly or implicitly make before he can act. They enter on the collectivity level as role definitions, wherein actions of role-incumbents tend to be specified in terms of one side or another of a dilemma. The variables also enter on the cultural level as aspects of value standards. In that value standards are rules governing action, and insofar as an actor is committed to a standard, he will habitually choose the horn of the dilemma specified by adherence to that standard. As a consequence, the variables also enter at the personality level.

In view of their history, derivation, and content, it seems justifiable to conclude that the pattern-variables represent a further and more elaborate specification of the aspects of society dealt with by *Gemeinschaft* and *Gesellschaft*.[26] In our judgment it is legitimate to speak of them as theoretical components of the more general types. On the basis of our analysis we feel that it is possible to take Parsons' first four variables, add Sorokin's familistic–contractual dichotomy, and Weber's rational–traditional pair, and conceive of them as subtypes of *Gemeinschaft* and *Gesellschaft* or sacred–secular. In so doing it is our judgment that all of the major implications and content of these two typologies are covered, and in addition the advantage of having more specific categories to work with is gained. The fit with the Durkheim, Cooley, and Redfied typologies is not

---

[26] Parsons has stated that he had been dissatisfied with the concepts *Gemeinschaft* and *Gesellschaft* in handling the professions, especially the doctor-patient relationship. However, four out of his five variables place this on the same side; namely, the *Gesellschaft* side. Only on the collectivity vs. self-orientation does it fall on the *Gemeinschaft* side. It is interesting to note, however, that the collectivity orientation in this relationship rests on an institutional rather than a motivational base. The collectivity orientation of the physician has become built into a set of institutionalized expectations, and hence it is to a physician's self-interest to act contrary to his own self-interest in an immediate situation (collectivity orientation)—but *not in the "long run."* The long-run orientation is self rather than collectivity, and hence in this sense all the variables fall on the *Gesellschaft* side. See Parsons, *The Social System*, p. 473.

as good because of the differences in construction and levels of abstraction, but nevertheless it seems obvious that there are basic similarities between all of the typologies treated here. Thus the things that can be empirically said about *Gemeinschaft* and *Gesellschaft* or sacred and secular at least have implications for the other typologies.

This brief review of some of the classic polar typologies has emphasized the role of the continuum in sociological thought. In light of the predominance of structural-functional theory with its emphasis on the social system, an analysis of the relationship between the two perspectives is in order.

The Social System and the Continuum

The central notion of what is commonly referred to as structural-functional theory is that of the social system.[27] Parsons has defined the social system in bare essentials as consisting of "a plurality of individual actors interacting with each other in a situation which has at least a physical or environmental aspect, actors who are motivated in terms of a tendency to the 'optimization of gratification' and whose relation to their situations, including each other, is defined and mediated in terms of a system of culturally struc-

[27] Structural-functionalism is in most respects indistinguishable from general sociological theory. Perhaps its primary importance lies in the fact that it focuses attention on social systems. In this regard Talcott Parsons must be thought of as the key proponent of the tradition. See especially his *Essays in Sociological Theory* (Glencoe: The Free Press, 1949), and *The Social System*. As an important base see also A. R. Radcliffe-Brown, *A Natural Science of Society* (Glencoe: The Free Press, 1957), and *Method in Social Anthropology* (Chicago: University of Chicago Press, 1958). For relevant views see R. K. Merton, *Social Theory and Social Structure* (Glencoe: The Free Press, 1949); Walter Buckley, "Structural-functional Analysis in Modern Sociology," in Becker and Boskoff, *Modern Sociological Theory*, pp. 236-259; Kingsley Davis, "The Myth of Functional Analysis as a Special Method in Sociology and Anthropology," *American Sociological Review*, 24 (December, 1959), pp. 257-773; and C. P. Loomis and Z. K. Loomis, *Modern Social Theories* (Princeton: D. Van Nostrand, 1961).

tured and shared symbols." [28] Expressed somewhat differently, Sorokin indicates that the social system exists in the "meaningful interaction of two or more human individuals . . . by which one partly
tangibly influences the overt actions or state of mind of the other." [29]

In the abstract sense, then, a social system may be perceived at
any level—from the direct, face-to-face, personal interaction of two
actors up to the indirect, enormously interlinked, and impersonal
interaction of a "society." The concept of the social system can be
used to make explicable and intelligible the behavior involved in
such diverse spheres as familial, community, educational, religious,
occupational, political, and military organizations. Or it can be used
in a more concrete and localized sense to analyze such social entities as a specific family, fraternity chapter, rural school, friendship
clique, factor, platoon, program, etc. A part of the efficacy of the
concept lies in the fact that the analytic observer is enabled to move
from the particular to the general and back again. It is equally legitimate to examine both American society and the relationship of a
physician and his patient as behavioral social systems. With equal
justification, one can turn his attention to the Catholic Church or
to a concretely representative component of that church by means
of the concept of systems.

When the behavior of many people living together is examined
as a system of relationships, it is found to be orderly; it has a pattern. It is the pattern, not the people, which is termed society. Society is a tissue of reciprocal activity, differentiated into a variable
number of systems, some of them quite distinct, highly structured
and persistent, others not so directly traceable but amorphous and
transient, and all interlinked to such a degree that one sees different systems according to the perspective taken. Whatever system
one is viewing, however—whether it be the master system (society)
or any of its component sub-systems (community, family, etc.)—
the elements which constitute it as a social system remain the same.
Stated simply, society and its parts are not made of different stuff;
on the contrary, certain persistent elements appear at any level of
orderly interaction. As a consequence, these elements may be conceived of as being organic components of social systems, and thus

[28] Parsons, *The Social System*, pp. 5-6.
[29] Sorokin, *Society, Culture, and Personality*, p. 40.

may be utilized as the basis for analysis of social behavior in general.

In delineating the major structural elements and key processes of the social system, as for example in the work of Parsons, it is presumed that the crucial factors around which concrete social systems vary have been laid here. Experience in such a diversified society as ours quickly teaches us that the social systems in which we can or must participate vary remarkably with respect to the aforementioned elements and processes. We are accustomed to sharp contrasts, and differences are normal. It is not unusual to find ourselves acting in the most diversified systems within a very limited span of time. For instance, we may find ourselves participating in a church wedding ceremony where the norms are traditionally and specifically defined with respect to how one dresses and what one says and does. Behavior in such a situation is prescribed to the point where any deviation would cause consternation. To illustrate further, we may participate in a system where the expression of sentiment is not only common but required, as in the case of continued affectual interchanges within a family. At the same time, however, we may hold an occupational role in a bureaucracy where any such display would not only be unseemly but actually taboo, because the system depends upon the absence rather than the presence of sentiment. Or again, we may find ourselves in a system where the ends or objectives are quite specific, as in the case of joining a group attempting to promote sidewalks for the new suburban area into which one has just moved. In contrast, we may also have a circle of friends or gang within which the objectives would be difficult to pin down because they are defined in such diffuse terms as fellowship, having a good time, or congeniality.

These few examples should suffice to indicate that there are many *opposites* with *in-between gradations* within any complex society. Thus, the elements of social systems which have been delineated may be viewed as a series of *continua* along which concrete systems vary. To visualize a continuum one need only think of two poles and the range between them, as in the case of black and white with all the possible shades of gray in between, or tall and short with all the gradations of height in between, or rich and poor with all the differentials of wealth intermediate to them. The notion of the continuum is a simple one, but vital to the understanding of comparative *similarities* and *differences,* for it constitutes the *dimension* along which entities may be compared. Comparison, the delineation of similarities and differences, is most easily accomplished by establishing the polar types as the outside limits within which actual cases vary. This is as true of social systems as it is of any other kind of object, event, activity, etc. In order to see with the greatest clarity the many types of social systems that are likely to be examined in this era, it is essential that we establish the most fundamentally different *types* of systems as the limiting cases, or polar types within which actual systems vary. For want of better labels we shall call these types *Gemeinschaft* and *Gesellschaft,* although they are actually synthetic derivatives from the family of polar types and from social systems analysis.[30] These are blanket terms defining the most general continuum along which all social relations fall.

Gemeinschaft and Gesellschaft in Modern Dress

As conceptualized here, *Gemeinschaft* and *Gesellschaft* refer to constructed types of social system that may be used as the *standards* or *models* against which all systems can be compared although few of them approach the pure type. The vast majority of social systems must be characterized as being, to some degree, mixtures of *Gemeinschaft* and *Gesellschaft* attributes. Even as mixtures, however, the type as a standard enables us to compare actual systems, not only to the type as a model, but to one another as being variable approximations to either pole of the continuum. Thus it is legitimate to say that one system is more *Gemeinschaft*-like than another, or to

[30] We run the risk here of confusion with the earlier Tönnies formulation. This is by deliberate choice and represents an attempt to remove the romantic and psychologistic overtones from *Gemeinschaft* and *Gesellschaft* by restructuring them in terms of contemporary systems analysis. The suppositions are that polar typologies would be more efficient if they incorporated the refinements of structural–functional theory and that the enrichment of systems analysis requires the longitudinal dimension implicit in the polar typological tradition.

state that certain *Gesellschaft*-like characteristics are present in a primarily *Gemeinschaft*-like system. Systems may be viewed as consisting of the following primary elements.[31]

Roles. The *Gemeinschaft* system consists of roles that are diffuse in structure, marked by similarity, based on ascription, and which must in the nature of the case be few in number. This is in sharp contrast to the *Gesellschaft* where the roles are functionally specific, diversified, based on achievement, and can be many in number.

The diffuseness of the role means that it is a general role wherein the relationship is broadly inclusive and is not limited to

[31] Some indication of why the particular elements used in this analysis, and in the analysis of planning social change (Chapter VII) were chosen is in order. Clearly all such selective and abstractive choices are to some extent arbitrary and reflective of the particular perspective and special purposes of the person making the selection. Given this partially arbitrary factor, however, there is a rationale underlying the set of elements we use in the explication of the social system. The test that is fundamentally used is that of "the going concern through time." In brief, the question we raise is: "What are the aspects of the social interactive process that must be present if a form of social organization is to be established and persist through time?" Our answer is that at a minimum there must be roles, beliefs, sentiments, goals, norms, power, sanctions, and facilities. These are prerequisite to the maintenance of a viable relationship through time on the part of a plurality of actors. We do not suggest that at a different level of abstraction it would not be possible to treat a larger or lesser number of elements as constituting a social system. These elements are constructs, and as such are merely meant to represent phenomena in the interactive process among which one can differentiate in order to delineate essential structural aspects of social systems.

It should be clear that adherence to this schema means that we do not utilize the standard distinction made between personal, social, and cultural systems. Our use of the preceding elements in effect fuses social and cultural systems so that we have a dichotomy of *action* systems, the personal and social. We take the view that it is necessary to abstract out cultural systems only for very limited and special purposes. As a general rule there is no advantage obtained through the theoretical formulation of the system trilogy of personal–social–cultural, especially in view of the fact that only two of these are systems of action. On the other hand the social system, as an action system, is only comprehensible as *a going concern* when the cultural aspects of behavior are thought of as *integral* to the social system. Again, this does not suggest that it is not desirable to abstract out cultural aspects of behavior in order to pursue particular kinds of inquiry. However, this is quite a different matter and not relevant to the following explication.

specific functions. The interpersonal attachment, with its intrinsic rights and obligations, is not delimited to some specific area of behavior or set of events, but consists in bonds transcending a wide range of particular situations. The rights and obligations are hence blanket rather than explicitly prescribed and delimited. The general similarity of roles within a *Gemeinschaft* is a reflection of this diffuseness or lack of specialization and the greater total involvement in the lives of others. The ascriptive base of the roles is an indication that "who people are" is of greater importance than "what they do." Ascribed roles are those to which people are assigned on the basis of such factors as age, sex, and social rank of family. Although these factors are beyond the control of the individual, nevertheless they are used by the members of a system to categorize him, and thus provide him with the appropriate roles. Finally, by the nature of the attachment, the *Gemeinschaft* cannot have more than a few roles. A proliferation of roles would mean an ultimate loss of diffuse attachments, blanket affectual commitments, and close interpersonal ties. This would imply the emergence of their opposites, and consequently the emergence of a *Gesellschaft*. The economy of expressive interests and relational rewards prevents our being deeply involved with very many people. We cannot be close to all people, consequently our allocation of blanket rights and obligations in roles is necessarily restricted to those with whom we are intimately involved in the interaction process. This constitutes the *Gemeinschaft*.

Perhaps the most readily observable area of difference between the *Gemeinschaft* and *Gesellschaft* lies in the role structure. The roles of the *Gesellschaft* are notably specific in function. That is, the rights and obligations involved are explicitly prescribed and delimited to restricted spheres of interaction. The person is only segmentally involved in the relationship, as in the case of providing a particular service or product beyond which he has no responsibilities to the other or others. Moreover, as a reflection of this functional specificity, the roles in the *Gesellschaft* tend to become diversified. Different people occupying different roles are called upon to make different contributions to the system. Thus a man is not "all things to all people," but is of special and limited significance to other members of the system. A bureaucracy, with its channels of communications and levels of decision making, is a classical example of the case in point. Although one cannot, even in the ideal case, imagine the complete elimination of ascription, it is nevertheless essential that achievement be the primary base of roles in the *Gesellschaft*. The emphasis is on "what people do," and the returns are allocated in terms of performance. When the requirements of the role are specified with regard to what the incumbent is supposed to do, there is a set of criteria that may be referred to in evaluating differential or competitive performance. Achievement, therefore, can be both recognized and rewarded. Finally, the *Gesellschaft* is capable of articulating many roles and thus complementing the activities of many people. The best single example is an elaborate division of labor with many people making minute contributions to a total product or economy, and nevertheless realizing the appropriate returns for their contribution. In such a role structure people can be personally independent and yet functionally interdependent in relation to many other "unknown" people.

Beliefs.   Our ideas about the world we live in or anything related to it constitute our beliefs. It has long been recognized that different types of knowledge, as well as the techniques and motivations for extending knowledge, are bound up with particular forms of social organization. The *Gemeinschaft* has a traditionally defined fund of knowledge handed down as conclusive and final; any effort to test the traditional knowledge, insofar as it implies doubt, is ruled out on moral grounds. In such a system thought is dogmatic, and the prevailing conceptions are treated as being the "real nature of things." There is no provision for doubt or the questioning of existent beliefs.

In contrast, the *Gesellschaft* also utilizes a fund of traditional knowledge, but does not look upon it as being either conclusive or final; indeed the tendency is to adjudge such knowledge inadequate to the demands of the future. The validity and reliability of knowledge is considered to be an open and testable question, not a commitment. There is no moral constraint involved in the investigation of the various aspects of the universe, and the *Gesellschaft* actually institutionalizes ways of attaining and codifying new knowledge. In such a system there is a direct concern with "how we know what we know" as well as with "what is it that we don't know." The mode of thought is primarily critical, pragmatic, and nominalistic. Consequently, beliefs in the *Gesellschaft* are continuously subject to modification and displacement in terms of new evidence and theories.

Sentiments.   Our expressive reactions, the ways we feel about the world we live in and its related aspects, constitute our sentiments. The *Gemeinschaft* always has a powerful expressive or affective component. The bonds of solidarity, intimacy, and sympathy, and the spontaneity of the action indicate a common emotional sphere where there is a pooling of sentiment. The common and typical experiences of the members have enabled them to develop similar feelings about those experiences and express them through common symbolic media—sentiments. These sentiments function as a set of established appreciative standards in terms of which people legitimately express themselves.

The *Gesellschaft* in the pure type would require affective neutrality, or the total absence of sentiment. Feeling would be absent due to the rational pursuit of ends in terms of expedient means. By the very nature of the case, however, ends are gratifying; that is, we have a stake in the attainment of them in terms of their want-satisfying qualities. We are not robots devoid of emotion; on the contrary, our feelings enter into even the most impersonal or rational activities. The total absence of sentiment in a system is a social impossibility. As a consequence, it is perhaps feasible to draw in the limits here and point out that in the closest approximations to the *Gesellschaft* we have flexible appreciative standards, diversified modes of expression, and a lack of consensus with regard to both "what we should feel" and "how feelings should be expressed." In sum, the sentiment system in *Gesellschaft*-like systems tends to be fragmentary and non-institutionalized.

Goals or Objectives.   In contrast to the area of sentiment where we find its expression characteristic of the *Gemeinschaft,* the explicit presence of goals or objectives is characteristic of the *Gesellschaft.* Social systems and relationships which are *Gemeinschaft*-like are those in which the relationship is an end in itself, as contrasted to those which are *Gesellschaft*-like, in which the relationships are means to ends. *Gesellschaft* is distinguished by rational action, and we refer to behavior as being rational when the appropriate means are most expediently adopted to the ends being sought, insofar as these ends are derived from the prevailing value systems. When we enter into relationships and utilize them as a means of achieving our own ends, the relationship constitutes a *Gesellschaft*. It is not value for its own sake, but merely for its utility or service.

The *Gemeinschaft,* on the other hand, is distinguished by a fusion of ends and means. The ends are obscure or, at most, diffuse in contrast to the specificity of the *Gesellschaft* case. The relationship, or system, is really an end in itself, and hence the behavior that goes into the maintenance of the relationship is difficult to segregate from any presumed purposes of that behavior. All activities, even those of economic production in a *Gemeinschaft*-like order, are ends in themselves. The more remote ends of living (ultimate goals) are taken as given; hence, the *Gemeinschaft*-like system exists on the basis of common understandings as to what is to be done, rather than on the basis of exchange of useful functions as is the case with the *Gesellschaft*.

Norms. The rules or guiding standards which prescribe what is socially acceptable or unacceptable constitute one of the crucial areas of difference between *Gemeinschaft*- and *Gesellschaft*-like systems. In the *Gemeinschaft* the norms are standardized, reflect a stable consensus, indicate a total commitment, and tend to be universal to the system. The standardization of norms is a product of repetition and the traditionalizing of certain forms. The stability of consensus with regard to the norms is evidence of their unquestioned acceptability. Total commitment of the members of a system to a set of norms indicates their belief in the moral legitimacy and intrinsic rightness of those norms. Universality of norms within a given system is evidence of the lack of deviance or mechanism of change. The normative order of a *Gemeinschaft* is stable and powerfully resistant to change.

The norms of a *Gesellschaft* are maintained on the basis of a shifting and precarious consensus and are characterized by deviationism, ambivalence, flexibility, and localization. The very existence of norms implies some measure of consensus, but in a *Gesellschaft* it is a precarious one because it is based upon such fickle notions as expediency, efficiency, opportunity, strategy, and similar concepts. The very character of the dominant norms precludes the sacredness of their content, and this encourages deviationism. Deviationism refers to the structured evasion of the manifest norms, and when practiced by enough members of the system the deviant pattern may become the normative pattern. General or unstructured deviationism within the *Gesellschaft* is not possible beyond the limits of minimal order. A state of normlessness, or *anomie*, refers to a distintegrated system or one relatively close to such a state. It is no longer a *Gesellschaft*, for it is no longer a social system. Ambivalence is a characteristic attitude of the members of a *Gesellschaft* in contrast to the total commitment of the *Gemeinschaft* case. Even moral rules are open to question. This means that the normative pattern of a *Gesellschaft* is flexible and susceptible to change. General norms universal to the system are less prominent than in the *Gemeinschaft*, and the vast majority of norms are localized with respect to the various segments or subsystems.

Power. This element of the social system differs markedly in allocation, distribution, and articulation in the *Gemeinschaft* and *Gesellschaft* forms, although both its influence and authority components may be present in either case. In the purest and most limited example of a *Gemeinschaft*—an erotic love relationship, for instance, wherein all other reference systems are ignored for at least a short time—one would find influence to be the only component of power present. The extent to which each lover could influence the other in terms of his or her wishes would be the measure of power. Such an idyllic *Gemeinschaft* would not long persist, however, for inevitably the intrusion of other role expectations representing memberships in other subsystems in the society would occur. For instance, the relationship might evolve into the institutionalized roles of husband and wife, which in turn represent differential access to the facility and reward structure of the system. Differences in male and female roles in society generally then become significant to this particular relationship. Thus one may properly speak of the authority of the husband as being over against that of the wife as part of the normative order. Established tradition grants certain rights and obligations to each of these roles as part of the marriage system, and any evasion of them constitutes a deviation from the normative pattern. Thus it appears that only in the incipient or formative period of a *Gemeinschaft* is it possible to have power manifest only through influence, although influence may remain as the primary mode of expression. When a *Gemeinschaft*-like system becomes persistent as a system, a traditional base of authority emerges. Authority identified with a particular role comes to carry the sanctity of tradition and thus acquires legitimation in the eyes of others.

Although both influence and authority are also present in the *Gesellschaft,* sharp and significant differences of their manifestation must be noted. In the *Gesellschaft* one must speak of the primacy of authority of office and law. The differentiated roles of the system are allocated different measures and types of authority. The authority resides in the role by normative definition rather than in the role incumbent. Moreover, rational-legalized norms may be referred to in order to determine the rights of various individuals in a situation. Thus the law, with its various enforcement mechanisms, may be invoked to insure the legitimate wielding of power. The dominant pattern consists, therefore, in explicitly presented and/or legally defined authority rights for the various status-roles of the system. It would be remiss, however, to ignore the inevitable operation of influence in anything except the purest *Gesellschaft.* Influence tends to take a different form here, however, in contrast to the *Gemeinschaft.* In the *Gemeinschaft,* due to the community of interest and fate, there is a likelihood of considerable sublimation of self-interest in deference to other-interest. As a consequence, influence exists primarily in terms of direct personal manipulative skills, for it would be awkward or unseemly to invoke the use of other kinds of facilities. In the *Gesellschaft* case, however, such limitations would not be the role. By definition, self-interest is primary; hence a much wider range of facilities could be legitimately utilized. Possessions, payoffs, superior knowledge, indebtedness for favor, and other such facilities would, along with the human-relational skills common to the *Gemeinschaft,* be found in the *Gesellschaft.*

In sum, power in the *Gemeinschaft* tends to be allocated and distributed on the basis of direct, intimate, interpersonal influence, and in terms of traditional definitions of roles. In contrast, in the *Gesellschaft* influence is primarily mediated through indirect, roundabout, extrapersonal facilities, and authority is vested in rational-legal norms as well as in contractually defined roles. As a consequence, the articulation of power in the *Gemeinschaft* is directly linked to the interpersonal nature of the role structure and cannot be diffused beyond the narrow limits of that system. In the *Gesellschaft*, on the other hand, we find the possibility of linking, and thus articulating, a highly elaborated role structure. The impersonality of the mechanisms of power provides the possibility of directing it through long chains of command or devious channels of role responsibility relative to a universalistic set of norms. The classic example of such a case of power articulation in the *Gesellschaft* form would be the modern political state. Such a power structure would be impossible under *Gemeinschaft* conditions.

Sanctions. The penalties and rewards which comprise sanctions vary in their form rather than function with reference to *Gemeinschaft* and *Gesellschaft* systems. The motivational relationship of penalties, with constraint of action, and rewards, with instigation of action, holds for both types of systems. The nature of these penalties and rewards, however, cannot help but reflect the different orientational, structural, and process characteristics of the diverse systems. The sanction pattern of the *Gemeinschaft* is informal, determined by custom, and repressive in its penalty provisions. In contrast the *Gesellschaft* pattern is formal, determined by law, and restitutive in its penalty provisions.

The informality of sanctions in a *Gemeinschaft* is an indication that they are an integral part of the day-by-day activities themselves rather than mechanisms of specific organizations. The intimacy, involvement, and commitment within the *Gemeinschaft* make the maintenance or furtherance of the relationship a reward in itself; conversely, any threat to the maintenance of the relationship would constitute a penalty in the eyes of the members.

The informality of sanctions leaves the way clear for custom to build and actually determine the time, place, and mode of their application. For instance, the violation of sacred norms within a *Gemeinschaft* would not draw forth merely random or *ad hoc* responses, but on the contrary would draw traditionally structured responses. Certain typical responses to certain typical violations would be the rule.

In the *Gemeinschaft*, penalties are instruments of repression of deviancy from the collective pattern. In the *Gemeinschaft*, orientations and conduct are much alike. People are homogeneous, mentally and morally; hence the *Gemeinschaft* is uniform and nonatomized in composition. This very homogeneity accounts for the stability and standardization of reaction against any tendency to evade or deviate from the normal ways of doing things. An offense against the common beliefs or sentiments within the *Gemeinschaft* is an offense against the common morality, and hence against the system as a whole. The reaction will be a collective reaction of relatively uniform character in the form of repressive action.

In turning to the *Gesellschaft*, once again the pattern is found to be opposite to the one just drawn. Sanctions within the *Gesellschaft* are formal in the sense that they are mechanisms employed rationally and universalistically by organizations having specific functions within the society. The ends sought are individual rather than collective, hence the relationship is a means rather than an end in itself. As a consequence, relational rewards and penalties do not have the same significance in the *Gesellschaft* as in the *Gemeinschaft*, for the loss of a relationship is the loss of a facility rather than the intrinsic objective. Rewards and penalties within the *Gesellschaft* must be figured more in terms of access to or denial of such things as goods and services, power, and prestige, rather than in social relational terms *per se* as in the *Gemeinschaft* case.

Law rather than custom is the source of application of sanctions. By law we mean a set of codified rules that carry some probability of enforcement by virtue of their legitimacy in the eyes of the participants and the presence of an enforcement agent. Law in this sense can refer to the rules of such organizations as the political state, a governmental bureau, a school, or a privately owned factory. Prescriptions for certain kinds of penalties for certain kinds of violations are provided for in codified rules that are universalistically applicable within the system. In the *Gesellschaft*, penalties are instruments of restitution rather than repression. The *Gesellschaft* is held together by the interdependence of its parts. The elaboration of the role structure stimulates individualism and differentiation. People in the *Gesellschaft* are heterogeneous; their mental and moral similarities are obscured by diversification of activity patterns. Spontaneous relations between individuals are thus replaced by contractual relations. Crime, consequently, is not an offense against common moral sentiments, but is an offense against personal rights. Offensive acts are not offenses against the common morality of the collectivity, but are infringements upon the equal rights of other individuals. For example, the vast majority of cases tried in the American courts each year are civil rather than criminal, and involve potential restitution to individuals rather than repression in the interest of the collectivity. This is simply the case of a *Gesellschaft*-like pattern being dominant, and therefore being characterized by restitutive action.

Facilities. In contemporary usage facilities constitute the resources that can be drawn upon as means to achieve the goals established within the system. Their proliferation and significance will therefore vary directly with the extent to which the social system is goal-oriented. From the preceding, it is obvious that the *Gemeinschaft* is normative-oriented, rather than goal-oriented. In the *Gemeinschaft* the relationship is an end in itself and hence it is the norms of maintaining that relationship that come sharply into focus rather than goals. Although it certainly has want-satisfying qualities, the *Gemeinschaft* lacks explicit objectives. The value of maintaining it, and the activity context within which it lies, goes unquestioned; therefore the aspects of maintenance are not formulated in terms of goals. For instance, it would be difficult for a typical family to state the objectives of its existence. The individual members might have various goals, but as a system the important thing would simply be a matter of continuing life as a family. In comparison, a Civil Defense unit would have no trouble in stating its objectives as a system, for they are explicitly formulated. This comparison uses examples of *Gemeinschaft* and *Gesellschaft,* and it is apparent that facilities are of much greater significance in the latter.

This is not to say that facilities are totally lacking in the *Gemeinschaft,* for the mere maintenance of the requisite activity calls for some measure of social and/or physical resources. The bulk of facilities required in *Gemeinschaft* forms will fall in the area of skills manifest in the meeting of social expectations. Roles in any system are defined in terms of expectations, hence any skills utilized in meeting those expectations would be classed as facilities. For example, the skills that a mother might possess in soothing ruffled feelings, the skills that a father might possess in disciplining the children, and those that the children might manifest in doing the chores, would all be conceived of as means of keeping the family going as usual. The means for implementing action in the *Gemeinschaft* are essentially the role performance skills utilized in meeting the normatively regulated expectations of others.

One of the fundamental orientations of the actor in the *Gesellschaft* is that of self-interest. The relationship is a means to his own personal ends. It is correct, therefore, to speak of the relationship itself as a facility. One enters into relations for the return or service involved, and terminates them when it is no longer needed or when more desirable substitutes can be found. The commitment is not to the relationship itself as in the case of the *Gemeinschaft*, but to the ends which it serves. For example, an employer will try to hire the most efficient workers in order to raise production, a dean will attempt to hire the most competent professor in order to improve the educational process, and a coach will attempt to proselytize the most skillful football players in order to win with greater regularity. In each instance the relationships involved are subordinated as means to the ends in view; hence they are facilities. The *Gesellschaft* is characterized, therefore, by a prevalence of relational facilities.

In addition to these relational facilities, one also finds a category of technical facilities in the *Gesellschaft* that is lacking in the *Gemeinschaft*. The diversification of roles inevitably brings about specialization. Specialization implies a greater depth of "know-how" with regard to some particular activity that cannot be possessed by the jack-of-all-trades. This leads to an inevitable development of more refined techniques and devices. It is no accident, for instance, that industrialization with its elaborate technology came about in conjunction with an increased division of labor and segmentalizing of economic roles. It could not have happened any other way. Technological development is responsible for the development of a greater range of artifacts which in turn can be used as facilities in the achievement of objectives. Thus the *Gesellschaft* is distinguished from the *Gemeinschaft* by the prevalence of technical rather than simple facilities.

This brief description of *Gemeinschaft* and *Gesellschaft* types in terms of systemic elements has been undertaken for two primary reasons. First, since the polar typological tradition has contributed heavily to the development of the sociological perspective over the years, it is believed that it is well worth salvaging and that a modernization of it through fusion with contemporary structural–functional theory may prove useful in the long run. Secondly, it is believed that comparative study, implicit in sociological research, will be greatly advanced in future years by *systems analysis*—the comparative study of social systems. This will probably require, as a major aspect of sociological orientation, a retention and refinement of the conception of *fundamental types of social systems*. These will be constructed types capable of functioning as bench marks and constituting the major outlines of the cognitive map within which the comparative study of actual and diverse systems can be efficiently pursued.

The Comparative Study of Social Systems

In the history of scientific enterprise the notion of system has played a persistent and gradually expanding part. It would not seem to be an overstatement to say that system has been a generic and fundamental idea in science. In recent years a number of proponents of the social system as a basic conceptual scheme have emerged and made contributions. It is assumed that the adaptation and consistent application of such a frame of reference would (a) stabilize the units of investigation, (b) standardize the perspective for viewing social phenomena, (c) facilitate the comparative study of diverse groupings, (d) expose general structural regularities in social phenomena, and (e) expose general functions of these structures in diverse settings.

In the light of these assumptions, it is clear that scholarly work will have to be undertaken in terms of two different but interdependent aims. First must come analysis of social systems in the abstract, so as to identify and theoretically articulate the components of systems that give the most promise of adequate empirical description of actual interaction patterns. This undertaking would involve the derivation from the conceptual scheme of theories about the structure and function of (a) social systems, (b) components of systems, and (c) the articulation of components, as well as theories about (1) the maintenance and (2) the development of systems.

Secondly, as a necessary and concomitant enterprise, it is evident that the comparative study of empirical social systems must be extended and expanded. It is inevitable that when one frees his curiosity from the particularities of nation or area, he will see many situations in other parts of the world comparable in certain respects to those originally arousing his interest. As a consequence, there will be a search for similarities and differences—for the general and recurrent in contrast to the merely particular and localized. The concern with that which is common to man under diverse circumstances constitutes the "seed bed" of the social sciences. The study of social institutions initiated and continues to lead the social sciences to emphasize a comparative point of view. The study of social, political, and economic systems as systems has similarly emphasized those components of Man's behavior which are persistent through time and space. It is only through the systematic making of comparisons that the social sciences can attain stable perspectives for the assessment of problems of social order and change. The acceleration of the processes of change throughout the world gives emphasis to the point that the social sciences must expand their manpower, extend their commitments, and intensify their investigation of the stable and repetitive forms and processes of social behavior.

For these reasons the comparative study of social institutions and systems requires further and rapid development. It is assumed that this objective already is implicit in all social scientific research, but there are real difficulties and limitations imposed upon social scientists, even of the highest competence, when they seek to widen the scope of comparative data in order to arrive at principles of more general significance. In part these problems are merely practical and can be resolved by more manpower, facilities, and financial support. In greater part, of course, they are methodological, theoretical, and empirical, and are intrinsically related to the state of development of the social sciences. A partial explanation of our lack of knowledge and understanding of diverse people and behavior presumably lies in the fact that we have not held constant our perspective for conceptualizing this behavior. Hence, comparability of the numerous empirical studies undertaken has been limited. The task here is one of examining the behavior of people of diverse cultural heritages in order to delineate the similarities and differences between them in terms of a basic and stable conceptual scheme. The formulation of these observed similarities and differences as empirical generalizations would constitute a delineation of the uniformities of behavior and add to the substantive corpus of sociological science. The notion of the societal continuum as developed within the various polar typologies constitutes one essential baseline for the advancement of comparative studies. Moreover, the merger of the typological and systematic styles or traditions of thought, as suggested in the preceding contemporary treatment of *Gemeinschaft* and *Gesellschaft,* constitutes another potentially significant resource for the achievement of comparative knowledge of social behavior.

—— 6

Types, Social Systems, and the Problem of Instigated Social Change

Polar type formulations such as those dealt with in the previous chapter have demonstrated the utility of the concept of the continuum in the comparative analysis of social structure. These polar types have established outer limits or standards by means of which intermediate structural forms, as empirical approximations or subtypes, can be comprehended from the perspective of the continuum. In so doing they have also contributed bench marks for the interpretation of processes of change. Such types of social system as *Gemeinschaft* and *Gesellschaft* are, of course, *action systems* despite the fact that they are traditionally defined in structural terms. The primacy of social structure in structural-functional formulations and in the comparative study of social systems does not preclude the possibility of useful and effective analysis of change, particularly when appropriate typologies are carefully constructed. Before proceeding with a typological formulation, however, brief commentaries on social structure and change would be pertinent.

137

Structural–Functionalism: Relevant Views

The fundamental concept in the perspective of structural-functional theory is the social system.[1] For most purposes the most significant analytical unit of the social system is the role, of which role expectations are the primary ingredient. Role may be defined as that organized sector of an actor's orientation which constitutes and defines his participation in an interactive process.[2]

Each individual is involved as a participant in a plurality of patterned, interactive relationships. This participation revolves around the two reciprocal perspectives inherent in interaction. Each participating individual is an object of orientation, and, insofar as this object significance derives from the individual's position in the social relationship, it is a status significance. Each individual is also oriented toward other actors, and in this capacity is not an object, but is acting, and therefore enacting, a role. The structure of the social system is constituted by a network of reciprocal role relationships.

Roles, of course, vary in their degree of institutionalization and the degree to which they are common to members of the society at large. A pattern governing action in a social system may be considered institutionalized insofar as it defines the main modes of the legitimately expected behavior of the persons acting in the relevant social roles, and insofar as conformity with these expectations is of structural significance to the social systems. Parsons conceives of in-

---

[1] For the systemic perspective, see in particular: Talcott Parsons, *The Social System* (Glencoe: The Free Press, 1951); Talcott Parsons, "An Outline of the Social System," in Talcott Parsons *et al.* (eds.), *Theories of Society* (Glencoe: The Free Press, 1961), pp. 30-79; A. R. Radcliffe-Brown, *A Natural Science of Society* (Glencoe: The Free Press, 1957); M. J. Levy, *The Structure of Society* (Princeton: Princeton University Press, 1952); G. C. Homans, *The Human Group* (New York: Harcourt, Brace, 1950); R. K. Merton, *Social Theory and Social Structure* (rev. ed.; Glencoe: The Free Press, 1957); N. J. Smelser, *Social Change in the Industrial Revolution* (Chicago: University of Chicago Press, 1959); and C. P. Loomis and Z. K. Loomis, *Modern Social Theories* (Princeton: D. Van Nostrand, 1961).

[2] Talcott Parsons, *The Social System*, pp. 38-39.

stitutions as constituting the main link between social structure and the actor, in that they are at the same time related to the functional needs of actors and to those of the system.[3] The link evolves from the normative–voluntaristic aspect of the structure of action. The roles that individuals play in a social system are defined in terms of goals and standards. From the point of view of the actor, his role is defined by the normative expectations of the members of the group as they are formulated in the cultural tradition.

These expectations are always an aspect of any situation within which an actor is acting. His conformity or deviation brings consequences in the form of approval and reward or condemnation and punishment. These expectations are not only aspects of culture, they are internalized as aspects of the actor's personality. In the process of socialization the actor internalizes, to varying degrees, the standards of the group so that they become motivating forces in his own conduct independent of external sanctions. The relation between role-expectations and sanctions is a reciprocal one. Sanctions to the actor are role-expectations to alter, and vice versa. Their institutionalization is always a matter of degree, based upon the variables affecting the actual degree of sharing values and standards, and those determining the motivational commitment to the fulfillment of expectations. Institutional behavior cannot be conceived of in terms of a rational model or self-interest terms, but it can be said that any individual can seek his own self-interest only by conforming to some degree to the institutionalized expectations. In social structure, then, one has a system of patterned expectations defining the *proper* behavior of actors in specified roles. This system is positively enforced both by the individual's own motives for conformity and by the sanctions of others. These well-established patterns of expectations in the perspective of a social system are our institutions. These institutions constitute the structurally stable element of social systems, and their prime function lies in defining the roles of the constituent individuals. Viewed functionally, institutionalized roles constitute the mechanisms by which varied human tendencies become integrated into a system capable of dealing with the problems of a society and its members.

[3] Talcott Parsons, *Essays in Sociological Theory* (Glencoe: The Free Press, 1949), pp. 34-36.

Social Change:
Theoretical Problems

The perspective briefly described above commonly carries the label of structural-functional. Of all the critical charges leveled at this type of approach, the one that it is indifferent to, or incapable of, handling change or problems of change is the most persistent and most frequently voiced. For instance, in a recent survey of theories of change, Martindale has suggested that theorists working from that perspective have "treated social and cultural change as of little general significance."[4] The most cursory review of the literature would indicate that this charge is manifestly off the mark, or at least seriously overstated. Its significance lies not in its validity, but in the fact that this view is not at all uncommon.

In a recent polemic advancing the "historicist" position and advocating the primacy of a "conflict" model in the assessment of change, Dahrendorf claimed that recent theoretical approaches in sociology have tended to analyze social structure in terms of immobility and have consequently assumed a utopian image of society. He suggests that over-concern with the social system has dulled our vision of change and stunted our problem consciousness. He comments that: "The extent to which the social system model has influenced even our thinking about social change and has marred our vision in this important area of problems is truly remarkable."[5]

In arguing the case for historical analysis, Bock has expressed the view that structural-functionalism is inadequate as an approach to the analysis of change on the basis of its premise that processes of change are deducible from an analysis of order or structure. He asserts that this premise or conviction stems from a reluctance to accept time and place events as classifiable data for the study of both

[4] Don Martindale, *Social Life and Cultural Change* (Princeton: D. Van Nostrand, 1962), p. 2.

[5] Ralf Dahrendorf, "Out of Utopia: Toward a Reorientation of Sociological Analysis," *American Journal of Sociology,* 64 (September, 1958), p. 126. For a similar view, see Evon Z. Vogt, "On the Concepts of Structure and Process in Cultural Anthropology," *American Anthropologist,* 62 (February, 1960), pp. 18-33.

persistence and change. Being hampered by an orientation that encourages the derivation of sources of change from the nature of the thing changing, structural-functionalism is not oriented toward the discernment of sources of change in happenings. Rather, Bock takes the view that "Processes of change are conceptual arrangeabilities of events." [6]

In criticizing the adequacy of the functional approach in dealing with social change, Geertz made the following succinct comment:

> The emphasis on systems in balance, on social homeostasis, and on timeless structural pictures, leads to a bias in favor of "well-integrated" societies in a stable equilibrium and to a tendency to emphasize the functional aspects of a people's usages and customs rather than their dysfunctional implications. [7]

Critics have also claimed that structural-functional analysis is couched in terms too general to explain the specific directions of change in any concrete society. Moreover, they aver, such specificity is beyond the province of structural analysis: such a mode of analysis can explain any concrete change only by reference to broadly general and hence inconclusive and inadequate causes or to forces or factors external to the system. [8]

In his editorial introduction to the recent Loomis and Loomis analysis of the sociological theories of Howard Becker, Kingsley Davis, George C. Homans, Robert K. Merton, Talcott Parsons, Pitirim Sorokin, and Robin Williams, Moore made the following comment on the style of their approach:

[6] K. E. Bock, "Evolution, Function, and Change," *American Sociological Review*, 28 (April, 1963), p. 229. For a more detailed exposition of "the historical view," see his provocative *The Acceptance of Histories* (Berkeley: University of California Press, 1956). Also see Howard Becker, *Through Values to Social Interpretation* (Durham: Duke University Press, 1950).

[7] Clifford Geertz, "Ritual and Social Change," *American Anthropologist*, 59 (February, 1957), p. 32.

[8] See, for instance, Dahrendorf, *op. cit.*, pp. 115-127; Bock, *op. cit.*, pp. 229-237; R. P. Dore, "Function and Cause," *American Sociological Review*, 26 (December, 1961), pp. 843-853; Wayne Hield, "The Study of Change in Social Science," *British Journal of Sociology*, 5 (March, 1954), pp. 1-10; David Lockwood, "Some Remarks on the Social System," *British Journal of Sociology*, 7 (June, 1956), pp. 134-146.

There are here no radical behaviorists, who "have made up their windpipes that they have no minds," or attitudes and aspirations. Yet they strike me as a rather "conservative" group with regard to the larger shape of things social. Fearing, perhaps, the "group mind" fallacy, the theorists seem to depict society as a kind of by-product of mindless functional necessities plus mindful and motivated individual actions almost solely at the interpersonal level. The "common value system" attributed to societies seems to have no politically powerful spokesmen, although we know better. And the values seem not to include deliberate, planned, and large-scale social change. The reality of such change tends to be treated as "exogenous," an unpredicted datum, and the equilibrium model used to trace through systemic consequences. The pursuit of consequences is not a trivial kind of labor. However, it does fall short of large issues—issues of scientific predictability as well as such practical questions as human survival and the capacity to tolerate change at explosive velocities—presented in the factual world of contemporary experience. Social revolutions no longer just happen, if they ever did. They are planned and executed, despite the real resistances that equilibrium models of society help to identify but not to protect.[9]

Since many of the most productive and distinguished theorists of our era are referred to in the preceding comment, it is indeed revealing with respect to the current state of affairs in sociological theory.

In recent years a series of analyses and commentaries has appeared in the literature that may be typified as revisionist or constructive with respect to the capabilities of structural-functional theory in handling change. These have ranged from quite defensive statements which underestimate present capability to suggestions for reformulations and new syntheses within the framework of existent theory. Implicitly or explicitly, these analysts have accepted the main trend of the development of sociological theory and have been exploring ways of extending and specifying theoretical capabilities with respect to problems of change.

In a recent analysis, Cancian focused on the problem of formalizing functional analysis in order better to adapt it to handling change. This analysis was based on the earlier presentation by Nagel of a formal definition of functional systems which, in turn, was

[9] W. E. Moore, "Editorial Introduction," to C. P. Loomis and Z. K. Loomis, *Modern Social Theories* (Princeton: D. Van Nostrand, 1961), p. xxiv.

based on Merton's explication of manifest and latent functions. Nagel did not explicitly consider the problem of functional analysis of change. His formal definition of a functional system, however, provided Cancian with a basis for outlining several specific ways in which functional analysis can be utilized in the study of change. Moreover, it led to the conclusion that most of the arguments about the so-called static nature of such analysis are based on semantic confusion and unimaginative and incorrect methods.[10] Fundamentally the burden was placed on the further development of methodology.

On the basis of an analysis of the social and political structure of traditional centralized empires and of the development of religions within them, Eisenstadt has argued that the institutionalization of any social system creates possibilities for specific and definable types of change, which develop not randomly but in specific directions primarily set by the process of institutionalization itself. "Our major point is that the institutionalization of any social system —be it political, economic or a system of social stratification or of any collectivity or role—creates in its wake the possibilities of change." [11] He reiterates the long established but frequently overlooked view that this creates the possibility of "anti-systems," or groups developing within the system with negative orientations toward its premises and values. Eisenstadt indicates that while the nature and strength of such anti-systems will vary, as between different institutional systems (*i.e.*, religious, economic, etc.) and between different types within each, and while they often may remain latent or inactive for prolonged periods of time, they nevertheless constitute important foci of change under facilitative conditions.[12] Perhaps the primary achievement of the Eisenstadt analysis was the effective illustration

[10] Francesca Cancian, "Functional Analysis of Change," *American Sociological Review,* 25 (December, 1960), pp. 818-827. Also see Ernest Nagel, "A Formalization of Functionalism," in his *Logic Without Metaphysics* (Glencoe: The Free Press, 1956), pp. 247-283; and Merton, *op. cit.*, pp. 19-84.

[11] S. N. Eisenstadt, "Institutionalization and Change," *American Sociological Review,* 29 (April, 1964), p. 235.

[12] *Ibid.*, p. 246. See also A. W. Gouldner, "Reciprocity and Authority in Functional Theory," In Llewellyn Gross (ed.), *Symposium on Sociological Theory* (Evanston: Row, Peterson, 1959), pp. 241-247; and Gideon Sjoberg, "Contradictory Functional Requirements and Social Systems," *Journal of Conflict Resolution,* 4 (June, 1960), pp. 198-258.

of the combination of systematic institutional analysis with the analysis of change in showing that the explication of change is inherent in the examination of concrete societies or parts thereof as social systems.[13] Again we have an indication that a systematic structural analysis is a prerequisite for anything approximating a compelling analysis of change.

As indicated previously, Bock is primarily a critic of the structural-functional approach. In his critique, however, he has issued the fundamentally important reminder that structure is also a *temporal* phenomenon. "Processes of persistence of tradition and processes of change in tradition are alike historical processes."[14] In a similar noting of the "ahistorical" character of modern sociology and sociologists, Shils makes the comment that: "On the whole, it may be said that neither concrete empirical sociology nor theoretical sociology has been especially well endowed with a 'sense of the past.'"[15] He takes note of a deficient appreciation of pastness as evidenced in the predominant conception of modern society as cut loose from tradition. In this he is critical of the relative absence of any sociological treatment of the nature and mechanisms of tradition. He goes on to make the following provocative comment:

> Pastness as the property of an object, of an individual action, of a symbol, or of a collectivity, has not yet been accorded a place in sociological theory. It need not remain so; and the correction of the formulations of the theory of action in a way that would do it justice should not be a hard task. The adaptation of the larger theory will be harder. Like much in the general theory, it will depend as much on a matrix of sensibility as on the deductive powers.[16]

Despite the superficial similarity of their approaches, and the concurrence of opinion as to the inadequacy of treatment of the temporal factor in contemporary sociological theory, Bock and Shils actually take radically opposed positions with respect to "the cor-

---

[13] Eisenstadt, *op. cit.,* pp. 235-247. See also W. E. Moore, "A Reconsideration of Theories of Social Change," *American Sociological Review,* 25 (December, 1960), pp. 810-818.

[14] Bock, "Evolution, Function and Change," p. 236.

[15] E. A. Shils, "The Calling of Sociology," in Parsons *et al., Theories of Society,* Vol. II, p. 1427.

[16] *Ibid.,* Vol. II, p. 1428.

rective." In the final analysis, Bock is advocating a reconversion of sociology into history and historical procedure. Shils, on the other hand, is suggesting the necessity of incorporating and coming to grips with the temporal dimension in systematic theory.

In a recent serious attempt to achieve a new synthesis of theoretical approaches to change, van den Berge tried to show that both functionalism and the Hegelian–Marxian dialectic present one-sided, but complementary and reconcilable, views of society. By an examination of what he conceives of as the basic postulates of functionalism and the dialectic, he imputes certain strengths and weaknesses to each which suggest a reformulation of both in minimal form. Van den Berge sees the problem as one of arriving at a theory of society that achieves an adequate balance between stability and the various sources of change, between consensus and conflict, and between equilibrium and disequilibrium. After primarily examining the Parsons version of structural-functionalism and the Dahrendorf version of the dialectic, he concludes that the two theoretical approaches show promise of a fruitful synthesis.[17]

One of the points of convergence suggested by van den Berge is that functionalism and the dialectic share an evolutionary notion of social change. Bock has referred to the functionalism *return* to evolutionism. This is an inaccurate appraisal, for structural-functionalism never left the broad framework of evolutionary thought. A distinction must be made between the discrediting or destruction of specific evolutionary formulations or theories (organicism, unilinear development, progress, etc.) in which structural-functionalism has played a fundamental role, and abdication of the general evolutionary view which structural-functionalism has never done. Indeed, in its evolution from earlier more fragmentary forms, social systems analysis has historically taken the evolutionary view seriously. The massive, two-volume *Theories of Society,* representative of the major individual contributions toward a theory of society and accompanied by relevant commentary, clearly indicates this historical stance. More important with respect to the problem under consideration here, Naegele makes the following summarizing comment:

[17] P. L. van den Berge, "Dialectic and Functionalism: Toward a Theoretical Synthesis," *American Sociological Review,* 28 (October, 1963), pp. 695-705.

The combination of an interest in the conditions of stability with an interest in the direction of transformation of social arrangements is made possible by the distinctions, implicit or explicit, made by the thinkers represented in this Reader.[18]

This assembly of the classical theoretical approaches to society in the *Theories of Society* volumes, however, carries a theme that is even more centrally relevant to the problem of a sociological perspective for continuity and change. That theme, which persistently runs through this literature constituting the foundations of sociological theory, is that of the *complication* of society and the inadequacy of any one model for its representation. Sociologists should not have to be reminded of the complexity of societal life, but in effect that is what this compilation does. Of course, this has particular relevance to the conceptualization of change. Change as variously conceptualized in cycles, spirals, straight lines, ascendencies, discontinuous alternation, and dialectic zigzags leaves us with a sense of inadequacy—and a low predictive ability. We have witnessed the downfall or limited applicability of the global, comprehensive, simplifying theories. The sweeping, broad-gauge, evolutionary, or cyclical theories have provided a relatively poor fit to data and have been of little explanatory value with respect to the changes of primary concern in contemporary life. An almost total rejection and abandonment of single factor explanations, uniform determinisms, and external (nonsocial) causes has also occurred. The rich and colorful vocabulary of change—*e.g.*, growth, decay, progress, development, lag, attrition, revolution, flux—has been shown to be sadly deficient with respect to many problems of change. The complexity of society and its processes of change remain even more visible today against the backdrop of these historical efforts to capture change conceptually in one model or another.

With regard to this problem, Moore remarks that:

> Between the global theories, which explain too little because they attempt too much, and the relativistic position that views all change as unique, there is a large middle territory. Within that spacious

terrain one may note the standardized internal dynamics of groups of various types, and identify the sources, forms, directions, and rates of change in types and segments of social systems. If the resulting theory is not exactly simple, neither is it wholly simple-minded.[19]

This statement leads us to the crux of the problem responsible for the rapid recent increase of anxiety, pessimism, and self-deprecation characterizing the many critics and revisionists of contemporary sociological theory. On the one hand, structural-functionalism—*e.g.,* incipient social systems analysis—has dominated the theoretical scene for several decades. The main drive, positive effort, and successful achievements of sociological theory have been concentrated in the build-up toward the capability of systems analysis. On the other hand, the theoreticians who have been most explicitly and continuously involved in that build-up have given limited *specialized* attention to the problem of transformation of systems—*e.g.,* to problems of continuity and change. The primary concentration has been on the *structure* of social systems, secondary attention has been devoted to *function,* and limited attention has been paid to *change* per se. The theoretical drive toward systems analysis has contributed to a paradoxical situation in the discipline. First of all, it is from the perspective of this build-up (along with the accompanying empirical accumulation) that the deficiencies, distortions, and general inadequacies of all extant theories of change have been noted. Secondly, the positive achievements of systems analysis make possible, and sensible, all of the current rash of criticism pointing out deficiencies in the handling of problems of change. Theoretical concentration has been on the system per se, and yet in the eyes of many, if not most, sociologists, the problem of change constitutes the fundamental problem of society. Therefore, the view prevails that any theory of society or its aspects or components should be competent to deal with problems of change. This raises the question as to whether social systems analysis (and its historical antecedents—structural analysis, functionalism, and structural-functionalism), is really as feeble, currently and potentially, in the area of

[19] Moore, "A Reconsideration of Theories of Social Change," p. 811.

change as it is reputed to be, and leads us to further consideration regarding this approach. We will examine this problem by setting forth some basic postulates of social systems analysis.[20]

Basic Postulates of Social Systems Analysis

Before examining the basic postulates, a distinction must be made between the social system as an intellectual construct or model and social systems as going concerns. All systems of real life, *e.g.*, a particular society, community, corporation, or family, are *open systems*. They are interacting with their environment, which includes other social systems, in many and varied ways. Empirically we recognize that these interactive foci or relational clusters which we view as social systems are always involved with and interlinked with other social systems. Their autonomy and isolation are always relative rather than absolute, and *de facto* they are always, to varying degrees and in widely varied ways, a part of a more extensive network of social relationships within which they are nested. For purposes of analysis, however, it is necessary to assume that, in the application of the intellectual construct of social system to particular real-life systems, the operation of the system is affected only by specifiable conditions previously established in the environment and by relations among the elements of the system obtaining at the time of the analysis. The domain of relevance of the construct social system is on the one hand broad enough to encompass all relational clusters conceivable as social systems despite variations in type, and on the other hand always so delimited that it never completely or perfectly represents the complexities, actualities, and uniqueness

[20] It is not suggested that these are *the* basic postulates in any absolute or exhaustive sense. It is suggested, however, that any more extensive or refined listing would have to include these or variant forms of them "accounting for" the sectors which they represent. Attention is also directed toward the list of postulates ascribed to structural-functionalism by van den Berge. There is considerable overlap in the two sets, although our concern is more directly with social systems. See van den Berge, *op. cit.*, p. 696.

of any social system as an active going concern. There is nothing unusual about this, since it is in the nature of all constructs and analysis. However, a failure consistently to recognize this has resulted in the imputation of certain difficulties to sociological analysis, particularly with reference to the problem of conceptualizing and explaining social change, that are not inherent in sociological analysis but, on the contrary, are reflective of the stage of development of that analysis. Within this context we will now proceed to examine what appear to be the basic postulates of social systems analysis.

Societies may be looked at holistically as systems of interrelated parts. Hagen has described the historical development of systems analysis as follows:

> As judged by the history of the physical, biological, and social sciences, study in any field is apt to begin with a none-too-ordered description of phenomena in the field, followed by a cataloguing of them on bases that seem to make sense. As understanding grows, the systems of classification become more closely related to the functioning of interacting elements. Gradually, generalizations about functioning are reached which are useful in predicting future events. As the generalizations gain rigor, they take the form of analytical models of the behavior of the elements being studied. They take the form, that is, of systems. When they do, a great increase in rigor and power is achieved.[21]

This is, in effect, a statement of an evolutionary view of the methodological development of the scientific disciplines. The developing capability of sociology with respect to the fruitful utilization of the intellectual construct of social system is simply an aspect of the broadly based extension of capability of the whole complex of scientifically oriented disciplines. The further extension of that capability is a necessary working assumption.

Any degree of complexity in a society implies that there are interactive foci within it which also may profitably be looked at as systems. The concept of the social system can be used at any level

---

[21] E. E. Hagen, *On the Theory of Social Change* (Homewood: Dorsey Press, 1962), p. 4. Also see his "Analytical Models in the Study of Social Systems," *American Journal of Sociology,* 67 (September, 1961), pp. 144-151.

from the dyadic relationship to the society at large. It is the structuring of the interaction so that it has some minimal degree of autonomy and social organization that justifies this flexible use of the notion of system.

All real-life systems are open systems in that they always have interchanges and relationships with other systems and the environment in general. Some degree of closure is characteristic of all systems, and they vary widely in the extent to which they are closed. However, none is entirely closed. All systems are relational foci clustered within a larger network of relationships. As such they are *accessible,* to varying degrees, to *input* through the linkages outside the system. The phenomenon of diffusion constitutes the most obvious case.

Social systems have a temporal dimension. Social systems are constituted out of symbolic interaction. Interaction has a duration, or time dimension, and this is a continuity possessing a past, present, and future. As these interactions are stabilized into institutional arrangements, the structure of the interaction can persist independently of any particular individuals. It is this persistence through time that gives our social institutions a degree of control over the future of any social system. A social system always projects both ways from the present. Goals, objectives, aspirations, and institutionalized ways of doing things constitute the core of projection into the future. Tradition, custom, accumulated knowledge, established values, and our institutional arrangements constitute the projection into the past. For any persistent social system the projection into the past tends to be much greater (of longer duration) than any reasonably predictable projection into the future. In other words, our goals and aspirations with respect to the future tend to be for the short run, in contrast to the long-run of history. This in itself is ample enough reason to require the inclusion of the past as a factor in general sociological formulations.

Social systems have a dialectic dimension. There are conflicts and contradictions inherent in social structure. The very old tradition of typing societies or relationships antithetically, *e.g., Gemeinschaft und Gesellschaft,* sacred–secular, mechanical–organic, etc., is reflective of a recognition of the coexistence of fundamentally different principles of social organization and normative order within the same system.[22] The primary utility of these polar type labels does not lie in the ability to attach one or another of them to a system as a blanket description; rather, it lies in the fact that through the paired opposites one can remain sensitized to the alternatives (and the range they encompass) persistent within the system. Predominant institutionalization of one alternative does not dispel its counterpart. The presence of incipient or established anti-systems within a social system constitutes a fundamental dynamic of change.

Social systems vary along the dimension of structural and functional differentiation. Again our lead comes from the polar typologies. All of them, e.g., rural–urban, primitive–civilized, status–contract, developed–underdeveloped, etc., carry with them the notion of the direct relationship between differentiation and complexity. The greater the differentiation the greater the complexity of the system. The greater the complexity the greater the probability of further differentiation. In his milestone work on social change, Smelser makes the following reference to differentiation:

> This implicit concept underlies much of our discourse about social development. We seldom ask, however, whether the *very process* of passing from a less differentiated to a more differentiated social structure possesses definite regularities, and whether the sequence itself produces phenomena which can be analysed systematically. It is my assertion that such regularities do exist, and can be extracted from societies in flux.[23]

The work that Smelser has done along these lines to date has had a significant impact upon our notions of general structural change.

A given state of the social system presupposes all previous states, and hence contains them, if only in residual or modified form. This might well be referred to as the principle of *structural continuity*. Social process is the dynamic aspect of any given social rela-

---

[22] See J. C. McKinney and C. P. Loomis, "The Typological Tradition," in J. S. Roucek (ed.), *Contemporary Sociology* (New York: Philosophical Library, 1958), pp. 557-582. For a different but related perspective, see Reinhard Bendix and Bennett Berger, "Images of Society and Problems of Concept Formation in Sociology," in Gross, *Symposium on Sociological Theory*, pp. 92-118.

[23] N. J. Smelser, *Social Change in the Industrial Revolution* (Chicago: University of Chicago Press, 1959), p. 2.

tion. If a social system is a network of social relations, it is also a *flow* of relationships through time. It follows that history is a continuity of such relationships—an evolutionary process in which, similar but not identical to the organic world, nature makes no leaps and in which the most difficult act is the attempt to break with the past. As long as the system persists, rather than moving into extinction, factors of both endogenous and exogenous change have operated *within* the framework of social *order* characterizing the system.

Change is immanent in the social system. Sorokin has commented on the principle of immanent change as follows:

> As long as it exists and functions, any sociocultural system incessantly generates consequences which are not the results of the external factors to the system, but the consequences of the existence of the system and its activities. As such, they must be imputed to it, regardless of whether they are good or bad, desirable or not, intended or not by the system. One of the specific forms of this immanent generation of consequences is an incessant change of the system itself, due to its existence and activity.[24]

Change is inherent in social systems since they are *action* systems. A great deal of behavior is future-oriented in the sense that it is directed toward objectives, gratifications, and the achievement of aspirations. At the level of individual behavior and role relations it involves many confrontations, recombinations, and adaptations. At a more complex level, one can refer to the inherently unstable condition of a social system consequent upon imperfect socialization and social control, ambiguities and looseness of role specification, conflict between institutions organized on different orientational bases (e.g., religious, economic, political, etc.), and the process of structural differentiation. Moreover, one can again note the conflict and change rooted in the process of institutionalization when it is viewed as a social form of problem-solving.

All systems are subject to exogenous (extrasystemic) change. Here again reference is to the fact that all persistent social systems are open systems. This means that no social system is entirely in

[24] P. A. Sorokin, *Social and Cultural Dynamics* (Boston: Porter Sargent, 1957), p. 639.

control of its own present and future. By virtue of its interrelationships and interdependencies with other systems, and by virtue of its
existence within a general environment, a social system is subject to
inputs and influences. The specification and tracing out of these is
essentially an empirical task and one of fundamental importance in
the assessment of rate and direction of change within a system.[25]

Social systems tend to persist in a moving equilibrium. Davis
makes the succinct comment that:

> It is only in terms of equilibrium that most sociological concepts
> make sense. Either tacitly or explicitly anyone who thinks about
> society tends to use the notion. . . . It is usually phrased in static
> terms, but as soon as the element of time is added it alludes to a
> moving equilibrium.[26]

The model of the dynamic equilibrium has change built into it,
although not to the degree that is satisfying to those seeking a
theory of change. However, it appears to be not only logically necessary but empirically correct to speak of the equilibrating tendency of
social systems. Moreover, it seems empirically warranted to speak
of a long-range tendency toward integration within systems. Dysfunc-
tions, tensions, stress, deviance, variance, inventions, innovations,
diffusions, and differentiation itself tend to be dealt with by the
established institutional structure and normative order. Adjustive
or adaptive responses are made within the system, and hence change
tends to occur gradually (in the historical sense of time), although
by no means evenly, in all sectors of the system. The very fact that
a system is always differentiated to some degree implies that change
will not take place with the same degree of probability in all sectors.
We are empirically well aware of the fact that change tends to take
place much more rapidly in the area of technological development

[25] For an extensive examination of the research in diffusion, see Elihu
Katz, M. L. Levin, and Herbert Hamilton, "Traditions of Research on the
Diffusion of Innovation," *American Sociological Review,* 28 (April, 1963),
pp. 237-252. For an exploration of the "linkages" of systems, see C. P.
Loomis, *Social Systems: Essays on Their Persistence and Change* (Princeton:
D. Van Nostrand, 1960).

[26] Kingsley Davis, *Human Society* (New York: Macmillan, 1949), p.
634.

than in the ideological sphere, in economic affairs in comparison to religious, etc. The assumption is typically made in the equilibrium model that any change has repercussions throughout the system. This must be understood as a working assumption and not a mechanical law. The direction, rate, and degree of dependent change are empirical problems with respect to any change. The repercussive assumption merely directs attention to the assessment of consequences; it does not in itself indicate anything about the extent of interdependencies involved in any particular change. This remains primarily an empirical problem, although it would undoubtedly be of considerable help to have a more systematic map of the primary sources of change.

The preceding premises and postulates relate to social systems analysis, and only partially to its intellectual precursors, e.g., structuralism, functionalism, and structural-functionalism. To use an evolutionary phrase, the discipline of sociology has now reached a stage in its development wherein it is clearly on the threshold of systems analysis. This is only possible because of the varied contributions of the many "feeder" or subsidiary lines of thought which are convergent with structural-functional theory at the systems level. The historical concentration on the delineation of structure and the widely varied attempts to explicate functionalism must be understood primarily as a phase in the development process of the discipline.

For example, Parsons takes a much more optimistic view of the disciplinary capacity to deal with problems of change today than at the time he wrote *The Social System*. On the basis of sociological developments in the past few years, he now believes that the problems of social change are:

> . . . soluble in empirical-theoretical terms. Above all we have at our disposal a conceptual scheme which is sufficiently developed so that at least at the level of categorization and of problem statement it is approaching the type of closure . . . which makes *systematic* analysis of interdependencies possible. We can define the main ranges of variability which are essential for empirical analysis, and the main mechanisms through which variations are propagated through the system. We can quantify to the point of designating deficits and surpluses of inputs and outputs, and here and there we

come close to specifying threshold values beyond which equilibrium will break down.[27]

It is clear that we now have the theoretical ability (or potential), and in many cases the methodological and empirical ability, to deal with conflicts, contradictions, deviance, variance, strain, dysfunction, innovation, invention, diffusion, adaptations, and repercussions within the loose framework of structural-functional analysis. As structural-functionalism is, through time and effort, "tightened up" and transformed into a full-blown style of social systems analysis, one can assume that approaches to these disparate types of problem and change can be better articulated. However, at least for the foreseeable future, one cannot assume that this will result in a general theory of change. On the contrary, the greater likelihood is the fuller development of complementary models of social change, in effect a pluralism of change models all related in one way or another to the structure and function, and the maintenance and development of social systems. These will have to reflect the several premises listed above with respect to change and systems analysis, and not merely the equilibrium premise. It may well be that the prime indicator of a movement up to the level of a genuine systems analysis will be that of the developed capacity to handle change in terms of the requirements implicit in the several systemic premises.

Social Change: Practical Problems

Clearly we do not have a general theory of change if what is meant by this is a theory that will encompass enduring shifts of a whole society from one state to another state. Moreover, such a theory is not immanent. It is at this point that a statement made by Moore is relevant. "The mention of 'theory of social change' will make most social scientists appear defensive, furtive, guilt-ridden, or frightened. Yet the source of this unease may be in part an unduly awe-stricken regard for the explicitly singular and implicitly capital-

[27] Talcott Parsons, "Some Considerations on the Theory of Social Change," *Rural Sociology,* 26 (September, 1961), p. 238.

ized word 'Theory.'" [28] The absence of a general and comprehensive theory may be discomforting, but in no sense is it catastrophic. Several theoretical approaches to change have been developed, and each in its own way is extremely useful. *None* of them has been more than partially exploited either methodologically or empirically. These theories concern subprocesses of change within and between systems, and none of them claims to encompass the general phenomena of change as such. These subprocesses or aspects of change are of great importance in their own right. Empirically the absence of anything resembling a general theory is neither as important nor as devastating as one might be led to believe by the self-effacing posture of many sociologists with respect to change. Sociology has provided a number of fairly high-level, empirically based, and interdependent propositions concerning social change. [29] It is obvious that we have many treatments of change in the literature which are satisfactory in an empirical sense, as well as theoretically respectable. These are treatments of limited or specified changes within the general system. In a recent survey, Boskoff described some of these theories and their areas of relevance. [30] The point here is that the search for a theory of social change may continue to contribute a fearsome challenge for the discipline of sociology, and to fire the imagination of particular sociologists, but the absence of such a theory does *not deter* the sociologist from treating change within systems and between systems in meaningful and theoretically useful ways. Moreover, it is precisely knowledge of change of this order and at this level which is actually or potentially of direct use to those in policy making and implementation positions with respect to the planning, instigation, and execution of change. The kinds of

28 W. E. Moore, "A Reconsideration of Theories of Social Change," p. 810.

29 For a brief, succinct, and yet comprehensive review of established generalizations related to social change, see W. E. Moore, *Social Change* (Englewood Cliffs: Prentice-Hall, 1963). Also note Bernard Berelson and G. A. Steiner, *Human Behavior: An Inventory of Scientific Findings* (New York: Harcourt, Brace and World, 1964), especially pp. 613-619.

30 Alvin Boskoff, "Social Change: Major Problems in the Emergence of Theoretical and Research Foci," in Becker and Boskoff, *Modern Sociological Theory*, pp. 260-302.

change that planners and "change agents" are interested in are the kinds of change that sociologists and other social scientists are theoretically and methodologically capable of dealing with.

In the light of these considerations regarding social structure and social change, we can again return to the problem of utilitarian construction and interpretation of types. A specific problem within the broad area of "instigated social change" has been chosen for a demonstrational analysis.[31]

Accessibility and the Instigation of Change

Most Latin American specialists agree that geographical accessibility is an important determining factor in the rapidity with which technological changes are incorporated. Thus Ralph Beals, in what he calls a frivolous note, says, "If I were to rate acculturative forces I have seen at work in various communities, I think I would suggest that one road is worth about three schools and about fifty administrators." [32] In his classical study of an area which in precolonial times had one homogeneous culture, Robert Redfield concludes that "Yucatan, considered as one moves from Merida southeastward into forest hinterland, presents a sort of social gradient in which Spanish, modern, and urban gives way to the Maya, Archaic, and primitive." [33] Notwithstanding the importance of geographical accessibility, several studies of Latin American communities have revealed that geographical accessibility is only one factor in cultural change. Studies have demonstrated that communities which have

31 For the original presentation of the material used in the following analysis, see C. P. Loomis and J. C. McKinney, "Systemic Differences Between Latin-American Communities of Family Farms and Large Estates," *American Journal of Sociology,* 61 (March, 1956), pp. 404-412.

32 Sol Tax, *Heritage of Conquest: The Ethnology of Middle America* (Glencoe: The Free Press, 1952), p. 232.

33 Robert Redfield, *The Folk Culture of Yucatan* (Chicago: University of Chicago Press, 1941), p. 13.

been described as folk or *Gemeinschaft*-like in some respects, may in other respects have urban or *Gesellschaft*-like elements, such as the impersonalization of relationships and utilitarian motives in interpersonal interaction. Therefore, it becomes necessary to consider accessibility in terms of some nongeographical dimensions. Specifically, this calls for examination of communities in terms of their attributes as social systems. In addition, in order to escape the limitations of the general, more blanket typologies such as *Gemeinschaft* or folk, it appears desirable to develop subtypologies.[34] An operational demonstration of type usage will be attempted in order to provide a theoretical comparison of intercultural accessibility of communities of family-sized farms and large estates.

First, however, a large-estate community and a family-farm community will be compared in terms of their concrete attributes as communities, and significant differences will be pointed out. On the basis of obvious distinctions, it appears necessary also to direct attention to the systemic attributes of large-estate and family-farm communities on a more general and abstract level. This is based on the assumption that the sharp differences apparent in the analysis of the two particular communities give evidence of the existence of two distinct *types* of social organization in rural Latin America. In the comparison of these social organizations, they are treated in terms of the theory of social systems, and, thereby, at least some of their theoretical systemic attributes are established. This procedure rests on the assumption that the establishment of the abstract systemic attributes would supplement the empirical evidence and promote comparative studies of what appear to be two fundamentally different types of social structure. If the social systems differ on both the empirical and the theoretical levels, it would seem likely that the problem of accessibility to cultural change is dual rather than unitary, and hence calls for different procedures in the strategy and instigation of change.

[34] For an earlier recognition of the need for subtypes of general typologies and for an earlier presentation of the technique used here, see C. P. Loomis and J. A. Beegle, *Rural Social Systems* (New York: Prentice-Hall, 1950), Chapter I and Appendix A.

The Social Systems
to Be Compared

The specific social systems compared are the large-estate community of Atirro, with sixty-five families, and the nearby community of family farms, San Juan Sur, comprising seventy-five families. Both these communities are located in the Turrialba Canton of Costa Rica. Although there is great variation in both communities of family farms and large-estate communities in Latin America, it is believed, on the basis of available evidence, that Atirro and San Juan Sur are, in general, fairly typical.

Before proceeding to the theoretical examination of these communities' systemic attributes, we shall point out what appear to be their salient empirical characteristics.[35] The following comparisons summarize obviously important empirical differences.

Physical Accessibility. Atirro is accessible by vehicle over a dirt road the year around, although walking is the most common means of locomotion. It is approximately six miles from the trade-center town of Turrialba, a place of 6,500 people. San Juan Sur, which is three miles from Turrialba, is accessible by vehicle only during the drier months of the year. Several horse trails lead to San Juan Sur.

Spatial Arrangements. Atirro is a "cluster" village, and the houses are closely grouped about the administrative building and coffee mill. San Juan Sur is a village strung along a trail, which makes it

[35] The selection of categories for description is always to some extent arbitrary. There was a principle of selection utilized in determining the categories for empirical description of the two communities. Since accessibility to change is at base the problem, descriptive categories were chosen that were directly relevant to or would provide essential information regarding the differential accessibility of the communities. Reference here is to physical, mental, and social accessibility. The assumption is that the instigation of change is dependent upon degree and type of accessibility.

For a comprehensive description of the communities under analysis here, see C. P. Loomis, *et al., Turrialba: Social Systems and the Introduction of Change* (Glencoe: The Free Press, 1953).

appear to be the less densely populated. Actually, the amount of farm land per person is the same—about two acres.

Mobility. The workers on the hacienda are quite mobile. At the time of enumeration, one-fourth of the residents had been in Atirro a year or less. The people of San Juan Sur are comparatively immobile. Only one family had lived in the community for less than a year.

Routine Activity. The yearly round of activities centering around the cultivation of coffee and cane is substantially the same in San Juan Sur as in Atirro. However, the individual farmer of San Juan Sur is not so inexorably bound to schedules and working hours as is the laborer in Atirro.

Social Class. San Juan Sur is not a highly stratified community, while the hacienda community Atirro is. In San Juan Sur, only one informal grouping does not extend over a wide range of ranks. Family and friendship and informal-group affiliation in San Juan Sur almost completely bridge variations in status. Hence the status differences do not result in classes.

In contrast, stratification on a class basis does exist in Atirro; there is a labor class, a skilled-supervisory class, and a proprietary class. Over two-thirds of the residents of Atirro could be designated as proletarian, whereas very few of the landless in San Juan Sur could be so classed. The landless in San Juan Sur are, for the most part, close relatives of owners and interact freely with owners in general. Ownership of land is a primary value and is clearly related to status, but it does not constitute an insuperable barrier to interaction. There are social barriers to interaction in Atirro based upon the relation to the land and its use.

Social Status. There are recognizable differences in status within both communities and in the function of the status system. In San Juan Sur most interaction takes place in the family and among family friends, and the social-status system apparently reinforces their goals and norms. For instance, farm ownership, a larger income, and central location in the family-friendship structure are positively associated with social status.

In Atirro, on the other hand, status is more closely related to the organization of the entire community. Atirro functions as much more of a unit than does San Juan Sur; hence the status system serves the function of controlling the interaction of individuals in functionally important roles in the community more than it does in San Juan Sur.

The Communication Structure. In Atirro, communication as reflected in visiting takes place more frequently within the classes than across class boundaries. In San Juan Sur the paths of communication cross almost all social-status distinctions.

Social Structure. In Atirro the most important social structures are the family units and the hacienda as an economic organization; in San Juan Sur only the family units are of real importance. The functional integration of the hacienda rests upon a division of labor, and the system is articulated daily. In contrast, San Juan Sur is articulated as a unit only on special occasions, such as fiestas and crises. The interaction within friendship groups in Atirro tends to follow the lines of status differentiation, in contrast to the extended family cliques of San Juan Sur. There is a diversity of normative orders in Atirro which achieves integration through interdependence of roles, statuses, and classes; in San Juan Sur the normative order is a matter of consensus.

Clique Structure. The cliques in San Juan Sur are composed largely of family groups, in which each member operates under the same general norms and places his family obligations above other bases for friendship. The ties of blood and marriage are chiefly responsible for the groupings. The cliques cannot be differentiated on the basis of outward characteristics; they appear to be basically similar. In Atirro, in contrast, there exist differences among cliques. Certain cliques are almost completely isolated. Class barriers operate to perpetuate differences between the cliques. This distinction between the two communities is emphasized by the fact that in San Juan Sur there is one informal community leader of dominant importance; in Atirro there are several.

Leadership. The five prestige or community leaders and all other persons of high rank in San Juan Sur were farm owners. In Atirro, neither the owner nor any other members of the proprietary class were designated by the community members as leaders. Instead, those designated were from the skilled-supervisory class. Their leadership, in part at least, is a function of their position in the hacienda organization. The actual leadership exercised by the owner of Atirro is evidently based upon (1) authority and power, (2) kinship relations, and (3) property holdings and wealth. In contrast, the outstanding leader in San Juan Sur owes his position primarily to personal attributes and achievements. He is a skilled and persuasive speaker, who knows how to get on with people in general.

Now that important empirical differences between the actual communities of San Juan Sur and Atirro have been pointed out, an examination of *type differences* in the light of social systems theory will be undertaken. It should again be noted that the more general a type, the greater the simplification of the empirical attributes, and the more specific a type, the greater is the number of general characteristics excluded from the construction. The general polar types such as the *Gemeinschaft–Gesellschaft* typology have unquestionably been of great heuristic value over the years. Yet for certain kinds of problems it seems advisable, indeed necessary, to take the components or aspects of the general types and treat them as variables. In view of their history, derivation, and content, it seems justifiable to conclude that Parsons' pattern-variables represent a further and more elaborate specification of the aspects of society dealt with by *Gemeinschaft* and *Gesellschaft*. On the basis of the analysis in the preceding chapter, it seems legitimate to refer to them as theoretical components of the more general types. Also on the basis of that analysis, it seems justifiable to conceive of Parsons' first four variables, Sorokin's familistic–contractual dichotomy, and Weber's rational–traditional pair as subtypes of *Gemeinschaft* and *Gesellschaft*. In so doing it would appear that all of the major implications and content of the general typology are covered, and in addition, the advantage of having more specific categories to work with is gained.

The Procedure

In an attempt to avoid some of the shortcomings of previous typological descriptions of communities, the following procedures have been adhered to: First, what appear to be the important subtypes of the major general types have been introduced as continua. Second, in the analysis the subtypes are used in the form of variable polar components of more general types. These subtypes, although varied and to a certain unavoidable degree overlapping, represent similar levels of abstraction. Third, we have used the concept of the social system and consequently are able to treat these subtypes as systemic attributes. This establishes the theoretical possibility of finding similar attributes in apparently different empirical groups. Fourth, the types are applied to only one social system or reference group at a time. No attempt is made to apply the types to many reference groups, such as the family, church groups, occupational groups, political systems, etc., simultaneously. The level of abstraction is thereby held constant. It should also be noted that the types are applied to *social* systems, not cultural systems or personality systems. Fifth, the types are applied to specific and comparable relationships between specific and comparable roles in specific social systems. Sixth, to standardize the typing of the relationships, a specific category of action is supplied.

In order to make the theoretical treatment of these systems pertinent to the problem of intercultural accessibility or to resistance to change, the type of change under consideration is that which requires community action, not merely normal or gradual infiltration of ideas or techniques. Reference is to *instigated change* involving the articulation of the entire community in a common course of action, such as proposals to introduce organized sanitation to prevent spread of communicable diseases, or quarantine regulations of sick persons with such diseases, or to set up community-wide cooperatives, schools, and the like.

The Social Relationships to Be Compared

In order to arrange for typing of communal action, a role in each community was chosen which articulated the power structure of the whole social system. On the large estate, Atirro, the role of the administrator was chosen as the subject, and the role of an immediate subordinate, the supervisor, was chosen as object. The administrator initiates action continuously to the supervisor, who is in daily contact with most families in the hacienda community.

Since the power structure of San Juan Sur is articulated only during fiestas and times of crisis, and since there are no formally elected or appointed governmental administrative officials, obviously there are no roles exactly comparable to those of the administrator and supervisor at Atirro. The local informal leader of the community, the *gamonal*,[36] most frequently initiates action in the community as a whole. The following will perhaps best provide an idea of the leadership of the *gamonal* in San Juan Sur:

> During a heavy rain in the wet season one of the children of San Juan Sur fell in a bridgeless river when returning from school. She was drowned. The river is now bridged because Sr. Torres rallied all villagers and their families to walk to the trade center town to demand that the *Jefe Politico* make funds available to bridge the river. This leader has led the community members in several such events.[37]

In our typology the *gamonal* is considered as subject, and a fellow community member whom he chose to help him is considered as object.

The Specific Category of Action

Several social scientists [38] who are Latin American specialists were asked to function as judges in the typing of the two com-

[36] Various terms are used for informal leaders in Latin America who may resemble ward heelers or public opinion leaders in the United States. *Gamonal, caudillo, quayacan,* and *cacique* are used, depending on the area.

[37] C. P. Loomis, paper read at Founders' Day Institute, Boston University, 1953.

[38] Antonio M. Arce, Eduardo Arze Loureiro, Reed Powell, Charles Proctor, Manuel Alers-Montalvo, and Roy Clifford typed Atirro and San Juan Sur. Olen Leonard and Wilson Longmore used the same procedure but typed other large-estate communities and communities of family-sized farms in Latin America known intimately to them.

munities under consideration. With two exceptions, each is intimately acquainted with Atirro and San Juan Sur. They responded to the schedule included here as Figure 1. The instructions that they followed, as well as the continua offered them, are seen in the figure.

On theoretical grounds we have accepted the *Gemeinschaft* and *Gesellschaft* types as the most general forms relevant to the problem at hand. Figure 2 indicates the subtypes or component continua which appear to be the chief constituents of these general types. In typing the relationships as presented in Figure 2, an attempt was made to communicate the meaning of the continua through characteristics of their poles. This was done by means of the illustrations contained in the schedule presented here as Figure 1.

The judges' reactions are portrayed schematically in Figure 2. Different profiles emerged for the two communities. These are marked F and H. The two systems tended to scale out toward opposite poles of the typology, sharp and significant differences being thereby established at the theoretical level on the basis of an intimate and detailed knowledge of two particular concrete organizations.

The Types and Relevance
to the Instigation of Change

Insofar as a specific manifestation of the employment of power in San Juan Sur tended toward the affective, particularistic, ascriptive, diffuse, traditional, and familistic poles, it becomes subject to the hypotheses and statements made about *Gemeinschaft* and related general-type communities.

In contrast, Atirro under comparable conditions tended toward the opposite poles of affective neutrality, universalism, achievement, specificity, rationality, and contractualism, and hence becomes subject to hypotheses and statements made about *Gesellschaft* and related general-type communities.

The profiles which emerged for Atirro and San Juan Sur at the level of theoretical systemic attributes in effect generalized these

FIGURE 1

The Schedule

(As Used by Latin American Specialists in Typing Relationships)

Instructions: Assume that in both the community of family-sized farms (San Juan Sur) and the large-estate community (Atirro) two leaders are organizing a reception for the national president, who has just informed the leader in the subject role that he will arrive on the next day. The roles which structure the interaction which is to be placed on the continua are the following: hacienda community—subject is the administrator and object the next subordinate, *e.g.,* the supervisor; community of family-sized farms—subject is the most powerful informal leader, the *gam-* *onal,* in San Juan Sur and the object whoever helps him most in the execution of the act. In both cases the initiator of the action is the subject, administrator on the hacienda community and *gamonal* in the community of family-sized farms.

Place an *H* on each continuum below for the above-described action between the specified roles for the event and situation as indicated, for the hacienda community. Place an *F* on each continuum to indicate how the interaction event and situation for the *roles* specified would compare in the community of family-sized farms.

NORMS OF ORIENTATION OF THE SUBJECT TO OBJECT

I.

Affectivity   Affective Neutrality

5	4	3	2	1	0	1	2	3	4	5

Note: Position No. 5 as the polar type represents action determined completely by emotions—love, hate, fear, and other emotions. Examples of interaction which would fall toward this pole are the following: mother as subject loving her child; Damon as subject pleading to die for his friend Pythias.

Position No. 5 as a polar type represents action completely devoid of feeling. Examples of hypothetical interaction which would fall close to this pole are the following: a robot commanding another actor; the hired gunman "cold-bloodedly" shooting his victim; a telephone operator giving the object the time of day at the response to a dial signal, etc.

II.

Particularism   Universalism

5	4	3	2	1	0	1	2	3	4	5

Position No. 5 as a polar type represents action governed only by the exigencies of the relationship

Position No. 5 as a polar type represents action governed entirely by norms of the reference system of the of the immediate subject to object (or other particular relationship of subject) permitting the norms of no other reference system to have any influence. Examples which fall toward this pole: in government where subject and object are related by kinship-nepotism; also favoritism; a mother (subject) protecting and bearing false witness before a judge (object) for her son who she knows has committed murder in "cold blood."

whole society. Examples which fall toward this pole: in government, where civil service rules and regulations, not kinship or friendship relations, guide action; a Damon or Pythias reports to the police his best friend as committing a murder which is known to no one else.

NORMS OF ORIENTATION PRESCRIBING ASPECTS OF OBJECT WHICH WILL DETERMINE ACTION AND SCOPE OF ACTION RELEVANT

III.

Ascription
(Quality)

Achievement
(Performance)

5	4	3	2	1	0	1	2	3	4	5

Position No. 5 as the polar type represents action determined completely by the qualities of the object—sex, age, race, etc., are the determinants on the level of the subject's action. Examples approaching this type: employing and paying women less than men are paid for the same work or vice versa; failure to obey fair employment practices laws.

Position No. 5 as the polar type represents action determined completely by the object's performance or potential performance. Examples approaching this type: subject paying object piece rates, disregarding race, creed, or any other quality, conforming to fair employment practices.

IV.

Diffuseness

Specificity

5	4	3	2	1	0	1	2	3	4	5

Position No. 5 as the polar type represents a situation in which the roles require that subject and object form a complete community of fate so that all of the object's being and existence is relevant to the subject. Examples approaching this type: the mother's range of interest in her child; the wife's interest in the husband.

Position No. 5 as the polar type represents a situation in which the role of the subject narrowly prescribes the scope of interest and responsibility of the subject for the object. Examples approaching this type: the subject's interest in the telephone operator as object in the act of telephoning; the patron of the prostitute as object and the prostitute as subject or vice versa; doctor (object) –patient (subject) relationship falls this side of continuum.

V.

Traditional   Rational

5	4	3	2	1	0	1	2	3	4	5

Position No. 5 as the polar type represents action entirely determined by customary ways and procedures coming down from the past. Examples approaching this type: where protocol, convention, or custom dictates action irrespective of its efficiency. Hypothetical case: The servant lets his beloved master be killed by thieves in the bedroom because tradition prohibits the servant from addressing the master directly in the bedroom.

Position No. 5 as the polar type represents action currently planned to maximize gratification to the subject and minimizing his expenditure of effort, time and money. Examples approaching this type: those between buyer and seller at the market place.

VI.

Familistic   Contractual

5	4	3	2	1	0	1	2	3	4	5

Position No. 5 as the polar type represents action in which the subject is motivated to affectivity, particularism, ascription, and diffuseness as typed above. If the relationship of the mother to the child is taken as an example for most cultures, all four items register toward the polar type. Whoever in the family is the task-assigner and disciplinarian may play a role which is placed lower on the affectivity continuum composing this "sponge" but meaningful type.

Position No. 5 as the polar type represents action governed by contract, such as those between buyer and seller in the market. The marriage contract (really a misnomer) does not belong here. Typically, such relations between subject and object are affectively neutral, universalistic, and functionally specific, and, if not involving the object himself in the contract (as a slave or serf) but rather his services or wares, are oriented to achievement or performance. Even in the latter case it may have this orientation. The doctor (subject)–patient (object) relationship falls on this side. Also it falls on this side for all continua above.

Source: C. P. Loomis and J. C. McKinney, "Systemic Differences Between Latin American Communities of Family Farms and Large Estates," *American Journal of Sociology*, 61 (March, 1956), pp. 410-411.

FIGURE 2

PROFILES TYPING THE NORMS OF ORIENTATION OF SUBJECT TO OBJECT IN AN ACTION CONTEXT

		Gemeinschaft subtypes	5	4	3	2	1	0	1	2	3	4	5	*Gesellschaft* subtypes
		Affectivity		F					H					Affective Neutrality
		Particularism			F					H				Universalism
		Ascription (Quality)		F					H					Achievement (Performance)
		Diffuseness		F							H			Specificity
		Traditional		F						H				Rational
		Familistic		F						H				Contractual

F designates the profile of the relationship of informal community leader and an assistant in a community of family-sized farms.

H designates the profile of the relationship of the manager to an immediate superordinate, the supervisor, in the large-estate community.

two specific communities into a typology applicable to a great variety of specific social organizations. The empirical descriptions which were developed apply to the two communities as individual cases. By complementing these case descriptions with a theoretical placement in a generally applicable typology, the two particular communities are made susceptible to all hypotheses and propositions characteristic of *Gemeinschaft* and *Gesellschaft* and related polar typologies. Atirro and San Juan Sur appear to be representative in form of communities commonly found in rural Latin America. If they are typical, the differences between them are significant in view of the ideological struggles going on in the world today concerning the relative merits of various forms of land tenure and settlement form. Even more important, if the communities of Atirro and San Juan Sur are actually representative of other large-estate and family-farm communities in Latin America, then we have solid grounds for saying that the large-estate community possesses a different order of accessibility, socially and culturally, than the family-farm community.

The type of social organization represented empirically by San Juan Sur is one in which economic productivity is low because the division of labor is little developed, the objectives of economic activity are more commonly the maintenance of status relations, social mobility is low, and because the customary forms of behavior are so fixed that they determine the manner and effects of economic performance. In contrast, the type of social organization represented here by Atirro is characterized by a more complex division of labor, a relatively open social structure in which class is significant but in which class barriers are not insurmountable, a situation in which social roles and economic reward are distributed primarily on the basis of achievement, and in which, consequently, innovations and the pursuit of self-interest are fully sanctioned.

These types of structure are typically identified with two different modes of orientation to knowledge. These two different orientations are crucially related to the matter of accessibility to change and hence to any proposed form of instigated change. It is now a standard view in the sociology of knowledge that different types of knowledge, as well as the techniques and motivations for extending knowledge, are bound up with particular forms of groups.

Gemeinschaft types of society have a traditionally defined fund of knowledge handed down as conclusive and final, they are not concerned with discovering new ideas or extending their spheres of knowledge. Any effort to test the traditional knowledge, insofar as it implies doubt, is ruled out on moral grounds. In such a group the prevailing methods are ontological and dogmatic; its mode of thought is that of conceptual realism. In contrast, *Gesellschaft* types of organization institutionalize techniques for the attainment and codification of knowledge. In such a group the methods are primarily epistemological and critical; the mode of thought is nominalistic.

Given such differences in structural types and modes of orientation, it is clear that the problem of instigating change, of whatever purpose or form, must be perceived of in very different ways for the two contrasting types of systems. Moreover, there appears to be ample justification for saying that the instigation of any change will necessarily have to follow different procedures, adapted to two distinctly different social structures. The success of the planning and execution of such change will in large part be determined by the extent to which it is appropriate to the system for which it is intended.

The specific and very limited problem that has been dealt with here with respect to these communities is part of a much larger problematic area, that of *social change*. If sociology is to play a key role in contemporary social research, then the major inquiries must be made in a world where the patterns of the past are under increased pressure from a dynamic future. From out of our heritage of diverse theoretical schemes for the analysis of change, the idea of the societal continuum remains as a fundamental point of reference. The dynamics of a societal continuum so formulated as to comprehend the concept of constant polarity and transitional society, in which empirical regularities, constant societal denominators, and universal norms can be recognized, cannot be sterile.

The general typologies and the related work of theorists attacking broad-scale problems are still relevant and of orientational utility to contemporary sociologists. It must be recognized, however, that general "sponge" types such as those we have utilized have inherent limitations with respect to the handling of many specific problems. The use of general types alone results in the obscuring rather than clarification of some specific problems. On the other hand, the use of highly concretized, specific types alone results in the loss of a meaningful frame of reference. To avoid this dilemma it seems feasible to use subtypes of general types and thereby retain the dual advantages of uncovering specific aspects of a problem and preserving theoretical articulation. Typification invariably involves simplification; therefore it is imperative that the task of typification be performed at a level relevant to the problem under investigation. The preceding exploration of the problem of instigated social change represents an attempt to utilize the theoretical contributions of a general typology and the empirical contributions of two selected cases in the typification of social organizations which are internationally the target of such change.

—7

Types, Continuity, and the Process of Planning for Change

The preceding discussion has concentrated on social systems, change, and the problem of instigated change. The methodological objective was to indicate the utility of typological formulations at different levels with respect to a specific problem touching upon these important sectors of social phenomena. We will now abstract out a limited component of the change process, planning, and subject it to typological analysis. We will construct a typology of the planning process in order to demonstrate that such a procedure contributes to an understanding of planning and its relation to social structure, continuity, and change. Before proceeding with the typology, additional commentary on social structure and change is in order.

Sociology, just as each of the social sciences, has its own particular focal point of analysis. The fundamental datum for the sociologist is interaction. In the generic sense, interaction refers to reciprocal and interdependent behavior among two or more components in a situation. Sociologists, by tradition, restrict their attention to interaction among human beings. This type of interaction is unique in that it takes place through communication by means of symbolic behavior. For interaction to take place there must be a plurality of persons, there must be reciprocal action between them, and communication through signs and symbols must take place.

Moreover, interaction has a duration or time dimension, and this is a continuity possessing a past, present, and future. Insofar as a future is necessarily involved, an anticipated state of affairs (consequences, goals, or ends) in part determines the character of the ongoing action. Consequently, interaction will have an object which cannot lie in the separate behaviors of the individuals involved, but lies in the reciprocal action itself. This will hold whether or not it is visible to the participating actors or to an independent observer. Therefore, interaction cannot be explained solely in terms of unit acts performed by participating actors, but stands as a legitimate order of existence in its own right.

Having postulated the preceding with regard to interaction, it is necessary to further propose that interaction can develop certain uniformities over time and hence become *systematized* by the *structuring* of action. Structure refers to the established patterns of interaction that tend to persist. Expressed in another way, structure is a general term having reference to all those attributes of interaction which enable one to view the *relationships* involved as composite or complex wholes made up of interdependent parts. In brief, behavioral systems emerge out of interaction, and we typify these as *social systems.* Just as all other disciplines of scientific orientation, sociology is concerned with the *orderliness* or uniformities involved in its particular class of phenomena, and it finds this order in the social system. The problems that cluster around the development, maintenance, and modification of that order may all be typified as problems of *social change.* These are not only problems of theoretical and empirical significance to the sociologist, they also constitute the *social problems* perceived by and of concern to the members, or some segment of the membership, of society. It is here that the routine or "bread and butter" concerns of the sociologist, indeed all social scientists, and the moral and practical concerns of the public become mutually implicated.

Historically, many sociologists have raised serious questions about the nature of the relationship between social scientists and society and the mutual responsibilities involved therein, perhaps none more provocatively than Louis Wirth. Wirth consistently expressed the view that social science cannot be, and should not pretend to be, disinterested in the problems of the world. It was his contention that a completely disinterested social science could not exist, since the values, beliefs, and rationalizations of the scientist not only influence his choice of frame of reference and problem area, but also influence the selection of relevant data, recording of observations, theoretical and practical inferences drawn, and the manner of presentation of results.[1] Wirth held the view that "Without valuations we have no interest, no sense of relevance, or of significance, and, consequently, no object."[2] Moreover, more than most sociologists, Wirth was aware of the consequences of ideas. He held that no matter how objective or disinterested one attempts to be, he cannot escape the fact that

> . . . every assertion of a "fact" about the social world touches the interests of some individual or group, one cannot even call attention to the existence of certain "facts" without courting the objections of those whose very *"raison d'etre"* in society rests upon a divergent interpretation of the "factual" situation.[3]

Consequently, whether the social scientist likes it or not he is involved with practical problems of the ongoing world; and since he is involved, he not only should but must be responsible for the consequences of his research. The implication of this position is that the task of science, particularly social science, should be to help solve the crucial social problems facing man as he lives in this world. Wirth's position was that until social scientists find a method of obtaining answers to critical problems, they cannot expect society to support their endeavors.

Whether or not the individual sociologist accepts the Wirth point of view—and it is clear that many do not—the fact remains that the discipline of sociology, along with the other social sciences, has something of value to offer the society which it studies. What it has to offer consists in the aggregate knowledge it has of the structure

[1] See Louis Wirth, "Preface" to Karl Mannheim, *Ideology and Utopia*, translated by Louis Wirth and E. A. Shils (New York: Harcourt, Brace, 1936), pp. xiii-xxxi; and Louis Wirth, "Ideological Aspects of Social Disorganization," *American Sociological Review*, 5 (August, 1940) pp. 472-482.

[2] Letter from Louis Wirth to Gunnar Myrdal, September 29, 1939. Reprinted in part in *American Dilemma* (New York: Harper and Brothers, 1944), Vol. 2, pp. 1063-1064.

[3] Louis Wirth, "Preface" to *Ideology and Utopia*, p. xvii.

and function of society, and of the problems that confront society in its efforts to maintain and develop itself in the process of change. It is clear that this knowledge lies in the public domain, not only nationally, but internationally. Consequently, whether or not the individual scholar wishes to be at the direct service of mankind, it is evident that the aggregate knowledge to which he has contributed is at such service.

If society, and of course any of its component social systems, is to maximize its probability of successfully coping with the problems confronting it, then it must utilize the best available knowledge in coming to grips with those problems. Coping with problems of continuity and change is dependent in part upon the ability to *anticipate*, which in turn is based upon the ability to mobilize relevant knowledge. It has long been recognized that the most rational way of confronting the future and the changes involved in it is to *plan* for it and thus attempt to gain at least some degree of control, however minimal, over the events yet to come. The existent and developing knowledge of the social sciences thus constitutes the basic underpinning of the activity now institutionalized as social planning.

Planning and Change

"To plan or not to plan is no real issue. Planning even of economic affairs has existed at all levels of our national life, both public and private, since the beginning of our history." [4] Planning is a normal and universal human activity which is manifest in different forms and explicit in varying degree in all persistent social systems. Planning is esentially the attempt to resolve the problems of the future by assessment of future consequences, as implicated in the activities and events of the present and our experience of the past. The process of planning is the process of delaying, organizing, and selecting a response appropriate to the anticipated situation in terms of the known alternative possibilities. Planning, just as any case of mobilization and utilization of knowledge, lies inside the process of conduct. It may be thought of as a process of pointing

[4] C. E. Merriam, "The Possibilities of Planning," *American Journal of Sociology*, 49 (March, 1944), p. 397.

out; to plan for something is to distinguish it before acting. In this sense planning, insofar as it involves some social unit or organization, is the social analogue of thinking at the individual level. Although a universal human activity, it has become explicit and institutionalized as an activity in its own right only in certain types of social systems. The continuum on which these types fall can be described in terms of the broad polar types, *Gemeinschaft* and *Gesellschaft*.[5]

The mainstream of history of Western society has been one of transition from *Gemeinschaft* to *Gesellschaft* form of organization. A part of the price paid for that transition is the loss of the integration characteristic of the *Gemeinschaft* structure. Since the modern sociologist perceives himself as primarily an analyst of society and not as a utopian remodeler of society, it makes no sense merely to urge a return to *Gemeinschaft*. A "back to *Gemeinschaft*" movement would be as impotent as most nativistic and romantic movements. The sociologist, perhaps above all others, is convinced that change has to take place within the framework of *the existent social structure*. This obviously means that the integration of knowledge characteristic of our *Gemeinschaft* era is unattainable. It does not necessarily follow, however, that integration of a different order, integrated knowledge compatible with the present social structure, cannot be attained. In its various forms and in its reliance on various subspheres of knowledge, planning in effect constitutes the social device for the attainment, however imperfectly, of the integration of existent knowledge and social structure. It is for this reason that planning has become an explicit, visible, and specialized activity within the *Gesellschaft*-like system and within the many subtypes of component social systems clustering toward that end of the polar continuum.

The relationship, in the general if not the operational sense, between planning and structural continuity is clear. Planning involves the attempt to maintain and develop social systems, and hence may be regarded as a rational component of structural continuity. In the small-scale system the planner may simply be one person,

[5] Ferdinand Tönnies, *Community and Society: Gemeinschaft und Gesellschaft*, edited and translated by C. P. Loomis (East Lansing: Michigan State University Press, 1957).

whereas in the large-scale system the planner may be an organization in its own right. Whatever the scale of these variations, planning itself, as a type of human activity, can be viewed best as a *method* of extrapolation. It is a way of speculating as to what a result may be, and then justifying the speculation by means of the result. The most substantial grounds upon which to base such a speculation consist in as complete a knowledge as possible of the existent structure, knowledge of the system in its present form as linked to the past. Projections on this basis are little theoretic leaps, but they require an understanding of the social system for which the plans are being made.

In this view, planning is neither ivory-tower speculation, intellectual star-gazing, nor utopian thinking. Essentially it is a practical and instrumental activity. Its criteria and style are pragmatic. Although concerned with the instigation, management, and realization of change, it has no general or theoretical problem of change. The paucity or inadequacy of theories of change, as described earlier, are matters of irrelevance to the planner and the planning operation. As institutionalized to a high degree in sectors of modern society, planning is always for the short run or for what might be called a "spacious present." In the historical sense of time, planning confines itself to very brief periods despite the use of such euphemisms as "long-range planning." Such planning typically has reference to periods in the range of five, ten, or in rare instances, twenty years. Moreover, there is no shortage of basic knowledge and no necessary shortage of data for the conduct of planning for change. On the contrary, there is a vast underuse and frequent misuse of existent relevant knowledge and data. In this regard it is suggested that sociology, like its sister social sciences and despite its theoretical deficiencies with respect to change, has a perspective to offer the planner. However commonplace, pedestrian, and nonesoteric this perspective may seem, it would appear to be essential to the planning process and hence utilitarian.

In examining the planning process, it is of course possible to dissemble it into various phases or components. Four phases will be distinguished here, and for purposes of convenience these will be referred to as Systemic Mapping, Evaluation, Decision-Making, and Implementation. When viewed in terms of a natural or chronological order, it is possible to see them forming a gradient in which sociology, and the social sciences generally, make their heaviest contribution in the beginning and successively lesser contributions as planning moves through the later phases. When planning is viewed as a *type* of human activity, distinguishable from other social forms, it becomes evident that these phases are subtypes of the planning process; as such they represent clusters of differentiated activities with some degree of independence. In effect we have constructed a *typology* of *planning* that is simultaneously chronological and analytical. In the chronological sense the underlying continuum is, of course, temporal: a natural history of activities, a beginning to an end. In the analytic sense the continuum is from knowledge to action, knowing to doing. In either case the types are based upon a close observation of the planning process as conducted in various spheres of national life, and represent a crude initial grouping of the multitude of diverse activities implicated in planning as a social institution. Here then is the typology.

Systemic Mapping

Of the phases of the planning process delineated here— systemic mapping, evaluation, decision-making, and implementation —it is evident that the latter three are highly dependent upon the former, although it is also evident that a breakdown in any one of the phases is destructive of the total process. Planning for a system calls for knowing a system. It is in this sense that systemic mapping constitutes the first and primary task of the planner. The quality and success of the other phases of the planning process relate directly to the degree of solid undergirding furnished by systemic mapping. Systemic mapping implies a general comprehension of the structure of the social system and an understanding of the functioning of its primary elements. Although it is not implied here that there is in sociology some universal agreement as to what the elements of a social system are, it is maintained that in the accumulative work of sociologists certain analytic units of behavior have been consistently dealt with. It is these units that are conceived of here as being the elements of the social system, and as such are the primary referents for the planner in the estimation of change.[6]

Roles. As indicated earlier the most significant analytical unit of social system is, for most purposes, the role. It is now traditional in sociology to view a social group as a structural-functional system formed by a network of interconnected roles through which interaction processes are maintained. It is the role, not the concrete individual, which is the conceptual unit in the social system. Each role carries with it a particular set of role expectations which any incumbent of the role is expected to fulfill. In our terminology, these role expectations are merely socially constructed typifications of interaction processes which are socially approved ways of confronting one another with respect to the management of typical problems. As such they are frequently institutionalized. Consequently they are differentiated and arranged in domains of relevances which in turn are evaluated and ranked in terms of prevailing standards of belief and value.

Role differentiation is undoubtedly the most fundamental characteristic of organized social systems in contrast to crowds, mobs, or abstract collectivities. Even the simplest preliterate tribal societies have minimal role differentiation in which distinctions are based upon at least age, sex, and leadership factors, both ascribed and achieved. With role differentiation evaluation inevitably occurs, and hence ranking takes place in the hierarchical sense of placing higher or lower valuation upon specific roles. All differentiation does not readily lend itself to hierarchical arrangement, however; it also refers to relations of functional interdependence, as in the division of labor wherein many roles can be conceived of simply as being different. There is, however, a strong tendency even in the occupational

---

[6] It should be noted that we, of course, use the same elements of the social system in the following discussion that we used in the earlier analysis of *Gemeinschaft* and *Gesellschaft*. In the earlier analysis we used the elements merely as vehicles to indicate the contrasts and differences between fundamentally different types of system. The focus was not upon the elements in the sense of offering a generic description of them. In the present analysis such a description is offered in order to specify the nature of the system within which and for which planning takes place. The two discussions are thus complementary rather than repetitive.

sphere for people to evaluate different roles in higher and lower terms. The competition and conflict over the highly valued roles is frequently an outstanding characteristic of complex systems, and a direct reflection of prevailing orientations. Knowledge of the role structure and its incumbents is clearly mandatory for any planner as a prerequisite for the achievement of a realistic strategy for approaching the future.

Beliefs.   Any given proposition about any aspect of the universe which is accepted as true may be called a belief. This condition of being accepted is essentially cognitive, although it may be strongly colored by emotion—in other words an expression of sentiment. In any case, it provides a cognitive view which may serve as the basis for voluntary action. The significance of beliefs is not dependent upon the intrinsic, objective truth of the particular proposition. Of course, beliefs vary in accordance with the norms or standards against which they are tested. There are false beliefs (contrary to demonstrable evidence), true beliefs (in accord with empirical evidence), and beliefs that are methodologically untestable (unverifiable in form). A particular belief may be based on accumulated factual evidence or upon prejudice, intuition, superficial appearances, or faith. Accordingly, there can be empirical beliefs and nonempirical beliefs. The nature of its derivation need not affect the potency of the belief itself. People may act just as energetically and determinedly on the basis of unverified or unverifiable beliefs as upon the basis of empirically sound beliefs. The belief that water will boil at a particular temperature under given conditions has compelling evidence behind it, but as a belief it does not compare in importance for action with such an unverifiable belief as, "the Emperor is divine." The belief on the part of a group that it is a chosen people may rest upon tenuous grounds, but it can unquestionably initiate more action than can a belief in the positive correlation of suicide rates and business cycle phenomena, which rests upon more tangible evidence. In brief, beliefs are formulations of what we think about the universe, its objects, and their relations. A belief system is a kind of cognitive mapping of the situation.

Any given social system is characterized by certain specific beliefs held by the majority of its members. These vary from system to system and are a component part of the outlook of the members. It is self-evident that a knowledge of what people believe is essential to the planner or planning today.

Sentiments.   Closely related to belief, and yet analytically separate in the social system, is the element of sentiment. Whereas beliefs embody thoughts, sentiments embody feelings about the world we live in. Beliefs are primarily *cognitive* and represent what we know about the world no matter how we know it. In contrast, sentiments are primarily expressive and represent what we feel about the world no matter why we feel it. As actors we are not merely rational or intellectual in our outlook, but also emotional. The sight of a brave matador facing the fierce bull in the bull ring brings tears of admiration to the Latin eye, and uncomfortable feelings of nausea to the Anglo, who would regard the Latin in this instance as cold-blooded, without proper sentiment. How barbarous to the Hindu with his deep sentiment against taking any life would be both the Latin in the bull ring and the Anglo with his DDT sprays. The organized expression of emotion may be called sentiment. As the above example illustrates, any particular sentiment is a generalized pattern of emotion, part socially and part physiologically determined, and expressed in action. It appears as a complex biological and social channelization of emotional drive. Sometimes, as in the case of mother love, it includes such a range of factors as fear, joy, sympathy, sorrow, and anger, all related (although with ambivalence) to the pattern of sentiment.

In the discussion of beliefs, the relationship between the belief system of a group and that group's objectives was observed. In the same sense, there is a relationship between the sentiment system of a group and that group's norms. The sentiments are the feelings themselves; the norms determine what the group considers a proper and appropriate way of displaying the feeling. How cold-blooded and without sentiment the Latin male, with his affectionate *embrazo* ready for his dear *amigo,* would regard the guarded handshake of two Anglo males. The friendship feeling itself, the real sentiment, has not been shown to be stronger or weaker in the Anglo or the Latin case. Latin norms provide a means for a warm, demonstrative greeting; Anglo norms prescribe more restraint.

Sentiments and beliefs are often quite intimately related, and not infrequently a belief may be an expression of sentiment. Sentiments cannot be kept active and functional except as they are formulated in beliefs, symbols, and rituals. The proper interpretation on the part of the planner of such manifestations of sentiment is of crucial significance in assessing the possibilities of planning outcomes.

Goals or Objectives. Goals or objectives are those changes which members or some segment of the membership of the social system expect to accomplish through the operation of the system. The goals and objectives can more easily be differentiated from other elements in social systems which specialize in instrumental action. Thus the military commander in a given battle operation draws upon his training and experience in the specialty of logistics to estimate the cost in men, materials, and other facilities of achieving a given specific objective. Logistics requires that the goals and objectives be sharply differentiated from the other elements, particularly the facilities and norms of the social system. This is an example of the case of instrumental or *Gesellschaft*-like activity.

In recent years an increasing number of organizations or social systems have been established to evaluate the organizational efficiency of other social systems. Such organizations exist under various titles, and their members may call themselves evaluation specialists, management engineers, social engineers, or various other designations. These evaluation specialists are usually employed by instrumental social systems, such as factories, business concerns, government bureaus, and the like. In all cases evaluation specialists must determine the goals of the system being evaluated in order to ascertain with what efficiency and to what extent these goals are achieved.

In social systems which characteristically engage in expressive activity, such as voluntary adult choral societies or children's play groups, the action itself tends to become an end or objective, a condition which makes it difficult indeed to differentiate between ends and sentiments and the other elements of the social system. Likewise, in social systems such as religious organizations which characteristically engage in moral or integrative actions, the ends are usually difficult to separate from other elements, especially the beliefs and norms. In fact, in certain rituals the norms of the act become ends. When great emphasis is placed upon protocol or etiquette a somewhat similar phenomenon occurs. The manner in which goals and objectives vary in their content and autonomy from system to system is of great importance to the sociologist, as well as to the planner who has the task of delineating them in an instrumental-type system.

The prevailing goals or objectives of a given system may be broad and diffuse, those of another system may be more functionally specific. The objectives of one system may emphasize change, those of another retention of the status quo. In part because of these variations, particular social systems become distinguishable. For example, a family may strive to provide all its members with a level of living compatible with prevailing standards, and this may be conceived as one of the family's objectives. A bank may direct its activities toward the goal of increasing its investment earnings, a common banking objective. A football team may strive to better its standing in the national ratings as prepared by sports writers and commentators, a not uncommon goal of "big-time" football. A mission may attempt to save souls by converting a number of non-believers each year, a normal missionary goal. In short, the different types of ends that characterize various social systems constitute a fundamental point of reference for the understanding of these systems. This is as true from the action point of view of the planner as it is from the academic point of view of the sociologist.

Frequently the expressed goals or objectives of a system are found by the observer to be far less important to an understanding of the operation of the system and the prediction of its behavior than certain latent functions; the latter may be of great significance in the actual motivation of the members but remain unspecified as goals and objectives by members. The members of a "home demonstration club," for example, may believe that the real goal of the organization is to improve their home-making skills. Careful analysis, however, may reveal that the more important and latent function of the club is the sociability it provides the members and their heightened self-esteem resulting from friendly conversational exchange. Also, in the analysis of social action the manifest goals must be compared with the unanticipated but actual results. Only through relating the expressed goals, latent functions, and actual results to the beliefs and sentiments of social systems can action be understood or predicted. The implications for the planner are manifold.

Norms. The rules or guiding standards which prescribe what is socially acceptable or unacceptable are the norms of a system. Norms govern the selection and application of means in the attainment of ends or goals. Norms are rules of procedure or, in everyday terminology, the "rules of the game." As such, they play a major part in establishing expectancy patterns for action in any given system. More inclusive than written rules, regulations, or laws, norms refer to all criteria for judging the character or conduct of individual action or any societal form or function. They constitute the standards determining what is right and wrong or good and bad in given situations with respect to relationships with others. A norm typically appears as a minimum standard or model to which a given social system expects its members to conform their behavior, costume, food, housing, and other aspects of life, depending upon the situation to which the norm is applicable. Some norms are general in nature and may not be violated by anyone; others apply only to particular actors and status-roles within the system. Particular norms may be especially crucial for special social systems. For instance, the norm of efficiency may be primary in the productive system; the norms of validity, reliability, and objectivity may be paramount in a scientific system; and the norms of fair play and good sportsmanship may be dominant in an athletic activity.

Any social system may be described with respect to one of its major dimensions as being "a normative order." The notion of system implies order; hence a major criterion, along with interaction, for delineating a system is simply the extent of consensus with respect to appropriate ways of doing things. Norms have a pervasive influence throughout the system by functioning as guides in the enactment of roles, and in determining the manner in which goals may be realized, power utilized, facilities allocated, sanctions applied, beliefs held, sentiments expressed, and status allocated, to name just a few of the normative functions. In brief, norms play a key role in the stable functioning of a social system. A simple but basic imperative for the planner is not to play the game unless he knows the rules of the game—the norms.

Power.   Power, in normal usage, refers to the ability or authority to control others. Power has many components, typically classified under the main rubrics of *authority* and *influence*. Authority may be defined as the right, as explicitly specified within the system, to control the action of others. Established authority always resides in a role, not in an individual as such. The individual derives his authority from his incumbency of the role, hence the meaning of "authority of office." For instance, the authority of the father, priest, president, coach, policeman, diplomat, or bank examiner resides in his office, and such authority cannot be taken with him when the office is abandoned. An unfrocked priest cannot deliver the sacraments, a deposed coach cannot direct game strategy, nor can an ex-diplomat implement foreign policy. Authority, therefore, always implies some degree of institutionalization—the standardization of expectancies with regard to the rights of an incumbent of a role.

Influence may be regarded as control over others which is personal-relational in nature. The capacity to control resides in the individual actor and his facilities rather than in a role, although the role in this case can be a facility. Influence may be based upon such factors as skill in manipulating people, social capital resting upon past favors, superior knowledge of the social system, wealth or reputation, or other outstanding qualities. A popular leader may wield enormous influence despite a lack of office; a mother in a patriarchal family where authority nominally resides with the father may actually control the family by virtue of a strong personality; a politician may hold the office but there may be a power behind the throne, someone controlling him and hence actually controlling the office. Thus influence is manifested in many ways and constitutes one of the less accessible aspects of a social system.

Every social system is in one respect a system of power relations with hierarchical superordination and subordination, and regulated exchanges between role incumbents. In planning for the future in a social system, the planner must either be at the top of this power hierarchy or have access to it. The latter is the case in complex systems where planning tends to become a specialized or staff function. In any event it is clear that the decision-making and implementation phases of planning are dependent in a determinate sense upon commitment of the power structure.

Sanctions. The term *sanction* refers to *rewards* and *penalties* meted out by a social system to its members in order to induce conformity to its norms and motivation toward its goals. Hence sanctions can be either positive or negative and are manifest in the potential satisfaction-giving or -depriving mechanisms at the disposal of the system. Positive sanctions are the *rewards* available to the members of the system. Rewards, of course, vary widely in their character, ranging from the purely symbolic to the material. By social definition they consist in what is worth having or striving for within the system. Negative sanctions are the *penalties* of the deprivation of such items as are socially defined as rewards at the disposal of the social system.

It would seem that the primary function of sanctions in a social system is that of *motivation*. Sanctions constitute the enforcement potential behind the norms of the system. Through reward the system encourages its members to strive for the highly valued returns of the system, and through penalties it discourages the violation of the norms. Sanctions, therefore, are important both from the standpoint of *instigation* of action and *constraint* of action within the system.

In planning for change it is imperative that this motivational structure be taken into consideration. There can be no major incongruity between the goals established in planning and the existent sanction system. In effect, the motivational pattern embedded in the sanction system has to be mobilized in support of the planning goals if there is to be any likelihood of their realization. Any marked inconsistency between planning goals and this motivational structure would indicate that these goals are utopian rather than realistic with respect to the system.

Facilities. Facilities may be defined as the means used within the system to attain *ends* in accordance with the norms of the system. Always implied in the attainment of an objective is the necessary control of *means*. As an ideal or model, facilities are nothing more nor less than means to some further goal and hence completely instrumental in character. In contrast, the reward as an ideal or model is an end in itself, an object of gratification in its own right, not linked to the attainment of a further goal, and clearly related to the expressive or emotional complex of behavior. Thus a car used as a taxicab in order to make money to buy other goods and services is a means, hence a facility; a car used for its pleasure-giving qualities and valued as a thing in itself has the character of reward. Realistically, the ideal or model facility and/or reward rarely exists. The taxicab might conceivably provide pleasure and pride to its owner, and render many nonfacilitative services as well as the facilitative function of earning money. Similarly, it is difficult to visualize the car which serves only as pleasure giving, without sometimes being simply a means by which the children could arrive at school, the father at his office, the guest at the train, and the mother at the hairdresser's.

Likewise, persons in roles generally nonfacilitative in character can upon occasion assume a role which becomes a temporary facility. A person in the role of friend, and valued for the most part purely as a friend, can shift into the role of mediator in the securing of a new job. Thus the person, playing a different role, temporarily becomes a facility, a means by which a new job is secured.

Put another way, facilities are *possessions* [7] which are significant as means to further goals. A possession may be defined as an entity which is transferable from one actor to another, or one system to another, through the process of exchange. This entity, the possession, is always a right or bundle of rights. It is never a physical object as such, but always consists in rights of *use, control,* or *disposal* of social or physical objects. For instance, one's land as a facility is a possession of rights of use, control, and disposal. It is not a facility for one's neighbor because he does not have such rights with respect to it. When one possesses a contract with a person it really signifies that one has certain rights to him as a facility. Hence, possessions can be of either relations (people) or objects (things), and in either case they refer to rights. When these possessions are used as means in the attainment of ends, they are facilities.

[7] Talcott Parsons, *The Social System* (Glencoe: The Free Press, 1951), p. 119.

From the standpoint of the planner, the problem is again one of mobilization. Insofar as planning is goal-directed, it is clearly dependent on control of the appropriate facilities if the goals are to be realized. In effect, facilities are the resources, human and otherwise, of the system; if planning is to have any meaning or consequence, it must encompass and ultimately articulate those resources. The extent to which facilities are at the disposal, accessible to, or susceptible to the control of the planner will in large part determine the operational achievement of the planning process.

This treatment of the social system may seem overly long from the standpoint of the planner and much too skimpy and generalized from the standpoint of the sociologist. It has been necessary, however, to delineate the main structural elements of social systems in order to emphasize four points. First, planning as a type of social activity takes place in and for social systems; hence the first task of the planner or planning organization is to "know the system" as it now exists. This means that the elements of the system constitute the planner's main reference points with regard to understanding the system as a persistent and continuing form of organization. Second, any projection of goals for a system and selection of means for the attainment of those goals must be in congruence with the structural and action possibilities in the present system. Third, it is precisely at this level that much planning goes astray, whether it is planning for urban renewal, rural electrification, population relocation, land redistribution, plant automation, economic development, or for any one of the many other areas of social enterprise for which we now customarily and explicitly plan. This is to say that insofar as planning is planning for people, an understanding of the contexts within which these people live and act is crucially related to realistic potential and achievement possibility of planning. Fourth, it is at this level that sociology, and the other social sciences in general, have the most to offer the planner. As disciplines concerned with the study of various phases of the social context, they have accumulated a not inconsiderable amount of theoretical and empirical knowledge about the systems or types of systems with which planners are concerned. With no assessment of guilt indulged in, it is necessary to say that by and large much of this information is *not* integrated into current planning processes. Until it is, much of the activity classifiable under the rubric of "planning for the future" will remain partially unrealistic and unduly abstract and arbitrary.

Despite the overriding importance of systemic mapping in the planning process, however, it must be pointed out that it merely constitutes the foundation. There are other phases of the process which have to be carried out before the rewards of planning can be realized.

Evaluation

Although we are referring to evaluation as a formal phase of an instrumental process, it is important to point out that evaluation as a type of activity is woven into the very fabric of social behavior. Evaluations are being made at all times and places as a normal part of symbolic interaction. Thus the structural elements of social systems are in part a product of and in part productive of evaluations. In the generic sense, evaluation is the process through which varying positive and negative priorities or values are assigned to the perceived object. Such diverse phenomena as goals, concepts, customs, persons, collectivities, or events can be and are symbolized aş objects in the normal conduct of human activity. Positive and negative values imputed to these objects, and choices of action related to these evaluations, are articulated routinely in the behavior sustaining a social system.

Evaluation in this broad sense enters into the minutiae of living. Each time an object is evaluated it may be appraised by separate participating members of the social system, so that at one level we have countless and continuing individual evaluations. Through communication, these individual evaluations become caught up in the social interaction process which sustains the social system. Social interaction is largely based upon communication, which in turn is a process by which information, decisions, and directions pass through a social system, and the ways in which knowledge, opinions, and attitudes are formed or modified.[8] Out of this interaction process within the system the goals are reiterated, the norms reviewed, the

---

[8] C. P. Loomis and J. A. Beegle, *Rural Social Systems* (New York: Prentice-Hall, 1950), p. 32.

roles articulated, the statuses assigned, the facilities allocated, and so on. The result is a continuous interactive consensus, a *systemic* rather than an individual evaluation.

Interactive or social consensus is not often synonymous with unanimity, although on the very abstract level systemic evaluations can tend to be broadly universal. For example, the concepts of freedom, health, monogamous marriage, and equal opportunity would probably meet with little dissent as values in most of the social systems in the United States. Conversely, poverty, cowardice, slavery, and weakness would probably be universally disapproved of in these same social systems.

Considerably less consensus is likely to prevail when the abstraction is made more concrete and an attempt is directed toward making it operational. Freedom, yes, but freedom for and from what? Freedom to preserve the status quo or to change the status quo? Freedom to protect property by zoning laws, or freedom for a man to build what he wants wherever he wants it located? When a generally accepted abstraction such as freedom is reduced to the concrete, subsystems within social systems are likely to form, each with its version of what constitutes freedom and how it should be protected. The evaluative process, then, can be seen as a priority and as a value-establishing and -maintaining activity. It enables the actors within a system to establish a common ground upon which the sorting out of the diverse action proposals can take place, and a working consensus can be established which gives order and purpose to the closely related and concrete activity of decision-making.

Evaluation in this broadest, or everyday sense is oriented chiefly to the past and present, less to the future. Assessment of "the American Way," for instance, often involves a comparison of the present with the ideas of the founding fathers. The difficulty of evaluating the events or objects of the future is demonstrated by the uncertainties surrounding the values attached to atomic power, space exploration, automation, formation of new nations, and aid to underdeveloped economies. Paradoxically, however, it is with respect to the future that evaluation takes on its more specialized functions and becomes a formal process in its own right. It is in *Gesellschaft*-like or instrumental systems that one finds evaluation institutionalized to some degree as a special activity. This means-ends linkage characteristic of the instrumental system requires a continuing evaluation of both means and ends and their proper relationship. For the planner this implies evaluation at two levels: evaluation of competing goals in order to determine those most appropriate for the system, and evaluation of alternative means (facilities) so as to select those most appropriate for the realization of those goals.

With respect to the evaluation phase of planning, the contribution of sociology and the other social sciences differs in type from that which they make in systemic mapping. In the latter case it is largely substantive and as frame of reference; with respect to the former it is largely methodological. Most social scientists are committed to the notion of adding to, extending, and furthering knowledge, but a far fewer number are committed to making evaluations. The so-called evaluation studies do not compare in rigor with those in the main body of the discipline. Nevertheless, action must proceed, organizations must work toward their goals, and programs must be mounted in the attack upon pressing problems. All of this means that instrumental systems have to carry on and do the best they can with the facilities at hand. The difference between merely "muddling through" and establishing a solid and reliable basis for decision-making lies in the quality of the evaluation. The methodologies of the social sciences, with or without the personnel, are partially transferable to the planning situation. The adaptation of such methodology will in the long run give the planner a higher degree of confidence in his evaluation and hence contribute positively to the decision-making process.

Decision-Making

It should again be noted that the four phases of the process of planning for change which have been delineated here are based upon an underlying continuum. This continuum might be variously described as one of knowledge to action, knowing to doing, or objective to normative. With the decision-making phase we move further from the knowledge or objective end of the continuum and closer to the action or normative polar point.

Decision-making may be defined as a process whereby alternate courses of action available are reduced so that action of some sort may proceed within the system. Whereas the evaluative process is largely oriented to the past and the present, decision-making is primarily oriented to the future. A decision based upon past mistakes and successes may still have to be modified to adjust to changed conditions. In addition, there is the factor of unpredictability in the future, the gamble that one set of circumstances and not another will prevail. Under these circumstances the commitment of the decision-makers is necessarily a limited and tentative one. The planning process never stops within an on-going system; therefore the input from systemic mapping and evaluation calls for a flexibility in the decision-making machinery which will enable it to modify, adjust, or even reverse earlier decisions.

This flexibility does not imply indecisiveness, vacillation, or naked expediency; it is merely indicative of a fundamental limitation of the formal planning process. The brute fact is that social systems do not exist in a vacuum; on the contrary, they coexist in a state of interdependency and interpenetration within a society which is a social system in its own right. Moreover, no society exists in pure separation from the rest of the world, although certain tribal societies come fairly close to being closed and isolated systems. For the mass of the world's societies, however, there exists the whole fabric of international relations, not merely in the political sense but also in a diffuse pattern of social transactions. Since planning in any manageable sense is always planning for *a* system and not for all systems simultaneously, obviously severe limitations are placed upon the ability of any particular social system to control its own destiny, through planning or any other social device. In a different context, Riemer has made a comment that is particularly appropriate here:

> Under the circumstances, we may do well to avoid the futile attempt of committing ourselves, once and for all, to a series of planning objectives of general validity. It seems called for, rather, to make the proclamation of ends and their specification in terms of tangible objectives and the choice of adequate social and technological instrumentalities part of the planning process itself.[9]

[9] Svend Riemer, "Social Planning and Social Organization," *American Journal of Sociology*, 52 (March, 1947), p. 511.

This bring us back to the point made earlier—that evaluation is largely concerned with the past and present and decision-making with the future. It may also be said that evaluation is primarily concerned with ends and decision-making with means. This is an apparent rather than real paradox. In thorough systemic mapping and evaluation the natural, most appropriate, feasible, or realistic goals for the system are turned up as aspects of the existent social structure. The major goals of the system are, in effect, a "given" for the decision-maker; it is his task to orient himself to these goals.

It is at the level of secondary or subsidiary goals and the choice from among alternate courses of action that the role of the decision-maker becomes vital. In the evaluation process it is typical that alternative courses of action are turned up, and these require that a choice be made from among them. Sometimes these choices must be made on fairly arbitrary grounds, or on the basis of very subtle shadings of difference. These decisions can also call for an acute sense of timing and skilled administration. It is no accident that the instrumental system, the type that has made the planning process explicit, has also institutionalized the decision-making or executive role in functionally diffuse or extensible terms. It is not the intent here to downgrade or disparage the importance of the decision-making role. The intent is to indicate that the truly big decisions are implicit in the social structure and can be extrapolated into structural continuity by means of systemic mapping and evaluation. The little, or implementive, decisions lie in the sphere of decision-making proper. This does not mean that they are unimportant. On the contrary, they represent vital vehicles of structural continuity and necessary instruments for the system in its continuous pursuit of its own ends.

Implementation

The distinction made here between decision-making and implementation may seem artificial and unnecessary. It is neither. The distinction must be made for two very simple but good reasons. In the first place, anyone can make a decision, but for a decision to have a likelihood of implementation it must be made by the right people within the system. Secondly, a mere random decision will not work; it must be a decision appropriate to the state of affairs within the system if it is to have any possibility of implementation. These matters may seem rather mundane and self-evident, but they both have direct bearing on planning as normally conducted in contemporary society.

With regard to the matter of the right people making decisions, we are inevitably led to certain considerations concerning power. In some social systems, such as armies or large factories, a comparatively few roles are vested with a great amount of power. The commanding officer of an army, or the president of a large manufacturing corporation, each with his group of advisors, has considerably more directly usable power than the incumbent of a leadership role in a more power-diffuse system. The roles which control and can commit the power in the power-concentrated systems also control most of the important, strategic level decision-making for that system. As the incumbent of the role has the authority for the decision, so he also has the responsibility for its soundness. The general or corporation executive who is discovered guilty of a few glaring errors in decision-making (e.g., loss of battles or profits) finds that he is expendable; a new general or new executive ready to try alternate methods of action is on hand to step into his shoes.

In a less obvious, but no less real way, power is coupled with decision-making in social systems where power is distributed on a diffuse basis among its members. When there is free decision-making among members of a social system, there tend to be a number of proposals and counter-proposals made before a decision is reached. A characteristic of decision-making in such power-diffuse groups is that of compromise. Among proponents of various views of more or less equal power, one can scarcely hope to gain acceptance of his proposal at the expense of the rejection of all others. The final decision is likely to be made up of bits and snatches from all those presented. Neither the decision nor its resultant consequences can be directly traced to one or a few persons, and the whole system is likely to share the blame or the credit for the results of the decision. Even in a power-diffuse social system, however, power is never distributed absolutely equally. The emergence of leadership and the development of alliances prevent the maintenance of a community of equals. A system can have a plurality of leaders, each wielding power of his own, who can marshal adherents for his proposal by threats, promises, or other persuasions. The struggle for the right to make the decision can be masked under many symbols or it can be an overt and bitter power struggle. Even under such circumstances the struggle may end in uneasy compromise, or in a complete standoff in which all the machinery of decision-making has been used but no decision results and matters stand as before.

The power-concentrated and power-diffuse systems briefly described above are easily recognizable as polar types. Most actual systems will fall somewhere in between on the continuum represented by the types. Planning as an established process can be carried on in either type of system. The planning operation, therefore, has to be articulated in very different ways in systems with differing power structures. In any case, however, if planning is to have any probability of implementation it must stand in one of two relationships to the power structure, of whatever form in the system. The planner (or planning body) must either be the *incumbent* (or incumbents) of the dominant power role (or roles) or must have *access* to that role (or roles).

Expressed simply, operation and planning cannot be separated if the latter is to have any long-run consequences for the former. In a small-scale system the administrative and planning functions can be vested in one role or a small number of roles. In such a system, operation and planning are easily integrated. In a large-scale system, however, operation and planning can frequently be cruelly separated in a complex role system. It is ironic that the development of large-scale organization has, on the one hand, facilitated the institutionalization of planning and, on the other, frequently segregated it from the power structure. This is not a small problem in view of the fact that large-scale organization is a dominant type in modern society, e.g., the industrial bureaucracy.

The point here is that even if it is necessary within a complex system to maintain planning as a functionally specific activity carried on by a suborganization, it is also necessary that the planners have access to the power structure. If, because of size and complexity, administrators and planners cannot be the same people, the former must be able to and willing to assimilate the work of the latter if there is to be any planning input into the system. The planner has to have more than the ear of the administrator; he must also have his comprehension and empathy if there is to be an implementation to planning.

The second point raised earlier, concerning decisions appropriate for the system, really calls for no special elaboration. The context of this entire chapter is oriented to that point. In various local, national, and international programs involving planning as a specific activity, we have accumulated a recent history of many tragic experiences. Oftentimes the failure cannot be traced to any lack of power to make decisions, or any failure to make those decisions, but to the brute fact that the decisions were incapable of implementation because they were inappropriate for the system. In brief, they were wrong for the system in structural continuity. Programs involving the instigation of economic, technological, educational, political, and civil change have foundered in the morass of social resistance and inertia. The decisions setting the stage for such failures were all too often made in the abstract or from too limited or specialized a perspective. The implication is clear with regard to the vital role of systemic mapping and evaluation.

The relationship of sociology and the other social sciences to the decision-making and implementation phases of planning is quite indirect and often negligible. The fundamental commitment of the scholar is to "knowing" and that of the planner to "doing." The basic contribution of the social sciences to planning for change lies in the area of contribution of knowledge. The contribution of the planner is in the skilled and selective use of that knowledge in mapping for the future. Clearly these activities cannot be completely segregated. Individual social scientists can pass over the line and reach the point where they think they know what ought to be; they then bring their disciplinary knowledge to bear upon the problem of changing what is to what they believe ought to be.[10] They may curtail their scholarly activities, or even cease to function as scholars, but their backgrounds have provided them with equipment useful in the planning process. It is no accident that one finds social scientists (or ex-social scientists, if preferred) involved in making and implementing policy in many

[10] Sol Tax, "Anthropology and Administration," in E. A. Hoebel *et al.* (eds.), *Readings in Anthropology* (New York: McGraw-Hill, 1955), p. 393.

sectors of national life and on the international scene. It would be difficult to assert that this transfer of role constitutes a loss to the society, since both roles are of functional importance.

The Pragmatic View

Social systems have no more important problem than that of change. Social systems develop by adjusting themselves to the problems before them. How can order and structure be preserved in a system and yet have the necessary changes take place? To bring about change is seemingly to destroy the existent order, and yet systems must change, for change is implicit in the action that constitutes society. How can society find a method for changing its own institutions? The answer here is in the pragmatic tradition.[11] The view is taken that planning is a natural type of behavior and is manifest in even the most elementary forms of persistent social life. As a type of behavior of considerable importance in certain types of systems, it in turn has its own distinguishable subtypes which have been delineated here as systemic mapping, evaluation, decision-making, and implementation. In the *Gesellschaft*-like or instrumental system, planning is elevated to the status of a method. When incorporated as a method of society and its component social systems, it follows that we should look upon it as the method for securing the changes most appropriate to both the existent and anticipated problems. As a method, however, it can have no thrust or effectiveness independent of the substance provided by the various fields of knowledge, particularly the social sciences. In this respect the special contribution of sociology lies in the area of the analysis of social structure and continuity.

[11] The general attitude expressed toward planning in this book in one sense represents a specialized adaptation of the work of G. H. Mead. See especially *Mind, Self and Society* (Chicago: University of Chicago Press, 1934); *Movements of Thought in the Nineteenth Century* (Chicago: University of Chicago Press, 1936); and *The Philosophy of the Present* (Chicago: Open Court, 1932).

———8

Toward a Codification of Typological Procedure

The realm of science, including social science, is composed of that which is common to various observers—the world of common experience as it is symbolically formulated. The experienced world consists of a realm of natural events that are no more the property of the observer than they are of the things observed. There is a necessary relationship between observer and observed; therefore the fundamental factor is the direct and common accessibility of both observer and observed. The completeness of the accessibility will vary, both with reference to object and observer, but the fact that it must be common is essential to the method of science and goes unquestioned.

The pragmatically inclined have been impressed by the fact that the scientist has no generalized problem of knowledge despite the fact that it is his particular business to know.[1] Knowing is not a matter of proceeding from the uncertain effects in the individual to the world beyond which is supposed to cause those effects— scientific research always posits an unquestioned world of existence within which its problems appear and are tested. Any part of this world may become problematic and therefore an object of the knowing process. For the researcher, to know is not to have existences and meanings given; it is the initiation of an inquiry into some part of the common world that has become problematic, an inquiry that

[1] G. H. Mead, *The Philosophy of the Act* (Chicago: University of Chicago Press, 1938), pp. x-xi.

necessarily proceeds through the formulation of hypotheses and their testing in the unquestioned world that surrounds the problem area. For the purposes at hand, the instruments, the controls, the laboratories, the fellow scholars (the verifiers) are parts of the un-problematic world that is "there" as a world of objects in which theories can be tested. Knowledge in a scientific sense is not contemplation, but discovery through hypotheses tested in action by "things" which are for the moment unquestionably real, although in other situations they can be a part of the problematic area.

An external world is objectively "there," independent of our experiencing of it. Expressed differently, research work is work of discovering, and we can only discover what is in existence.[2] Although external objects exist independently of the experiencing individual, they possess certain characteristics by virtue of their relations to his experiencing of them that they would not otherwise possess.[3] These characteristics are their *meanings* for us. As suggested here, the independence of data is frequently interpreted as a metaphysical affirmation of a real world independent of observation and speculation. There is no such necessary implication in scientific methodology. A metaphysical affirmation is of a reality that is final, whereas in the scientist's procedures no such finality is contemplated. On the contrary, his procedures contemplate continued modification and reconstruction in the light of facts and events emerging in ceaseless novelty. Data are isolated elements in a world of things, and their isolation is overcome by the scientist's hypothesis. He cannot stop with the data. They do not speak for themselves, but are a phase of the investigation involved in his cognitive advance. The problem for the scientist is not simply a matter of "seeing" what is "out there." Seeing in any meaningful sense depends upon our looking, and looking will inevitably reflect a whole system of interests, theories, and purposes that will lead us to seek one character rather than another in the object or matter under consideration. For the researcher, data are always taken rather than given. Observation is not merely a matter of opening one's eyes or ears, or turning on one's

---

[2] G. H. Mead, *The Philosophy of the Present* (Chicago: Open Court, 1932), p. 7.

[3] G. H. Mead, *Mind, Self and Society* (Chicago: University of Chicago Press, 1934), p. 131.

instruments; rather it is always directed in terms of some sort of problem and expresses some sort of an interest.[4] However tentative, and however uncertain he may be of its reliability and validity, the scientist persistently will effect a relationship between data, bringing them into some sort of an ordered whole. This gives them at least a provisional reality, a meaning, not attached to them as mere data.

In creating this ordered whole, even provisionally, the scientist is postulating a uniformity of nature. On a pragmatic basis we can continue to explain the world in terms of uniformities, and to do so with confidence because the assumption has always worked.[5] As an aspect of explanation the results looked for by science are uniformities, and it states them in terms of probabilities. As an aspect of this pragmatic view and probabilistic approach, we have the process of typification and the production of typologies.

All typification consists in the pragmatic reduction and equalization of attributes relevant to the particular purpose at hand for which the type has been formed, and involves disregarding those individual differences of the typified objects that are not relevant to such purpose. There is no such thing as a type independent of the purposes for which it was constructed. This purpose resides in the theoretical or practical problem which, as a result of our selective interest, has emerged as questionable from the unquestioned world in the background. Typologies are subordinate to the aims of research, namely the establishment of uniformities of explanatory value. Typologies are *instrumental* in the research process; they are fictional in the sense that they have been constructed. The reference of the type to the problem for whose solution it has been constructed, its *problem relevance*, constitutes the meaning of the typification. Thus typologies should be constructed so that they aid in the analysis of specific bodies of data. The *extension* of the area of applicability of the type simultaneously involves the extension of problem relevance and the analysis of relevant data. Typologies must be understood as representative of a pragmatic research methodology and thus subject to evaluation in terms of the accuracy of predictions which result from their utilization. An empirical error criterion is

[4] G. H. Mead, *Movements of Thought in the Nineteenth Century* (Chicago: University of Chicago Press, 1936), pp. 281-282.

[5] *Ibid.*, pp. 6-7.

the fundamental criterion in typological procedure, as it is in research methodology generally. It is clear that some particular typology can be used in the study of several different social systems or processes. This requires, however, that the goodness of fit of the typology to each set of data must be evaluated. By the very nature of their construction, typologies cannot have a perfect fit to any set of data. The better the fit, however, the greater the probability that the typology will be useful in the subsequent analysis.[6]

The construction of types is an aspect of scientific methodology generally and is not confined to any particular science; it is a procedure applicable to the data of any science, although obviously more characteristic of some than of others. This device has played an undeniable role in the growth of social science knowledge despite the fact that it retains many of its methodological ambiguities. The literature abounds in types, and yet whatever standardization exists in their construction is largely implicit. Despite the almost universal use of types within the social sciences, the problem of standardizing the procedures for their construction remains largely untouched.

Controversy has swirled around the concept of type since the time of Weber, and we continue to have excellent, although invariably ambiguous, discussions of typology in the literature.[7] These discussions continue to focus primarily on the ontology of types

---

[6] The emphasis which Weber placed upon the "fictionality" (comparable in meaning to "abstract") of typologies can be interpreted as evidence of a pragmatic orientation and should not be permitted to obscure the fact that the ultimate criterion in his methodology is an empirical error criterion. See Max Weber, *The Methodology of the Social Sciences,* edited by E. A. Shils and H. A. Finch (Glencoe: The Free Press, 1949), p. 93 *passim.*

[7] Among the more provocative recent discussions are Paul F. Lazarsfeld, "Philosophy of Science and Empirical Social Research," in Ernest Nagel, Patrick Suppes and Alfred Tarski (eds.), *Logic, Methodology and Philosophy of Science* (Stanford: Stanford University Press, 1962), pp. 463-473; Don Martindale, "Sociological Theory and the Ideal Type," in Llewellyn Gross (ed.), *Symposium on Sociological Theory* (Evanston: Row, Peterson, 1959), pp. 57-91; C. G. Hempel, "Typological Methods in the Natural and Social Sciences," *Proceedings,* American Philosophical Association: Eastern Division, 1 (1952), pp. 65-86; and J. W. N. Watkins, "Ideal Types and Historical Explanation," *The British Journal for the Philosophy of Science,* 3 (May, 1952), pp. 22-43.

rather than the development of their pragmatic utility as tools.[8] Whatever else a constructed type may be, it is clear that it is a conceptual tool. Despite its varied use over the years, it is possible to discern an underlying consensus which has enabled us to define the constructed type as a *purposive, planned selection, abstraction, combination and (sometimes) accentuation of a set of criteria with empirical referents that serves as a basis for comparision of empirical cases.* The elements and relations actually found in historical and contemporary social life supply the materials out of which the conceptual tool is constituted. These are identified, selected, articulated, and simplified into the constructed type on the basis of some idea of the social scientist's as to the nature of social reality and on the basis of the purposes of his inquiry. The question remains as to *how* this is done. An exploratory approach to this problem will be made here by means of a demonstrational analysis. This analysis consists of an explication of a procedural sequence in type construction. It is not implied that this particular sequence encompasses the range of typological procedures. The implication is that other procedures and sequences will have to be similarly explicated if the general process of type construction and utilization is to be properly delineated and recognized.

Unfortunately, it is not possible to turn to the work of those who have used typologies in the past to gain a clear idea of the steps involved. There is no standardized procedure used by all typologists. However, given the work of the past and an extension of this work in the light of relatively simple sociological methods, it is possible to develop a series of typological operations or procedural steps that may help to make explicit both the utility and the limitations of constructive typology in sociology and in the social sciences generally. In order to make the set of operations explicit, a single illustrative case will be used throughout.

[8] Recent exceptions would include A. H. Barton, "The Concept of Property Space," in P. F. Lazarsfeld and Morris Rosenberg (eds.), *The Language of Social Research* (Glencoe: The Free Press, 1955), pp. 40-53; A. D. Grimshaw, "Specification of Boundaries of Constructed Types Through Use of the Pattern Variable," *The Sociological Quarterly*, 3 (July, 1962), pp. 179-194; and Milton Bloombaum, "A Contribution to the Theory of Typology Construction," *The Sociological Quarterly*, 5 (Spring, 1964), pp. 157-162.

Delineation of the Problem Situation

The typologist, as all social scientists, works with some substantive area of inquiry. He faces an empirical as well as a theoretical problem. For the purpose of developing an illustration, let us pose the very broad sociological problem of assessing the degree of war guilt of various segments of the German society during World War II. Let us further pose the more limited problem of the typologist as the following: "What was the role of the German intellectual in the conduct of the aggressive acts of World War II?" This is an empirical question, but in an effort to answer it the typologist will pose, and be largely concerned with, more abstract and more theoretically relevant problems. First, however, he will concern himself with other steps.

Familiarization with the Relevant Available Data

In our example, the typologist would immerse himself in the particularities of the German situation. The facts and interpretations provided by the historian give a descriptive account of this situation. Some knowledge of German traditions, recent German events, and modern German behavior patterns is essential before proceeding further.

Since the literature implied by the breadth of the problem (its scope of relevance) is vast, it would, of course, be necessary to seek salient leads. For example, some of the work done in studying the German youth movement would be relevant. With a small number of basic types Becker carried out a penetrating study of the movement.[9] The basic concepts were sacred–secular, cult-sect–denomination-ecclesia, and charisma.

Becker hypothesized that the German youth movement came

[9] Howard Becker, *German Youth, Bond or Free* (New York: Grove Press, 1946).

into being because the ends and prospective life situations of its adherents had been defined by adults in patterns that were in sharp and observable contrast with the things adults actually did. There was a readily distinguishable difference between what parents said should be done and their actual deeds. Parents were seen to practice expediency under the guise of sanction and tradition. They visibly utilized affective outlets that they verbally condemned. Youthful idealism, fed on idealized patterns of the past, was rudely shaken by the harsh reality of adult deviousness. This demanded a redefinition of life by confused youth.

This dissent and rejection of adult values and standards gave rise to like-mindedness and resulted in the emergence of youth conventicles which later fused into sects. It became possible for rebels to join forces against a despised way of life. There was an emotional and collective youth reaction against the insincerities of rapid secularization. The emergence of hundreds of groups manifesting certain basic similarities of conduct was typed as the German youth movement.

Becker then delved into the important relationship between the youth movement, youth tutelage, Hitler youth, and ultimately the Nazi movement itself. Becker was able to show very clearly how the youth movement was perverted by the Nazis. The loose framework of fellowship (conventicles and sects) was eventually converted into a highly organized ecclesia. This was in direct contrast to the avowed aims of the early leaders and participants. Youth movement became youth tutelage, and a huge para-military organization emerged that was in sharp contrast to the early romanticism and anarchism. The external manifestations of the youth movement such as the dress, the roaming, the nest, the camp, the leadership principle, and the songs were borrowed by the Nazis and utilized as means to the accomplishment of specific ends. These were the Nazi ends of converting and utilizing youth in their system of control and expansion.

The phenomenon of perversion of a movement, the invidious use of tutelage for doctrinaire purposes, the buttressing of one movement by depicting it as the ideal realization of a powerful folk movement, the erection of a devised sacred society, are all of significance in understanding the Nazi movement and the continued strength and appeal of its ideology. Contrasting interpretations of this same phenomenon and analyses of other salient features of German society should be absorbed before attempting an approach to the specific problem.

Derivation of Hypotheses About Relationships and Sequences

On the basis of this knowledge of twentieth century German characteristics and the Hitlerian movement, the typologist might be led tentatively to hypothesize a very limited involvement of the German intellectual in the Hitlerian regime and its aggressive acts. In order to arrive at this tentative hypothesis, it will be necessary for him to turn to a more abstract level of analysis while at the same time keeping in mind the specifics of the historical situation with which he is dealing. When he turns to the sociological conceptual framework for the analysis of social systems and the role played by particular segments of populations in social systems, he develops a more abstract statement of his original problem. In so doing, he is able to generate a specific hypothesis relevant to his original empirical problem and at the same time make a more general statement, only one example of which is represented by his empirical problem.

In the particular example we are using, for instance, he may define the intellectual as the professional man of knowledge, with further specification of the kinds of individuals included in the class.[10] He will also classify the Hitlerian social system according

[10] For an example of the type of materials of relevance here, see Florian Znaniecki, *The Social Role of the Man of Knowledge* (New York: Columbia University Press, 1940). Znaniecki's study of the types of men of knowledge asks the broad question: What social function does the man of knowledge perform in all cultures and at all times? Znaniecki arrived at four types of men of knowledge who function under certain typical cultural conditions. Technologists, sages, schoolmen, and explorer-creators—each survive and serve their times with a specific type of knowledge. The Znaniecki formulation of course has no direct applicability to the problem in question here, but would constitute a part of the essential background. See also Logan Wilson, *The Academic Man* (New York: Oxford University Press, 1942).

to some scheme such as the following: charismatic, affectual, traditionally oriented, prescribed-sacred, and antirationalistic.[11] At this higher level of abstraction, he would hypothesize that in such a social system there would be relatively little emphasis on the general role of knowledge, and consequently the intellectual, as the professional man of knowledge, would probably be relegated to a minor and passive role in the social system.[12] The hypothesis at the general level would thus be: In a charismatic, affectual, traditionally oriented, prescribed-sacred, and antirationalistic social system intellectuals will play a relatively minor and passive role in the central activities of the social system. At the more specific empirical level in which the typologist is originally interested, he would state his hypothesis as follows: The intellectual was an impotent factor in the Hitlerian order.

Delineation of Empirical Uniformities and Pragmatic Reduction to Type

The class of intellectuals having been roughly blocked out as consisting of professional men of knowledge, the typologist then attempts to define the attributes of this class. These attributes are

---

[11] A summary statement such as the following one by Mühlmann can be very revealing: "We Germans have a barely concealed inclination for a romantic espousal of the cause of *Gemeinschaft* (culture, feeling) against *Gesellschaft* (civilization, intellect)." W. E. Mühlmann, "Sociology in Germany: Shift in Alinement," in Howard Becker and Alvin Boskoff (eds.), *Modern Sociological Theory* (New York: Dryden Press, 1957), p. 662.

[12] It would be of some importance here to check materials in the pre-Hitler period. In this regard Paul Honigsheim, as early as 1926, discerning a crisis in German higher education had related it to the diminution of *Gemeinschaft* and its replacement by an undesirable *Gesellschaft*. He developed a typology of individuals involved in the educational process. The types of professors—savant, aristocratic state employee, industrial capitalist, *literatus* or journalist, prophet, and the organizer—are discursively related to characteristic backgrounds, followers, and to the trends in the educational process. Paul Honigsheim, "Die Gezenwartskrise der Kulturinstitute in ihrer soziologischen Bedingheit," in Max Sheler (ed.), *Versuche zu einer Soziologie des Wissens* (Leipzig: Duncker und Humblot 1926), pp. 426-450.

empirical uniformities of the class, but they are chosen so as to be most *significantly representative* of the intellectuals' behavior with respect to the social system. He chooses those attributes that stand out as being the most obvious or the most crucial with respect to this relationship between the class of intellectuals and the type of social system being dealt with.[13] He defines those attributes in pure, possibly even exaggerated form, and then imputes to them the character of *system*.[14] In other words, he assumes for the purposes at hand that they belong together and hence are representative of the system of behavior called intellectual under the type of social conditions postulated. The type then is an hypothesized compound of empirically observed, but selected and purified attributes of the class being studied.

The attributes included within the construct "impotent German intellectual" in the present example might be (1) strong nationalism, (2) great respect for the traditions of the German armed

[13] "You will find that you often get the best insights by considering extreme types, or from thinking of the opposite of that with which you are directly concerned. If you think about despair, then also think about elation; if you study the miser, then also the spendthrift. That is also a general characteristic of anchor projects, which, if it is possible, ought to be designed in terms of 'polar types.' The hardest thing in the world is to study one object, but when you try to contrast objects, you get a sort of grip on the materials and you can then sort out the dimensions in terms of which comparisons are made. You will find that the shuttling between attention to these dimensions and to the concrete types is very illuminating. This technique is also logically sound, for without a sample, you can only guess about statistical frequencies anyway: what you can do is to give the range and the major types of some phenomenon, and for that it is more economical to begin by constructing 'polar types,' opposites along various dimensions. This does not mean of course that you will not strive to gain and to maintain a sense of proportion, with the hope of obtaining some lead on the frequencies of given types. One continually tries, in fact, to combine this quest with the search for indices for which one might find or collect statistics." C. W. Mills, "On Intellectual Craftsmanship," in Gross, *Symposium on Sociological Theory*, p. 43.

[14] For a criticism of the tendency of users of typologies to "slide" from *nominal* to *real* definitions without empirical testing, see Hans Zetterberg, "On Axiomatic Theories in Sociology," in Lazarsfeld and Rosenberg, *op. cit.*, pp. 539-540.

forces, (3) fear of Russia so great that the Nazis appear to be the lesser evil, (4) the view that the outside world and not German docility is responsible for the rise of Hitler, (5) political inactivity, (6) opposition to the Nazis expressed only in verbal grumbling rather than in more determined ways, (7) rejection of collaboration with working-class groups that oppose the Nazis, (8) pride in intellectuality as an end in itself, and (9) self-pity.[15]

The question might legitimately be raised at this time as to whether or not this type of intellectual might actively collaborate in Hitler's programme. The working assumption here is that they would not. Intellectuals who actively collaborated in the Nazi movement could easily possess *some* of the attributes of the type, since these same attributes (as individual attributes) could characterize other types of intellectuals or the intellectual as a general type. As a *composite,* however, it is assumed that this *set* of attributes manifest in intellectuals would be conducive to inactivity rather than activity and nonparticipation rather than participation. Such an assumption is necessary at this stage of the inquiry but is subject to empirical check. Such a check should be made prior to the final or interpretive phase of the inquiry.

It should be noted, of course, that if the type is to be constructed at a more abstract level so as to be relevant to the more general hypothesis stated earlier, some of the nine attributes specified would either be dropped or be stated in a less idiosyncratic form. For instance, great respect for the traditions of the German armed forces might be deleted or restated as great respect for all traditions of the national state. Such an abstract definition of the type would tend, in most cases, to increase the general utility of the type in a number of empirical cases at the cost of its degree of precision in any one case. Before considering the matter of utility, however, there are two other typological steps to be taken.

[15] This type is "borrowed" from Howard Becker, "Propaganda and the Impotent German Intellectual," *Social Forces,* 29 (March, 1951), pp. 273-276. The type is used *illustratively* here. The intent is to clarify the procedural steps of typology, and the substantive material involved is purely illustrative.

Simplification of the Type with Regard to the Attribute Sphere from Which It Is Drawn [16]

It is evident that, given the ideal nature of the constructed type and the usual diversity of empirical cases, there will be less than complete correspondence between the constructed type and the empirical class to which it refers. In fact, the degree of deviation from the type (and the distribution of that deviation in the class population) is as important as any other data in the ultimate evaluation of the utility of the type. However, given this deviation, there are certain to be *at least* two kinds of empirical cases: those that fit the type and those that do not. In fact, in the case under discussion, if we assume that each of the nine attributes used in defining the type is a dichotomy, there is the logical possibility of twenty-nine kinds of empirical cases, or 512 kinds of intellectuals, only *one* kind of which is the constructed type. Of course, if the attributes are actually variables assuming more than two values each, the number of kinds of intellectuals, so defined, is much greater.

Thus, before going to the empirical data for a rigorous examination of the correspondence between the type and the actual intellectuals, it is well to decide, on the basis of a general knowledge of the relevant data and a limited number of complete cases, whether all of the attributes included in the type are needed. Of course, it is also possible at this stage to locate additional crucial definitive attributes not originally included in the type. If it appears that two or more of the attributes are very highly correlated, some may be dropped. For instance, if all those who exhibit pride in intellectuality as an end in itself also exhibit self-pity, there is no need to carry

[16] The discussion by P. F. Lazarsfeld in "Some Remarks on the Typological Procedures in Social Research," *Zeitschrift fur Sozialforschung.* 6 (Alcan/Paris, 1937), pp. 119-139, is relevant here. See also A. H. Barton, "The Concept of Property Space in Social Research," in Lazarsfeld and Rosenberg, *op. cit.*, pp. 40-53.

both attributes in the type definition. Also, if it is found that some attribute included in the type on rational rather than empirical grounds is not found in the empirical cases, it can be dropped. Of course, this sort of simplification of the type definition can also take place after the empirical data have been more rigorously examined, but much effort will be saved if simplification can take place at this time.

Adaptation of Available Theories and Principles to Give a Tentative Explanatory Accounting of the Type

The original definition of the type was based on a consideration of the current state of knowledge and existent theory in the relevant areas of inquiry.[17] However, it is both possible and highly desirable to go beyond the level of asking what role a particular type of person is likely to play in a particular type of social system. It may be possible, for instance, to develop a *series* of hypotheses on the basis of a more rigorous examination of the role of various types of occupations and professions in different kinds of Western social systems. Such an examination might lead us to hypothesize, for instance, that intellectuals placed in different segments of the social system would behave somewhat differently. Thus we would be led to stating hypotheses about the *degree of approximation* of various *types* of German intellectuals to our constructed type of impotent German intellectual.

It will be seen from the above that there is necessarily a constant interplay between the fifth and sixth steps in the type construction process, between simplification of the type with regard to the attribute sphere and the adaptation of available theories and principles. When these two steps have been completed, the next step is obvious.

[17] The difficulties involved in relating types to generalized analytical theory are explored in detail by Talcott Parsons in *The Structure of Social Action* (2nd ed.; Glencoe: The Free Press, 1949), pp. 601-639.

Empirical Verification of the Type: Examination of the Rate of Incidence and Degree of Approximation

It is at this point that the often-acknowledged and more often implicit split between those sociologists who are primarily methodologically-oriented and those who are primarily substantively-oriented comes to light. It is also unfortunately true that it is at this crucial point that many of those who have used constructed types become rather vague and elusive. Let us examine what this step involves.

We have noted that, given the nine attributes used in our example, and assuming that each is a simple dichotomy, there are 512 kinds of intellectuals logically possible. We have also suggested that, where possible, this list of attributes should be reduced in number. But even if it is reduced to six, there are still sixty-four possible kinds of intellectuals. Let us assume that we *have* reduced the number to six, and let us further assume that we have found empirical cases of only half of these, or thirty-two kinds of intellectuals, one of which is our primary constructed type. In order to get this far, of course, we must also assume that we have adequate measures of the attributes for an adequate sample of intellectuals.

One of our first tasks will be to record the relative incidence of the constructed type. Since we have purposely made the definitive attributes of the type rather extreme, there is unlikely to be a high proportion of intellectuals who will be the pure type of impotent intellectual. Whether we have retained only our simple original hypothesis that German intellectuals would be found to be impotent, or have developed more refined hypotheses about different *kinds* of intellectuals, we are immediately faced with the problem of measuring the degree of approximation to the constructed type.

It is not sufficient simply to indicate that so many of the empirical cases fit the type and so many do not. One of the advantages of following the earlier steps is that one is able at this point to go beyond such a gross statement to a more refined analysis of the data. If the attributes of the type are adequately defined, we will know at this point how many cases exhibit *each* of these attributes, and we will thus be able to examine the total distribution of attributes within our sample of cases. It will then be possible to indicate not only how many cases do not fit the type precisely but also the degree to which they deviate from it (*how many* attributes they do not exhibit), and the pattern of these deviations (*which* attributes they do not exhibit). Given this information, it is possible to use the logic of scaling procedures to gain added insight into the relationship between the type and the empirical data. Using the attributes as items in a scale, we can then analyze these items with respect to their interrelationships.

There are, in effect, six items in our scale or seven points (or scale values). It is rather clear that here we have a scale of no higher order than an ordinal scale. Thus, there would be limits on the kind of analysis we can utilize. But either of the familiar techniques devised by Likert and Guttman could be used, and they would contribute much to our understanding of the type and the data. Using the Likert criteria, for instance, we would be able to see if all of the attributes "hang together" in the sense that each is related to the total configuration in a linear fashion. It should give us pause if we found, for instance, that there was more pride in intellectuality in those intellectuals who exhibited few or none of the other attributes than there was in those who exhibited many of them.

It is highly probable that we do not have a unidimensional scale in the Guttman sense, but it might be very valuable and revealing to investigate this matter. For instance, is it true that *all* those who exhibit self-pity also exhibit strong nationalism and great respect for the traditions of the German armed forces, but only *some* of them are politically inactive? Is it possible that there is not only a rank ordering of intellectuals with respect to their approximation to the constructed type but also a related rank ordering of the attributes of the type according to their incidence in the population of intellectuals? Is it possible that different kinds of intellectuals (differentially placed in the social system) tend to be particular scale types—that is, do they systematically exhibit some of the type attributes but not others? These are exciting and intriguing questions, but they are not very often considered by the typologist. To do so would indeed be difficult, but to fail to do so leaves all too many questions unanswered and much of the utility of typology untapped.

Even if the typologist must settle for a simple score computed by assigning a plus one to all type attributes and a zero to their lack, the problem of degree of approximation must be faced. Howard Becker, in using this type, interviewed approximately 600 intellectuals and never found one that manifested all nine attributes contained within the type.[18] As suggested above, such a finding raises a question regarding the adequacy of the original type attributes. It also opens the possibility of reducing the number of attributes in the original type and/or constructing other types, thus taking into account different kinds of intellectuals. Moreover, it must be acknowledged that the adequacy of the measure of approximation is an important factor in determining the utility of the typology. It is also important to recognize that a careful consideration of the problem of degree of approximation is crucial for the final step of type construction.

Interpretation

If the typologist has found that the type occurs with great frequency, he may conclude that the German intellectuals played only a minor role in the aggression, and that no other types representing the class need be constructed or examined.[19] However, it was suggested earlier that it is probable that the type incidence will not be sufficient to warrant any general statements on the basis of this type alone. As has been suggested, it may be that a number of clear-cut scale types have been isolated representing degrees of approximation to the pure constructed type. It is equally (or more) probable that a number of so-called nonscale types will have appeared. A careful examination of these may disclose that they are actually cases of a qualitatively different kind of intellectual rather

[18] See his "Propaganda and the Impotent German Intellectual."

[19] This would be true if it had been empirically established that representatives of the type had in fact been inactive in the Hitler programme.

than being quantitative approximations of the original constructed type. It may be that one or more additional types will have to be constructed using other attributes not included in the original type. Thus a series of types of intellectuals might be formed, each of them emphasizing certain aspects which the intellectual has in common with other intellectuals, because these aspects each have some relevance to the problem at hand. Numerous types can be formed and frequently have to be formed in connection with one particular problem. Conversely, a particular type, after construction, can be found to be relevant to a whole series of problems. In this way a type becomes *established* and is utilized as a referent in widely varied interpretive activity. In each instance, however, the *relevance* of the typification to the problem under consideration has to be *demonstrated* rather than taken for granted.

It must be noted here that the interpretive phase of the inquiry is of crucial significance. The breadth of latitude here is in part responsible for the controversy that surrounds the usage of types. Conversely, it is this breadth of latitude that gives typologies their frontier-breaking quality in inquiry. Conclusions with regard to the initial hypothesis must be handled with care and with special attention to counter-argument. In general, typological formulations can give one a compelling rather than conclusive case. It is unlikely that other interpretations of the hypothesis will have been eliminated by the mere establishment of the typology. Such a case, however, is not at all unusual in social research; indeed it may be thought of as "typical."

The important point to be made here is that the construction of the original type, the collection of data making possible the comparison of empirical cases with this type, and the evaluation of the degree of approximation of these cases with the type have shed additional light on the class of objects being studied (in this case German intellectuals). It has indicated the degree of adequacy of the generalization (or hypothesis) implicit in the original constructed type, and it has pointed the way toward a clarification of the deviations from this type. In so doing, the process has helped to give system to a body of historical data, thus making it pertinent to the sociological enterprise.

The Summing Up

It would seem evident that the primary function of types is to identify, simplify, and order the concrete data so that they may be described in terms that make them comparable. They function in this way at any level of abstraction, and hence can be utilized with respect to problems varying from limited to great breadth of scope. In effect, a type constitutes a reduction from the complex to the simple; hence the careful construction and use of types, as an intermediate procedure, can potentially make many large-scale problems accessible to more refined methodology and technique. The construction of a type or series of types helps us to know more precisely what mechanisms or structural relations are being postulated with respect to a problem area, sometimes calling attention to the need for further clarification of the operational meaning of relevant definitions and statements. The type assists in the discovery of inconsistencies between the empirical data and the theories used to explain them. It thus lays the basis for the further elaboration of theory and frequently suggests further empirical studies in a problem-complex. The type aids in handling complicated, simultaneous interrelations among a relatively large number of variables in a *preliminary* way, prior to the development of the operational possibility of handling them more rigorously with respect to any particular problem. Indeed, a primary role of the constructed type would seem to be that of a sensitizing device. Its use allows social scientists cognitively to map broad areas of social phenomena through the systematic tapping of historical and secondary data. This can quite conceivably result in increased precision of analysis in many areas in the social sciences, particularly in such areas as macrosociology, where the problems are currently often beyond the scope of the more rigorous experimental and quantitative techniques.

Selected Bibliography

ABEL, Theodore. *Systematic Sociology in Germany* (New York: Columbia University Press, 1929). A useful "background" statement on the sociological context within which the process of typification drew explicit attention as an aspect of methodology.

ADAMS, Richard. "A Change from Caste to Class in a Peruvian Sierra Town," *Social Forces*, 31 (March, 1953), pp. 238-244. The author suggests that the case history of social change from caste to class in Muquiyauyo is part of a typical pattern of change in many areas of South America.

ALLPORT, G. W. and VERNON, P. E. "A Test for Personal Values," *Journal of Abnormal and Social Psychology*, 26 (October-December, 1931), pp. 231-248. A report on the results of a test designed to determine the validity of Edward Spranger's six personality types. It is an excellent demonstration of how quantitative procedures can be adapted to ideal types.

ANDERSON, C. A. and BOWMAN, Mary Jean. "A Typology of Societies," *Rural Sociology*, 16 (September, 1951), pp. 255-271. A multi-dimensional typology of total societies is developed by correlating various indices such as occupation, rank, and kinship with the modalities of rigidity and diversity.

BARTH, Ernest A. T. "Air Force Base-Host Community Relations: A Study in Community Typology," *Social Forces*, 41 (March, 1963), pp. 260-264. Develops two typologies, one based on the structure of the ten communities studied and the other on

217

the interaction processes between each community and its Air Force Base.

BARTON, Allen H. "The Concept of Property Space in Social Research," in P. F. Lazarsfeld and Morris Rosenberg, editors, *The Language of Social Research* (Glencoe: The Free Press, 1955), pp. 40-53.   The concept of property space has been developed over the years by Paul F. Lazarsfeld. This article summarizes a collection of examples of the application of the concept of property-space to social research operations.

√   BECKER, Howard. "Constructive Typology in the Social Sciences," in H. E. Barnes, Howard Becker, and F. B. Becker (eds.), *Contemporary Social Theory* (New York: D. Appleton Century, 1940).   One of the leading exponents of the typological procedure discusses and illustrates the meaning of "constructive typology." He seeks to show its relevance to the social sciences generally, and also demonstrates specific application to sociology. This is an important article for the student of typologies.

BECKER, Howard. "Culture Case Study and Ideal–Typical Method," *Social Forces,* 12 (March, 1934), pp. 399-405.   An examination of the relationship between history and sociology with special reference to the place of the ideal–typical method. The article emphasizes the contribution of Max Weber in this area.

BECKER, Howard. *German Youth: Bond or Free* (New York: Grove Press, 1946).   A study of the German youth movement based upon the utilization of types of social structure, organization, and leadership.

BECKER, Howard. "Sacred and Secular Societies: Considered with Reference to Folk-State and Similar Classification," *Social Forces,* 28 (May, 1950), pp. 361-376.   A review of the meaning and importance of the concepts "sacred" and "secular," as well as an outline of the types and subtypes of sacred and secular societies.

BECKER, Howard. *Through Values to Social Interpretation* (Durham: Duke University Press, 1950).   Contains important material on the nature of constructive typologies in the social sciences. The author also demonstrates the applicability of typologies to sociological inquiry by elaborating a typology of sacred and secular societies.

BEFU, Harumi and PLOTNICOR, Leonard. "Types of Corporate Unilineal Descent Groups," *American Anthropologist*, 64 (April, 1962), pp. 313-327. An effort to construct a typology of unilineal descent groups in which several subtypes are distinguished according to the structure and function of the group.

BELLAH, Robert N. "Religious Evolution," *American Sociological Review*, 29 (June, 1964), pp. 358-374. Posits and describes five ideal-typical stages in the evolution of religion.

BENDIX, Reinhard. "Bureaucracy: The Problem and Its Setting," *American Sociological Review*, 12 (October, 1947), pp. 493-507. An analysis of large-scale organizations in which the types of democratic and authoritarian administrations are contrasted.

BENDIX, Reinhard. "Concepts and Generalizations in Comparative Sociological Studies," *American Sociological Review*, 28 (August, 1963), pp. 532-539. Discusses the bearing of comparative studies on sociological concepts, with special reference to constructed types (Bendix calls them "paired-concepts").

BENDIX, Reinhard. "Max Weber's Interpretation of Conduct and History," *American Journal of Sociology*, 51 (May, 1946), pp. 518-526. A discussion of the dilemmas Weber encountered in using ideal types as a methodological solution to the problem of reconciling the historically unique and individual actions of men with the wider determining structures of history that shape these actions.

BENOIT-SMULLYAN, Emile. "Status, Status Types, and Status Interrelations," *American Sociological Review*, 9 (April, 1944), pp. 151-161. A discussion of three types of status—economic, political, prestige—and their interrelationships.

BERGER, Peter. "The Sociological Study of Sectarianism," *Social Research*, 21 (Winter, 1954), pp. 467-485. A critique of various definitions of sectarianism and the construction of a new typology of the sect. This typology is then adapted to the American religious scheme.

BITTNER, Egon. "Radicalism and the Organization of Radical Movements," *American Sociological Review*, 28 (December, 1963), pp. 928-940.   Drawing on Weber, author attempts to develop "radicalism" as a theoretically pure type and to relate this concept to some of the organizational problems of radical movements.

BLOOMBAUM, Milton. "A Contribution to the Theory of Typology Construction," *Sociological Quarterly*, 5 (Spring, 1964), pp. 157-162.   An attempt to demonstrate a procedure for derivation of types from theory. Presents a formalized version of Durkheim's theory of the division of labor and then deduces the characteristics of *mechanical* and *organic* groups from the interrelated set of propositions constituting the theory.

BOSKOFF, Alvin. "Postponement of Social Decision in Transitional Society," *Social Forces*, 31 (March, 1953), pp. 229-234.   An effort to formulate a dynamic typology that can handle the process of sociocultural change. A specific type, the transitional society, is presented.

BOSKOFF, Alvin. "Structure, Function, and Folk Society," *American Sociological Review*, 14 (December, 1949), pp. 749-758.   An effort to integrate Odum's folk-regional sociology with the structural-functional framework. A societal typology based on degree of complexity and technical social organization is developed.

CADWALLADER, Mervyn. "Three Classes of Social Change," *Pacific Sociological Review*, 1 (Spring, 1958), pp. 17-20.   The author rejects the notion that social change can be conceptualized on a unilineal dimension and suggests three types of change—evolutionary, innovating, and compound—which correspond to three types of social organization—reproducing, nonreproducing, and mixed.

CARLIN, Edward A. "Schumpeter's Constructed Type: The Entrepreneur," *Kyklos,* 9 (1956), pp. 27-43. A comparative analysis of Schumpeter's entrepreneur type and Weber's charismatic leader as they are related to the problems of social change.

CHEIN, Isidore. "Personality and Typology," in P. L. Harriman (ed.), *Twentieth Century Psychology* (New York: Philosophical Library, 1946), pp. 94-115. Reprinted from *Journal of Social Psychology,* 18 (August, 1943), pp. 89-109. Chein presents a critique of some of the traditional objections of psychologists to the typological approach in studying personality. He suggests criteria to evaluate typological systems and applies these criteria to the personality types of Jung, Spranger, and Freud.

DANZIGER, K. "Ideology and Utopia in South Africa: A Methodological Contribution to the Sociology of Knowledge," *The British Journal of Sociology,* 14 (March, 1963), pp. 59-76. An effort to demonstrate empirically the relationship between a person's position in the social structure and his concept of the future.

DAVIS, Arthur. "Bureaucratic Patterns in the Navy Officer Corps," *Social Forces,* 27 (December, 1948), pp. 143-153. Starting with Weber's bureaucratic type, the author discusses the military variant of this type with special emphasis on authority and tradition.

DERBER, Milton, CHALMERS, W. E., and EDELMAN, Milton. "Types and Variables in Local Union-Management Relationships," *Human Organization,* 21 (Winter, 1962-63), pp. 264-270. A discussion of the procedures and problems involved in constructing a typology of union-management relations. The authors then demonstrate the utility of factor analysis in constructing a threefold typology.

DURKHEIM, Emile. *The Division of Labor,* translated from the first French edition, 1893, by George Simpson (Glencoe: The Free Press, 1947). The first work of a theoretician who continues to wield enormous influence. Utilizes the "mechanical" and "organic" societal types as well as the "repressive" and "restitutive" law types in a functional analysis.

DURKHEIM, Emile. *Suicide,* translated from the 1930 French edition (first edition 1897) by J. A. Spaulding and George Simpson (Glencoe: The Free Press, 1950). A classic typological study that still serves as a model in research design with respect to the articulation of theory and empirical inquiry.

EISTER, A. W. *Drawing Room Conversion: A Sociological Account of the Oxford Group Movement* (Durham: Duke University Press, 1950). The typological method is applied to the study of social movements and illustrated by an analysis of the Oxford Group movement.

FALARDEAU, Jean C. "The Parish as an Institutional Type," *The Canadian Journal of Economic and Political Science,* 14 (August, 1949), pp. 353-367. The author attempts to clarify the institutional nature of the parish by pointing out its typical historical pattern and the deviation from this pattern in the modern urban society.

FARBER, Bernard. "Types of Family Organization: Child-Oriented, Home-Oriented and Parent-Oriented," in Arnold Rose (ed.), *Human Behavior and Social Processes* (Boston: Houghton Mifflin, 1962), pp. 285-307. A revision of the Burgess institutional vs. companionship family typology is constructed to examine the relationship between degree of marital integration and severity of family crises.

FEI, Hsiao-Tung. "Peasantry and Gentry: An Interpretation of Chinese Social Structure and Its Changes," *American Journal of Sociology,* 52 (July, 1946), pp. 1-17. A discussion of the Chinese social structure suggesting a typology of the peasantry and gentry classes.

FEUER, Lewis S. *The Scientific Intellectual: The Psychological and Sociological Origins of Modern Science* (New York: Basic Books, 1963). A study of the historical development of the scientific intellectual as a social type. Surveying a wide range of historical and cultural cases where scientific activity has emerged, the author argues that the significant underlying factor is a hedonistic-libertarian ethic.

FICHTER, Joseph. "The Marginal Catholic: An Institutional Approach," *Social Forces,* 32 (December, 1953), pp. 167-173. Starting from a general typology of church participants, the author gives an excellent elaboration of one of the subtypes, the marginal participant.

FOREMAN, P. B. "Negro Lifeways in the Rural South: A Typological Approach to Social Differentiation," *American Sociological Review,* 13 (August, 1948), pp. 409-418. An effort to refine the structural analysis of the rural South by substituting a general concept such as "caste" with a more specific typology.

Fox, J. R. "Sibling Incest," *The British Journal of Sociology,* 13 (June, 1962), pp. 128-150. The works of Westermarck and Freud provide the basis for two types of sibling relationships. The relationship between these types and the severity of sibling incest tabus is examined cross-culturally.

FRANCIS, E. K. "The Adjustment of a Peasant Group to a Capitalistic Economy: The Manitoba Mennonites," *Rural Sociology,* 17 (September, 1952), pp. 218-228. A study of the assimilation process in which types of the parent society and host society are compared.

FRANCIS, E. K. "Toward a Typology of Religious Orders," *American Journal of Sociology,* 55 (March, 1950), pp. 437-449. A typology of religious orders distinguishing the community of religiosi (*Gemeinschaft*) from the religious order properly speaking (*Gesellschaft*). The historical development of religious orders is examined within the context of this typology.

FREEMAN, Linton C., FARARO, Thomas J., BLOOMBERG, Warner, and SUNSHINE, Morris H. "Locating Leaders in Local Communities: A Comparison of Some Alternative Approaches," *American Sociological Review,* 28 (October, 1963), pp. 791-798. From an analysis of several approaches to the problem of locating leaders in a community, the authors suggest that at least three distinct types of leaders can be found: "institutional leader," "effector," and "activist."

FREEMAN, Linton C. and WINCH, Robert. "Societal Complexity: An

Empirical Test of a Typology of Societies," *American Journal of Sociology,* 62 (March, 1957), pp. 461-466.   Using the factor analysis technique on forty-eight societies selected from Murdock's Cross-Cultural Area Files, the authors attempt to empirically validate the *Gemeinschaft-Gesellschaft* typology.

FRIEDMAN, John. "Cities in Social Transition," *Comparative Studies in Society and History,* 4 (November, 1961), pp. 86-103. Argues that villages and cities are too radically different to be represented as opposite poles on a single continuum and delineates some common characteristics of cities.

GERTH, Hans. "The Nazi Party: Its Leadership and Composition," *American Journal of Sociology,* 45 (January, 1940), pp. 517-541.   The emergence of the Nazi Party in Germany is analyzed in terms of the charismatic and bureaucratic types of dominance.

GOLDHAMER, Herbert and SHILS, E. A. "Types of Power and Status," *American Journal of Sociology,* 45 (September, 1939), pp. 171-182.   The authors make extensive use of the typological approach in their analysis of power and status.

GOLDKIND, Victor. "Sociocultural Contrasts in Rural and Urban Settlement Types in Costa Rica," *Rural Sociology,* 26 (December, 1961), pp. 365-380.   Proposes a fourfold typology for the classification of settlements in Costa Rica.

GOODE, W. J. "A Note on the Ideal Type," *American Sociological Review,* 12 (August, 1947), pp. 473-474.   The author presents a brief discussion of pertinent issues concerning the ideal type, emphasizing the works of Becker and Parsons.

GORDON, C. Wayne and BABCHUK, Nicholas. "A Typology of Voluntary Associations," *American Sociological Review,* 24 (February, 1959), pp. 22-29.   An effort to develop a typology of voluntary associations along an instrumental-expressive continuum.

GOULDNER, Alvin. "Attitudes of 'Progressive' Trade Union Leaders," *American Journal of Sociology,* 52 (March, 1947), pp. 389-

392. Two polar types of trade union leadership are discerned: the "business unionist" and the "progressive" leader. A brief account is then given of the progressive leader's attitudes and the social pressures to modify these attitudes.

GRIMSHAW, Allen D. "Specification of Boundaries of Constructed Types Through Use of the Pattern Variable," *The Sociological Quarterly*, 3 (July, 1962), pp. 179-195.   A refinement of Parson's "pattern-variables" into a more limited constructed typology. This involves recognizing both the social system and the pattern-variables as constructed types. It also means establishing boundary lines for the social system and cut points for the pattern-variables.

GROSS, Neal. "Cultural Variables in Rural Communities," *American Journal of Sociology*, 53 (March, 1948), pp. 344-350.   Certain aspects of Redfield's folk-society typology are applied to four rural contemporary communities in the United States. While the findings tend to support Redfield's hypothesis, important limitations in the analysis are suggested.

HABENSTEIN, Robert W. "Sociology of Occupations: The Case of the American Funeral Director," in Arnold Rose (ed.), *Human Behavior and Social Processes* (Boston: Houghton Mifflin, 1962), pp. 225-247.   The social organization of funeral directing is presented in terms of the typical "local funeral home" vs. the typical mass mortuary.

HACKER, Helen. "Arnold Rose's 'A Deductive Ideal-Type Method,'" *American Journal of Sociology*, 56 (January, 1951), pp. 354-356.   A critical examination of the possibility of applying the deductive ideal-type method to the structural-functional approach of Parsons, Merton, and others.

HALL, Oswald. "Types of Medical Careers," *American Journal of Sociology*, 55 (November, 1949), pp. 243-253.   The distinctive types of medical careers are identified according to the doctor's relationship with his patients, other doctors, and with the various medical institutions.

HALL, Richard. "The Concept of Bureaucracy: An Empirical Assessment," *American Journal of Sociology,* 69 (July, 1963), pp. 32-40.   From a review of the literature identifies six dimensions by which an organization may be classified as more or less bureaucratic, and attempts to construct scales for each.

HEBERLE, Rudolf. *Social Movements* (New York: Appleton-Century-Crofts, 1951).   Typological analysis of social movements starts with Weber's typology of motivation and reduces the motives of individuals in joining and supporting a social movement to four pure types.

HEMPEL, Carl. "Typological Methods in the Natural and Social Sciences," *Proceedings,* American Philosophical Association; Eastern Division, 1 (1952), pp. 65-86.   A provocative article outlining the logical and methodological character of typological concepts. The analysis is advanced from the standpoint of the methodological procedures of the physical sciences.

HILLER, E. T. *The Strike* (Chicago: University of Chicago Press, 1928).   An effort to study the strike as a cycle of typical events that take place in a more or less regular and predictable way.

HILLERY, George A., Jr. "Villages, Cities, and Total Institutions," *American Sociological Review,* 28 (October, 1963), pp. 779-791.   Develops a typology (composed of the "vill" and the "total institution") for more adequately differentiating among various human groupings often lumped together under the term "community." Holds, however, that these types are not "ideal" but more in the nature of "empirical abstractions," since "each component of each model is found in all of the case studies employed in the analysis."

HONIGSHEIM, Paul. "The Roots of Soviet Rural Social Structure: Where and Why It Has Spread," *Agricultural History,* 25 (July, 1951), pp. 104-114.   An effort to demonstrate the historical continuity in Russian rural organization. It is further suggested that this same type of organization is found among the peoples of eastern Europe.

HOPPER, Rex. "The Revolutionary Process," *Social Forces,* 28

(March, 1950), pp. 270-279. An attempt to synthesize earlier works in the area of revolutionary movements. The author sets forth four developmental stages of a revolution, pointing out the typical processes and leadership patterns at each stage of development.

Horowitz, Irving L. "A Formalization of the Sociology of Knowledge," *Behavioral Science,* 9 (January, 1964), pp. 45-55. An effort to bring more order into the sociology of knowledge through the utilization of some constructed typologies which Horowitz worked out. Also contains some commentary on other typologies which have been used in dealing with the subject matter of this area.

Hubbard, Harold and McDonagh, Edward. "The Business Executive as a Career Type," *Sociology and Social Research,* 47 (January, 1963), pp. 138-146. Following Raymond Mack's typology of occupations and occupational roles, the authors construct and empirically examine a seven-dimensional typology of the business executive.

Hughes, E. C. "Personality Types and the Division of Labor," *American Journal of Sociology,* 33 (March, 1928), pp. 754-768. Using the works of Durkheim as his basis, Hughes classifies personality types according to the individual's position in the division of labor. This is an important statement on the relationship between personality and occupations.

Jacoby, Arthur P. and Babchuk, Nicholas. "Instrumental and Expressive Voluntary Associations," *Sociology and Social Research,* 47 (July, 1963), pp. 461-471. A study of four voluntary associations which suggests that the instrumental-expressive continuum earlier advocated by Gordon and Babchuk is a valid one for classifying these associations.

Johnson, Benton. "On Church and Sect," *American Sociological Review,* 28 (August, 1963), pp. 539-549. Contains a critique of Troeltsch's typology and suggests a revision of it so that it is applicable to a broader range of contexts.

Klapp, O. E. "Heroes, Villains and Fools, as Agents of Social Control," *American Sociological Review,* 19 (February, 1954), pp. 56-62.   Examines the collective process of typification which results in the delineation of "social types."

LANDECKER, Werner S. "Types of Integration and Their Measurement," *American Journal of Sociology,* 56 (January, 1951), pp. 332-340.   Four types of social integration are stated and defined: the cultural, the normative, the communicative, and the functional. The author attempts to demonstrate how each of these types varies on a continuum of its own.

LAZARSFELD, Paul F. "Philosophy of Science and Social Research," in Nagel, Suppes and Tarski (eds.), *Logic, Methodology and Philosophy of Science* (Stanford: Stanford University Press, 1962), pp. 463-473.   The author criticizes the philosophers of science for failing to utilize contemporary social research in their formal analysis. He illustrates this critique by pointing out the need to examine important issues in the area of typological analysis.

LAZARSFELD, Paul F. "Some Remarks on the Typological Procedures in Social Research," *Zeitschrift fur Sozialforschung,* 6 (Alcan/ Paris, 1937), pp. 119-139.   An effort to clarify the logic of typological operations and improve the use of types in practical research. An early description of the now familiar attribute or property space.

LAZARSFELD, Paul F. and BARTON, Allen. "Qualitative Measurement in the Social Sciences: Classification, Typologies, and Indices," in Daniel Lerner and H. D. Lasswell (eds.), *The Policy Sciences* (Stanford: Stanford University Press, 1951), pp. 155-192.   A systematic analysis of some of the research procedures used in measuring qualitative data. It is an important statement on the logic of formulating typologies.

LEE, Shu-Ching. "China's Traditional Family: Its Characteristics and Disintegration," *American Sociological Review,* 18 (June, 1953), pp. 272-280.   A brief and generalized description of the familistic type of social organization closely associated with the traditional Chinese family.

LEEDS, Anthony. "Brazilian Careers and Social Structure: An Evolutionary Model and Case History," *American Anthropologist,* 66 (December, 1964), pp. 1321-1347. Presents the "static-agrarian" and "expansive-industrial" constructed types, assumed to occur in this order in societal evolution, and utilizing anthropological data, discusses the consequences of acculturation between societies approaching them.

LERNER, Daniel. *The Passing of the Traditional Society* (Glencoe: The Free Press, 1958). A study of social change in six Middle Eastern nations. The analytic tool used in this study is a typology of life styles—the traditional, the transitional, the modern—based on literacy, urbanism, media participation and empathy.

LINTON, Ralph. "Nativistic Movements," *American Anthropologist,* 45 (April-June, 1943), pp. 230-240. The presentation of a fourfold typology of nativistic movements and an analysis of the various conditions under which these types may be observed.

LOOMIS, C. P. "The Nature of Rural Social Systems: A Typological Analysis," *Rural Sociology,* 15 (June, 1950), pp. 156-174. A familistic *Gemeinschaft*-contractual *Gesellschaft* polar typology is constructed and applied to various social systems such as an Amish family, a government bureau, and a ditch association.

LOOMIS, C. P. and BEEGLE, J. A. *Rural Social Systems* (New York: Prentice-Hall, 1950). A book representing a convergence of the thought of Tönnies, Sorokin, and Parsons in particular and one that uses the *Gemeinschaft-Gesellschaft* typology as a basic referent.

LOOMIS, C. P. and McKINNEY, J. C. "Systemic Differences Between Latin American Communities of Family Farms and Large Estates," *American Journal of Sociology,* 61 (March, 1956), pp. 410-411. An attempt to delineate fundamentally different types of social structure in the same general sphere and in close proximity.

Lowenthal, Leo and Guterman, Norbert. "Portrait of the American Agitator," *Public Opinion Quarterly*, 12 (Fall, 1948), pp. 417-429.   An outline of some of the "distinguishing characteristics of the American agitator," and an examination of the social and psychological factors which enable him to flourish.

Mack, Raymond C. "Occupational Determinateness: A Problem and Hypothesis in Role Theory," *Social Forces*, 35 (October, 1956), pp. 20-25.   Proposes a twofold typology for describing occupations and occupational roles which is based on the degree of determinateness found in the occupation or occupational role.

Martin, James G. "Ideal and Typical Social Norms," *Sociological Inquiry*, 34 (Winter, 1964), pp. 41-47.   Distinguishes between these two types of norms and discusses the importance of this distinction to selected subject areas of sociological relevance.

McCord, Joan and Clemes, Stanley. "Conscience Orientation and Dimensions of Personality," *Behavioral Science*, 9 (January, 1964), pp. 18-29.   Delineates four types of conscience orientation and attempts to relate them to certain personality characteristics.

McKinney, J. C. "Constructive Typology and Social Research," in J. T. Doby, *et al.* (eds.), *An Introduction to Social Research* (Harrisburg: Stackpole Co., 1954), pp. 139-198.   An earlier treatment of the methodology and procedure of typing. Assesses the relation of typing to other methodological devices.

Merton, R. K. "Bureaucratic Structure and Personality," *Social Forces*, 18 (May, 1940), pp. 560-568.   The utilization of Weber's typology of bureaucracy to suggest problems of dysfunction and ambivalence for the bureaucrats as well as the clientele. Merton points out that the bureaucratic structure is the source of various types of conflict.

Merton, R. K. "Social Structure and Anomie," *American Sociological Review*, 2 (October, 1938), pp. 672-682.   An essay on how the relationship between the cultural goals and the institutional means of a society leads to various nonconforming patterns. These nonconforming patterns are examined within a typology of modes of individual adaptation.

MILLER, S. M. "The American Lower Class: A Typological Approach," *Social Research*, 31 (March, 1964), pp. 1-22.   An attempt to reformulate the broadly and sometimes vaguely defined concept of "lower class" into four types of lower-class individuals.

MILLS, C. Wright. "The Competitive Personality," *Partisan Review*, 13 (September-October, 1946), pp. 433-441.   A brief discussion of the decline of the "captains of industry" and the emergence of new personality types in the business world attuned to the needs of bureaucracy and salesmanship.

MINER, Horace. "The folk-Urban Continuum," *American Sociological Review*, 17 (October, 1952), pp. 529-537.   A review of criticisms of the folk-urban continuum and a discussion of its advantages and limitations for research and theory.

MINTZ, Sidney W. "The Folk-urban Continuum and the Rural Proletarian Community," *American Journal of Sociology*, 59 (September, 1953), pp. 136-143.   A critical discussion of Redfield's failure to utilize plantation communities in his folk typology of Yucatan. The author suggests that plantation communities have distinctive organizational features that necessitate constructing an independent type.

MIZRUCHI, Ephraim H. and PERRUCCI, Robert. "Norm Qualities and Differential Effects of Deviant Behavior: An Exploratory Analysis," *American Sociological Review*, 27 (June, 1962), pp. 391-399.   The authors sift out four characteristics of norms from data dealing with drinking pathology and use them to construct an eightfold typology of norms along a prescriptive-proscriptive dimension.

MOBERG, David. "Potential Uses of the Church-Sect Typology in Comparative Religious Research," *International Journal of*

Comparative Sociology, 2 (March, 1961), pp. 47-59.   A brief summary of Troeltsch's church-sect typology, discussing a number of pertinent criticisms.

MORRIS, Richard. "A Typology of Norms," *American Sociological Review,* 21 (October, 1956), pp. 610-613.   An elaboration of polar types—the absolute-conditional norms—which resembles Becker's sacred-secular typology.

NAHIRNY, Vladimir C. "Some Observations on Ideological Groups," *American Journal of Sociology,* 67 (January, 1962), pp. 397-405.   Contends that neither the traditional typologies for the classification of groups nor the more recent pattern variables are adequate for the classification of the character of social relations found in what the author refers to as ideological groups.

NASH, Dennison and SCHAW, Louis. "Personality and Adaptation in an Overseas Enclave," *Human Organization,* 21 (Winter, 1962-63), pp. 252-263.   A threefold classification of personality types—autonomous, transitional, and traditional—relative to the problem of immigrants adapting in a new country. The typology emerged from analyzing TAT protocols of Japanese farmers in Cuba.

ODUM, H. W. "Folk Sociology as a Subject Field for the Historical Study of Total Human Society and the Empirical Study of Group Behavior," *Social Forces,* 39 (March, 1953), pp. 193-223.   A general review of "folk sociology," with frequent references to the role of types and typological procedure.

PARK, Robert E. "Human Migration and the Marginal Man," *American Journal of Sociology,* 33 (May, 1928), pp. 881-893. This is Park's classic statement of a personality type which emerges from migration and cultural contact. In certain respects, the concept "marginal man" is an extension of Simmel's earlier typology of "the stranger."

PARSONS, Talcott. *Structure of Social Action* (Glencoe: The Free Press, 1949).   Contains a critical analysis of the typological method with special reference to Weber's contribution on the subject. Also includes a cogent analysis of Tönnies' *Gemein-schaft* and *Gesellschaft*.

PARSONS, Talcott. *The Social System* (Glencoe: The Free Press, 1951). Contains in systematic and generalized form the main outlines of a conceptual scheme for the analysis of the structure and processes of social systems. Abounds in types.

PASSIN, Herbert and BENNETT, J. W. "Changing Agricultural Magic in Southern Illinois: A Systematic Analysis of Folk-Urban Transition," *Social Forces*, 22 (October, 1943), pp. 98-106. This paper is an empirical application of Redfield's folk-urban typology to social change in a rural American community. Attention is focused on the polarities of isolation and homogeneity versus mobility and heterogeneity.

PEPPER, George B. "A Re-examination of the Ideal Type Concept," *American Catholic Sociological Review*, 24 (Fall 1963), pp. 185-201. A discussion and critique of Weber's and Parsons' use of ideal-type concepts in examining the notion that constructed typologies are useful in social theory only as preliminary devices, and must eventually give way to operational formulations.

PETERSON, Richard A. "Dimensions of Social Character: An Empirical Exploration of the Riesman Typology," *Sociometry*, 27 (June, 1964), pp. 194-207. Presents evidence which suggests that Riesman's types of inner-direction and other-direction are not uni- but multi-dimensional. Also provides a fairly exhaustive listing of the studies which have been concerned to date with Riesman's typology.

PETERSON, William. "A General Typology of Migration," *American Sociological Review*, 23 (June, 1958), pp. 256-266. Brings together into a fourfold typology some of the more significant analyses of both internal and external migration.

PORTERFIELD, Austin. "Suicide and Crime in Folk and in Secular Society," *American Journal of Sociology*, 57 (January, 1952), pp. 331-338. Rates of suicide and crime on both the state and local level are related to a hypothetical folk-secular polar typology. An index of "non-nativity" is provided to establish the polar points for the folk-secular continuum.

REDFIELD, Robert. "The Folk Society," *American Journal of Sociology,* 52 (January, 1947), pp. 293-308.   Here we find one of the few efforts by anthropologists to explicitly formulate a typology. Redfield presents a series of features found in the ideal folk society and states that the opposite characteristics constitute the ideal urban society.

REDFIELD, Robert. *The Folk Culture of Yucatan* (Chicago: University of Chicago Press, 1941).   A comparative study of a city, town, village, and tribe within the framework of the folk-urban typology.

REDFIELD, Robert. "Natural History of Folk Society," *Social Forces,* 31 (March, 1953), pp. 224-228.   Discusses various research applications of the folk society typology emphasizing its significance in understanding the historical development of civilization.

RIESMAN, David. *The Lonely Crowd* (New Haven: Yale University Press, 1950).   An attempt to relate character types—tradition centered, inner-directed, and outer-directed—to the long term movements of population curves.

ROSE, A. M. "A Deductive Ideal-Type Method," *American Journal of Sociology,* 56 (July, 1950), pp. 35-42.   The author argues that the success of economics with the deductive ideal-type method can be extended to the field of sociology. He discusses the procedure involved and illustrates his case from a number of areas such as race relations, family and social stratification.

SAHLINS, Marshall D. "Poor Man, Rich Man, Big Man, Chief: Political Types in Melanesia and Polynesia," *Comparative Studies in Society and History,* 5 (April, 1963), pp. 285-303.   The development of the abstracted or ideal types of "Big Man" and "Chief" in order to analyze certain differences in political structures between Polynesia and Melanesia.

SCHWARTZ, Richard D. and MILLER, James C. "Legal Evolution and Societal Complexity," *American Journal of Sociology,* 70 (September, 1964), pp. 159-169.   An effort to relate the development of certain legal structures to a society's position on the folk-urban continuum.

SELZNICK, Philip. "Institutional Vulnerability in Mass Society," *American Journal of Sociology,* 56 (January, 1951), pp. 320-331. This article implicitly utilizes the typological approach by elaborating the characteristics of a mass society and their relationship to specific institutional areas. The author also suggests a typology of mass organizations.

SHUETZ, Alfred. "Concept and Theory Formation in the Social Sciences," *Journal of Philosophy,* 51 (April, 1954), pp. 257-273. An analysis of methodological issues of the social sciences which necessitate the utilization of Verstehen and ideal types. Shuetz approaches the problem from a phenomenological point of view.

SHUETZ, Alfred. "The Stranger," *American Journal of Sociology,* 49 (May, 1944), pp. 499-507.   A phenomenological analysis of the typical situation confronting a stranger as he attempts to interpret the cultural patterns of the new group.

SIU, Paul. "The Sojourner," *American Journal of Sociology,* 58 (July, 1952), pp. 34-44.   Building on Simmel's and Park's earlier work on the stranger and the marginal man, the author constructs another social type found in situations of racial and cultural contact.

SJOBERG, Gideon. "The Preindustrial City," *American Journal of Sociology,* 60 (March, 1955), pp. 438-445.   Sjoberg asserts that there are important differences between the preindustrial city and the industrial city. He seeks to clarify this distinction by means of a typological analysis focusing attention upon the ecological, economic and social aspects of the preindustrial city.

SJOBERG, Gideon, "The Rural-Urban Dimension in Preindustrial, Transitional, and Industrial Societies," in Robert E. L. Faris, ed., *Handbook of Modern Sociology* (Chicago: Rand McNally, 1964), pp. 127-159.   Provides a brief listing with some commentary of nearly all the rural-urban typologies along with a proposed reformulation. Then uses this "reformulated" rural-urban typology to discuss patterns of behavior in the three constructed types of societies mentioned in the title.

SOROKIN, Pitirim A. *Social and Cultural Dynamics,* 4 vols. (New York: American Book Co., 1937-1941).   The master work of the erudite and prolific Sorokin. Contains a wide variety of types; see especially the "idealistic-ideational-sensate" triad.

SOROKIN, Pitirim A. "Variations on the Spencerian Theme of Militant and Industrial Types of Society," *Social Science,* 36 (April, 1961), pp. 91-99.   A re-presentation with some elaboration of Spencer's typology, with Sorokin arguing that it represents one of the soundest typological generalizations of sociology.

STANLEY, Manfred. "Church Adaptation to Urban Social Change: A Typology of Protestant City Congregations," *Journal for the Scientific Study of Religion,* 2 (Fall, 1962), pp. 64-73.   A schematic analysis of congregations in New York City, emphasizing the problem of adaptation to changes in the urban environment. A typology which indicates the inadequacy of former distinctions such as rural, suburban, and city churches.

STEPHENSON, William. "A Statistical Approach to Typology: The Study of Trait Universes," *Journal of Clinical Psychology,* 6 (January, 1950), pp. 26-38.   A psychologist suggests that ideal types in personality studies can be approached by concentrating on universes of traits, rather than a few highly generalized traits.

STINCHCOMBE, Arthur. "Agricultural Enterprise and Rural Class Relations," *American Journal of Sociology,* 67 (September, 1961), pp. 165-176.   Types of agricultural enterprises (such as the manor, plantation, and family-size tendency) are related to patterns of class relations. An excellent example of using typological procedure to compare stratification structures.

STINCHCOMBE, Arthur. "Bureaucratic and Craft Administration of

Production: A Comparative Study," *Administrative Science Quarterly*, 4 (September, 1959), pp. 168-187. The author makes a comparative analysis of mass production and construction industries, pointing out the failure of bureaucracy to develop in the latter. He then revises Weber's model of bureaucracy, indicating that it is a subtype of rational administration while professionalization is another main subtype.

STONEQUIST, Everett. *The Marginal Man* (New York: Charles Scribner's Sons, 1937). An elaboration of Park's concept of marginal man with comparative case studies from various parts of the world.

TÖNNIES, Ferdinand. *Community and Society Gemeinschaft und Gesellschaft*. Translated and edited by C. P. Loomis (East Lansing: Michigan State University Press, 1957). A translation of Tönnies' classic work on the *Gemeinschaft-Gesellschaft* typology. Supplemented by introductory comments of Sorokin, Heberle, McKinney, and Loomis.

VAN DEN BERGHE, Pierre. "The Dynamics of Racial Prejudice: An Ideal Type Dichotomy," *Social Forces*, 37 (December, 1958), pp. 138-141. Racial prejudice can be polarized around two ideal-types—"paternalistic" and "competitive"—each characterized by a cluster of interrelated features. It is also suggested that the typology can be applied to other forms of prejudice.

WARNER, W. Keith and MILLER, Sidney J. "Organizational Problems in Two Types of Voluntary Associations," *American Journal of Sociology*, 69 (May, 1964), pp. 654-657. The authors present and attempt to empirically apply a twofold typology of voluntary associations ("consummatory" and "instrumental") based on the purposes of the associations.

WATKINS, J. W. M. "Ideal Types and Historical Explanation," *British Journal for the Philosophy of Science*, 3 (May, 1952), pp. 22-43. The author criticizes the sociologistic approach to ideal types, arguing that the only meaningful ideal types in historical explanation are psychologically oriented.

WEBER, Max. *The Methodology of the Social Sciences.* Translated and edited by E. A. Shils and H. A. Finch (Glencoe: The Free Press, 1949). Contains the best translation extant of Weber's treatment of the "ideal type."

WEBER, Max. *Theory of Social and Economic Organization.* Translated by A. M. Henderson and Talcott Parsons and edited by Talcott Parsons (Glencoe: The Free Press, 1947). This important work contains Weber's classic statements on such topics as the typology of social action, the typology of social organization, and the typology of authority.

WEBER, Max. *The Protestant Ethic and the Spirit of Capitalism.* Translated by Talcott Parsons (London: Allen and Unwin, 1930). A classic work in historical sociology. The primary concern is with the "historical individual," but clearly uses supporting generalizing types.

WINCH, Robert E. "Heuristic and Empirical Typologies," *American Sociological Review,* 12 (February, 1947), pp. 68-75. The author's discussion of the distinction between heuristic and empirical typologies suggests that while empirical typologies have been neglected, they have a potential value for the social sciences. This potential can be realized by means of factor analysis.

WIRTH, Louis. "The Problem of Minority Groups," in Ralph Linton (ed.), *The Science of Man in the World Crisis* (New York: Columbia University Press, 1945), pp. 347-372. A typology of minority groups dealing with the kinds of relationships between minorities and dominant groups and focusing on the kinds of behavior characteristically associated with these types of relationships.

YOUNG, Frank W. and Ruth C. "Occupational Role Perceptions in Rural Mexico," *Rural Sociology,* 27 (March, 1962), pp. 42-52. The authors hold that their findings are at variance with the usual derivations of the folk-urban continuum and suggest that certain Western biases concerning its unidimensionality and polarity of attributes, among others, are built into it.

YUAN, D. Y. "The Rural-Urban Continuum: A Case Study of Taiwan," *Rural Sociology*, 29 (September, 1964), pp. 247-260. Examines the relationship of certain demographic and social variables defining urbanism to a rural-urban continuum constructed for Taiwan, and on the basis of results, suggests a slight modification of this typology.

Index